GOMORRAH

GOMORRAH

ROBERTO SAVIANO

Translated from the Italian by
Virginia Jewiss

MACMILLAN

First published 2007 by Farrar, Straus and Giroux, New York

First published in Great Britain 2007 by Macmillan
an imprint of Pan Macmillan Ltd
Pan Macmillan, 20 New Wharf Road, London N1 9RR
Basingstoke and Oxford
Associated companies throughout the world
www.panmacmillan.com

ISBN 978-0-230-01776-4 HB
ISBN 978-0-230-70367-4 TPB

Originally published in Italian 2006 as
Gomorra: viaggio nell'impero economico e nel sogno di dominio della camorra
by Arnoldo Mondadori Editore S.p.A., Milan.

1 3 5 7 9 8 6 4 2

A CIP catalogue record for this book is available from
the British Library.

Printed and bound in Great Briatin by
Mackays of Chatham plc, Chatham, Kent

Visit **www.panmacmillan.com** to read more about all our books
and to buy them. You will also find features, author interviews and
news of any author events, and you can sign up for e-newsletters
so that you're always first to hear about our new releases.

To S., damn it

Comprehension . . . means the unpremeditated, attentive facing
up to, and resisting of, reality—whatever it may be.
—Hannah Arendt

Winners have no shame, no matter how they win.
—Niccolò Machiavelli

People are worms and they have to stay worms.
—from a wiretapped conversation

The world is yours.
—*Scarface*, 1983

CONTENTS

© 2007 Jeffrey L. Ward

PART ONE

PART ONE

THE PORT

The container swayed as the crane hoisted it onto the ship. The spreader, which hooks the container to the crane, was unable to control its movement, so it seemed to float in the air. The hatches, which had been improperly closed, suddenly sprang open, and dozens of bodies started raining down. They looked like mannequins. But when they hit the ground, their heads split open, as if their skulls were real. And they were. Men, women, even a few children, came tumbling out of the container. All dead. Frozen, stacked one on top of another, packed like sardines. These were the Chinese who never die. The eternal ones, who trade identity papers among themselves. So this is where they'd ended up, the bodies that in the wildest fantasies might have been cooked in Chinese restaurants, buried in fields beside factories, or tossed into the mouth of Vesuvius. Here they were. Spilling from the container by the dozen, their names scribbled on tags and tied with string around their necks. They'd all put aside money so they could be buried in China, back in their hometowns, a percentage withheld from their salaries to guarantee their return voyage once they were dead. A space in a container and a hole in some strip of Chinese soil. The port crane operator covered his face with his hands

as he told me about it, eyeing me through his fingers. As if the mask
of his hands might give him the courage to speak. He'd seen the bodies fall, but there'd been no need to sound the alarm. He merely lowered the container to the ground, and dozens of people appeared out
of nowhere to put everyone back inside and hose down the remains.
That's how it went. He still couldn't believe it and hoped he was hal-
lucinating, due to too much overtime. Then he closed his fingers,
completely covering his eyes. He kept on whimpering, but I couldn't
understand what he was saying.

Everything that exists passes through here. Through the port of Naples.
There's not a product, fabric, piece of plastic, toy, hammer, shoe,
screwdriver, bolt, video game, jacket, pair of pants, drill, or watch that
doesn't come through the port. The port of Naples is an open wound.
The end point for the interminable voyage that merchandise makes.
Ships enter the gulf and come to the dock like babies to the breast,
except that they're here to be milked, not fed. The port of Naples is
the hole in the earth out of which what's made in China comes. The
Far East, as reporters still like to call it. Far. Extremely far. Practically
unimaginable. Closing my eyes, I see kimonos, Marco Polo's beard,
Bruce Lee kicking in midair. But in fact this East is more closely
linked to the port of Naples than to any other place. There's nothing
far about the East here. It should be called the extremely near East,
the least East. Everything made in China is poured out here. Like a
bucket of water dumped into a hole in the sand. The water eats the
sand, and the hole gets bigger and deeper. The port of Naples handles
20 percent of the value of Italian textile imports from China, but
more than 70 percent of the quantity. It's a bizarre thing, hard to understand, yet merchandise possesses a rare magic: it manages both to
be and not to be, to arrive without ever reaching its destination, to
cost the customer a great deal despite its poor quality, and to have little tax value in spite of being worth a huge amount. Textiles fall under

quite a few product classifications, and a mere stroke of the pen on the shipping manifest can radically lower price and VAT. In the silence of the port's black hole, the molecular structure of merchandise seems to break down, only to recompose once it gets beyond the perimeter of the coast. Goods have to leave the port immediately. Everything happens so quickly that they disappear in the process, evaporate as if they'd never existed. As if nothing had happened, as if it had all been simply an act. An imaginary voyage, a false landing, a phantom ship, evanescent cargo. Goods need to arrive in the buyer's hands without leaving any drool to mark their route, they have to reach their warehouse quickly, right away, before time can even begin—time that might allow for an inspection. Hundreds of pounds of merchandise move as if they were a package hand-delivered by the mailman. In the port of Naples—330 acres spread out along seven miles of coastline—time undergoes unique expansions and contractions. Things that take an hour elsewhere seem to happen here in less than a minute. Here the proverbial slowness that makes the Neapolitan's every move molasses-like is quashed, confuted, negated. The ruthless swiftness of Chinese merchandise overruns the temporal dimension of customs inspections, killing time itself. A massacre of minutes, a slaughter of seconds stolen from the records, chased by trucks, hurried along by cranes, helped by forklifts that disembowel the containers.

COSCO, the largest Chinese state-owned shipping company, with the world's third-largest fleet, operates in the port of Naples in consort with MSC, a Geneva-based company that owns the world's second-largest commercial fleet. The Swiss and Chinese decided to pool together and invest heavily in Naples, where they manage the largest cargo terminal. With over 3,000 feet of pier, nearly a million and a half square feet of terminal, and more than 300,000 square feet of outdoor space at their disposal, they absorb almost all the traffic in transit for Europe. You have to reconfigure your imagination to try to understand the port of Naples as the bottom rung of the ladder of

Chinese production. The biblical image seems appropriate: the eye of the needle is the port, and the camel that has to pass through it are the ships. Enormous vessels line up single file out in the gulf and await their turn amid the confusion of pitching sterns and colliding bows; rumbling with heaving iron, the sheet metal and screws slowly penetrate the tiny Neapolitan opening. It is as if the anus of the sea were opening out, causing great pain to the sphincter muscles.

But no. It's not like that. There's no apparent confusion. The ships all come and go in orderly fashion, or at least that's how it looks from dry land. Yet 150,000 containers pass through here every year. Whole cities of merchandise get built on the quays, only to be hauled away. A port is measured by its speed, and every bureaucratic sluggishness, every meticulous inspection, transforms the cheetah of transport into a slow and lumbering sloth.

I always get lost on the pier. Bausan pier is like something made out of LEGO blocks. An immense construction that seems not so much to occupy space as to invent it. One corner looks like it's covered with wasps' nests. An entire wall of bastard beehives: thousands of electrical outlets that feed the "reefers," or refrigerator containers. All the TV dinners and fish sticks in the world are crammed into these icy containers. At Bausan pier I feel as if I'm seeing the port of entry for all the merchandise that mankind produces, where it spends its last night before being sold. It's like contemplating the origins of the world. The clothes young Parisians will wear for a month, the fish sticks that Brescians will eat for a year, the watches Catalans will adorn their wrists with, and the silk for every English dress for an entire season—all pass through here in a few hours. It would be interesting to read someplace not just where goods are manufactured, but the route they take to land in the hands of the buyer. Products have multiple, hybrid, and illegitimate citizenship. Half-born in the middle of China, they're finished on the outskirts of some Slavic city, brought to perfection in northeastern Italy, packaged in Puglia or north of

Tirana in Albania, and finally end up in a warehouse somewhere in Europe. No human being could ever have the rights of mobility that merchandise has. Every fragment of the journey, with its accidental and official routes, finds its fixed point in Naples. When the enormous container ships first enter the gulf and slowly approach the pier, they seem like lumbering mammoths of sheet metal and chains, the rusted sutures on their sides oozing water; but when they berth, they become nimble creatures. You'd expect these ships to carry a sizable crew, but instead they disgorge handfuls of little men who seem incapable of taming these brutes on the open ocean.

The first time I saw a Chinese vessel dock, I felt as if I were looking at the production of the whole world. I was unable to count the containers, to quantify them. I couldn't keep track of them all. It might seem absurd not to be able to put a number on things, but I kept losing count, the figures were too big and got mixed up in my head.

These days the merchandise unloaded in Naples is almost exclusively Chinese—1.6 million tons annually. Registered merchandise, that is. At least another million tons pass through without leaving a trace. According to the Italian Customs Agency, 60 percent of the goods arriving in Naples escape official customs inspection, 20 percent of the bills of entry go unchecked, and fifty thousand shipments are contraband, 99 percent of them from China—all for an estimated 200 million euros in evaded taxes each semester. The containers that need to disappear before being inspected are in the first row. Every container is duly numbered, but the numbers on many of them are identical. So one inspected container baptizes all the illegal ones with the same number. What gets unloaded on Monday can be for sale in Modena or Genoa or in the shop windows of Bonn or Munich by Thursday. Lots of merchandise on the Italian market is supposedly only in transit, but the magic of customs makes transit stationary. The grammar of merchandise has one syntax for documents and another for commerce. In April 2005, the Antifraud unit of Italian Customs, which had by chance launched four separate operations nearly simultaneously, sequestered 24,000 pairs of jeans intended for the French market; 51,000 items from Bangladesh labeled "Made in Italy"; 450,000 figurines, puppets, Barbies, and Spider-men; and another 46,000 plastic toys—for a total value of approximately 36 million euros. Just a small serving of the economy that was making its way through the port of Naples in a few hours. And from the port to the world. On it goes, all day, every day. These slices of the economy are becoming a staple diet.

The port is detached from the city. An infected appendix, never quite degenerating into peritonitis, always there in the abdomen of the coastline. A desert hemmed in by water and earth, but which seems to belong to neither land nor sea. A grounded amphibian, a marine metamorphosis. A new formation created from the dirt, garbage, and odds and ends that the tide has carried ashore over the years. Ships empty their latrines and clean their holds, dripping yellow foam into the water; motorboats and yachts, their engines belching, tidy up by tossing everything into the garbage can that is the sea. The soggy mass forms a hard crust all along the coastline. The sun kindles the mirage of water, but the surface of the sea gleams like trash bags. Black ones. The gulf looks percolated, a giant tub of sludge. The wharf with its thousands of multicolored containers seems an uncrossable border: Naples is encircled by walls of merchandise. But the walls don't defend the city; on the contrary, it's the city that defends the walls. Yet there are no armies of longshoremen, no romantic riffraff at the port. One imagines it full of commotion, men coming and going, scars and incomprehensible languages, a frenzy of people. Instead, the silence of a mechanized factory reigns. There doesn't seem to be anyone around anymore, and the containers, ships, and trucks seem animated by perpetual motion. A silent swiftness.

I used to go to the port to eat fish. Not that nearness to the sea means anything in terms of the quality of the restaurant. I'd find pumice stones, sand, even boiled seaweed in my food. The clams were fished up and tossed right into the pan. A guarantee of freshness, a Russian roulette of infection. But these days, with everyone resigned to the taste of farm-raised seafood, so squid tastes like chicken, you have to take risks if you want that indefinable sea flavor. And I was willing to take the risk. In a restaurant at the port, I asked about finding a place to rent.

"I don't know of anything, the houses around here are disappearing. The Chinese are taking them . . ."

A big guy, but not as big as his voice, was holding court in the center of the room. He took a look at me and shouted, "There still might be something left!"

That was all he said. After we'd both finished our lunch, we made our way down the street that runs along the port. He didn't need to tell me to follow him. We came to the atrium of a ghostly apartment house and went up to the fourth floor, to the last remaining student apartment. They were kicking everyone out to make room for emptiness. Nothing was supposed to be left in the apartments. No cabinets, beds, paintings, bedside tables—not even walls. Only space. Space for cartons, space for enormous cardboard wardrobes, space for merchandise.

I was assigned a room of sorts. More of a cubbyhole, just big enough for a bed and a wardrobe. There was no talk of monthly rent, utility bills, or a phone hookup. He introduced me to four guys, my housemates, and that was that. They explained that this was the only apartment in the building that was still occupied and that it served as lodging for Xian, the Chinese man in charge of "the palazzi," the buildings. There was no rent to pay, but I was expected to work in the apartment-warehouses on the weekends. I'd gone looking for a room and ended up with a job. In the morning we'd knock down walls, and in the evening we'd clean up the wreckage—chunks of cement and brick—collecting the rubble in ordinary trash bags. Knocking down a wall makes unexpected sounds, not of stones being struck but of crystal being swept off a table onto the floor. Every apartment became a storehouse devoid of walls. I still can't figure out how the building where I worked remained standing. More than once we knowingly took out main walls. But the space was needed for the merchandise, and there's no contest between saving walls and storing products.

The idea of cramming apartments full of boxes dawned on some Chinese merchants after the Naples Port Authority presented its security plan to a delegation of U.S. congressmen. The plan calls for the port to be divided into four areas: cruise ships, pleasure craft, commercial vessels, and containers, with an evaluation of the risks in each area. After the security plan was made public, many Chinese businessmen decided that the way to keep the police from feeling they had to intervene, the newspapers from writing about it constantly, or TV crews from sneaking around in search of a juicy story was to engulf everything in total silence. A rise in costs was another reason for making the merchandise more inconspicuous. Having it disappear into rented warehouses in remote parts of the countryside, amid landfill and tobacco fields, would have meant a lot of additional tractor-trailer traffic. This way, no more than ten vans, stuffed to the gills with boxes, go in and out of the port daily. Just a short trip and they're in the garages of the apartment houses facing the port. In and out, that's all it takes.

Nonexistent, imperceptible movements lost in the everyday traffic. Apartments rented. Gutted. Garage walls removed to make one continuous space. Cellars packed floor to ceiling with merchandise. Not one owner dared complain. Xian had paid them all: rent and compensation for unauthorized demolition. Thousands of boxes brought up in the elevator, which was rebuilt to move freight. A steel cage with tracks and a continuously moving platform. The work was concen-

trated in a few hours, and the choice of merchandise was not accidental. I happened to be unloading during the first days of July. The
pay is good, but it's hard work if you aren't used to it. It was hot and
humid, but no one dared ask about air-conditioning. No one. And not
out of fear of punishment or because of cultural norms of obedience
and submission. The people unloading came from every corner of the
globe: Ghana, Ivory Coast, China, and Albania, as well as Naples,
Calabria, and Lucania. No one asked because everyone understood
that since merchandise doesn't suffer from the heat, there was no reason to waste money on air-conditioning.

We stacked boxes of jackets, raincoats, Windbreakers, cotton
sweaters, and umbrellas. It seemed a strange choice in the height of
summer to be stocking up on fall clothing instead of bathing suits,
sundresses, and flip-flops. Unlike the warehouses for stockpiling merchandise, these storage apartments were for items that would be put
on the market right away. But the Chinese businessmen had forecast
a cloudy August. I've never forgotten John Maynard Keynes's lesson
on the concept of marginal value: how, for example, the price of a bottle of water varies depending on whether it is in the desert or near a
waterfall. That summer Italian enterprises were offering bottles by
the falls while Chinese entrepreneurs were building fountains in the
desert.

After my first few days of work, Xian spent the night at the apartment. He spoke perfect Italian, with a soft *r* that sounded more like a
v. Like the impoverished aristocrats Totò imitates in his films. Xian
Zhu had been rebaptized Nino. In Naples, nearly all the Chinese who
have dealings with locals take Neapolitan names. It's now such common practice that it's no longer surprising to hear a Chinese introduce
himself as Tonino, Nino, Pino, or Pasquale. Nino Xian didn't sleep;
instead, he spent the night sitting at the kitchen table making phone
calls, one eye on the TV. I'd lain down on my bed, but I couldn't get
to sleep. Xian's voice never let up, his tongue like a machine gun, firing through his teeth. He spoke without inhaling, an asphyxiation of

words. His bodyguards' flatulence saturated the house with a sickly sweet smell and permeated my room as well. It wasn't just the stench that disgusted me, but the images it evoked. Spring rolls putrefying in their stomachs and Cantonese rice steeped in gastric juices. The other tenants were used to it. Once their doors were closed nothing existed for them but sleep. But for me nothing existed except what was going on outside my door. So I went and sat in the kitchen. Communal space. And therefore also partly mine. At least in theory. Xian stopped talking and started cooking. Fried chicken. All sorts of questions came to mind, clichés I wanted to peel away. I started talking about the Triad, the Chinese Mafia. Xian kept on frying. I wanted to ask him for details, even if only symbolic ones—I certainly didn't expect a confession about his affiliation. Presuming that the criminal investigations were an accurate reflection of the reality, I revealed my familiarity with the Chinese underworld. Xian put his fried chicken on the table, sat down, and said nothing. I don't know if he thought what I was saying was interesting. I never did find out if he belonged to the Triad. He took a few sips of beer, then lifted one buttock off his chair, took his wallet out of his pants pocket, flipped through it, and pulled out three bills. He spread them out on the table and placed a glass on top of them.

"Euro, dollar, yuan. Here's my triad."

Xian seemed sincere. No other ideology, no symbols or hierarchical passion. Profit, business, capital. Nothing else. One tends to think that the power determining certain dynamics is obscure, and so must issue from an obscure entity: the Chinese Mafia. A synthesis that cancels out all intermediate stages, financial transfers, and investments—everything that makes a criminal economic outfit powerful. For the last several years every Anti-Mafia Commission report has highlighted "the growing danger of the Chinese Mafia," yet in ten years of investigations the police have sequestered only 600,000 euros in Campi Bisenzio near Florence. A few motorcycles and part of a factory. Nothing compared to the economic force capable of moving the hundreds of millions of euros in capital that American analysts kept writing about. Xian the businessman was smiling at me.

"The economy has a top and a bottom. We got in at the bottom and we're coming out on top."

Before he went to bed Nino Xian made me a proposal for the following day.

"You get up early?"

"It depends . . ."

"If you can be on your feet at five a.m. tomorrow, come with us to the port. You can give us a hand."

"Doing what?"

"If you have a hooded sweatshirt, it'd be a good idea to wear it." Nothing more was said. Nor did I insist, eager as I was to take part. Asking too many questions could have compromised Xian's invitation. There were only a few hours left to rest, but I was too anxious to sleep.

I was ready and waiting downstairs at five on the dot, along with the others: one of my housemates and two North Africans with graying hair. We crammed into the van and headed to the port. I don't know how far we went once inside the port, or what back alleys we took; I fell asleep, my head against the window. We got out near some rocks, a small jetty jutting out into the gorge, where a boat with a huge motor—it seemed too heavy a tail for such a long, narrow craft—was moored. With our hoods up we looked like members of some ridiculous rap group. The hood I'd thought was to hide my identity turned out instead to be protection against icy sprays, an attempt to ward off the migraine that nails you in the temples first thing in the morning on the open sea. A young Neapolitan started the motor and another steered. They could have been brothers they looked so much alike. Xian didn't come with us. After about half an hour we drew up to a ship. I thought we were going to slam right into it. Enormous. I could barely tilt my head back far enough to see the top of the bulwarks. Ships in open water let out iron cries, like felled trees, and hollow sounds that make you swallow constantly, your mucus tasting of salt.

A net filled with boxes dropped jerkily from the ship's pulley. Every time the bundle knocked against our boat, it pitched so severely that I was sure I would fall into the water. The boxes weren't that heavy, but after stacking thirty or so in the stern, my wrists were sore and my forearms red from the corners jabbing them. Our boat took off and veered toward the coast just as two others drew up alongside the ship to collect more boxes. They hadn't left from our jetty, but all of a sudden there they were in our wake. I felt it in the pit of my stomach every time the bow slapped the surface of the water. I rested my head against the boxes and tried to guess their contents from their smell, to make out what was inside from the sound. A sense of guilt crept over me. Who knows what I'd taken part in, without making a decision, without really choosing. It was one thing to damn myself intentionally, but instead I'd ended up unloading clandestine goods out of curiosity. For some reason one stupidly thinks a criminal act has to be more thought out, more deliberate than an innocuous one. But there's really no difference. Actions know an elasticity that ethical judgments ignore. When we got back to the jetty, the North Africans climbed out of the boat with two cartons each on their shoulders, but I had a hard enough time standing without wobbling. Xian was waiting for us on the rocks. He selected a huge carton and sliced the packing tape with a box cutter. Sneakers. Genuine athletic shoes, the most famous brands, the latest models, so new they weren't yet for sale in Italy. Fearing a customs inspection, Xian preferred unloading them on the open sea. That way the merchandise could be put on the market without the burden of taxes, and the wholesalers wouldn't have to pay import fees. You beat the competition on price. Same merchandise quality, but at a 4, 6, 10 percent discount. Percentages no sales rep could offer, and percentages are what make or break a store, give birth to new shopping centers, bring in guaranteed earnings and, with them, secure bank loans. Prices have to be lower.

Everything has to move quickly and secretly, be squeezed into buying and selling. Unexpected oxygen for Italian and European merchants. Oxygen that enters through the port of Naples.

We loaded the boxes into vans as other boats docked. The vans headed toward Rome, Viterbo, Latina, Formia. Xian had us driven home.

Everything had changed in the last few years. Everything. Suddenly and unexpectedly. Some people sense the change without understanding it. Up till ten years ago, bootleggers' boats plowed the Bay of Naples every morning, carrying dealers out to stock up on cigarettes. The streets were packed, cars were filled with cartons to be sold at corner stalls. The battles were played out among the Coast Guard, customs, and the smugglers. Tons of cigarettes in exchange for a botched arrest, or an arrest in exchange for tons of cigarettes stashed in the false bottom of a fleeing motorboat. Long nights, lookouts, whistles warning of a suspicious car, walkie-talkies ready to sound the alarm, lines of men quickly passing boxes along the shore. Cars speeding inland from the Puglia coast, or from the hinterlands to Campania. The crucial axis ran between Naples and Brindisi, the route of cheap cigarettes. Bootlegging was a booming business, the Fiat of the south, the welfare system for those the government ignored, the sole activity of twenty thousand people in Puglia and Campania. It was also what triggered the great Camorra war of the early 1980s.

The Puglia and Campania clans were smuggling cigarettes into Europe to get around government taxes. They imported thousands of crates from Montenegro every month, invoicing 500 million lire—roughly $330,000—on each shipment. Now all that has broken up. It's no longer worth it for the clans to deal in contraband cigarettes. But Antoine Lavoisier's maxim holds true: nothing is lost, nothing is created, everything is transformed. In nature, but above all in the dynamics of capitalism. Consumer goods have replaced the nicotine habit as the new contraband. A cutthroat price war is developing, as discounts mean the difference between life and death for agents, wholesalers, and merchants. Taxes, VAT, and tractor-trailer maximums are the deadwood of profit, the real obstacles hindering the circulation of merchandise and money. To take advantage of cheap labor, the big companies are shifting production to the east, to Romania or Moldavia, or even farther—to China. But that's not enough. The merchandise is cheap, but it enters a market where more and more consumers with unstable incomes or minimal savings keep track of every cent. As unsold merchandise piles up, new items—genuine, false, semifalse, or partly real—arrive. Silently, without a trace. With less visibility than cigarettes, since there's no illegal distribution. As if they'd never been shipped, as if they'd sprouted in the fields and been harvested by some unknown hand. Money doesn't stink, but merchandise smells sweet. It doesn't give off the odor of the sea it crossed or the hands that produced it, and there are no grease stains from the machinery that assembled it. Merchandise smells of itself. Its only smell comes from the shopkeeper's counter, and its only endpoint is the buyer's home.

We left the sea behind and headed home. The van barely gave us time to get out before it returned to the port to collect more cartons, more merchandise. I nearly fainted getting into the elevator. I took off my sweatshirt, soaked with sea and sweat, and threw myself on my bed. I don't know how many boxes I'd carried and stacked, but I felt as if I'd unloaded shoes for half of the feet of Italy. I was exhausted, as if it were the end of a long, hard day. My apartment mates were just waking up. It was still early morning.

ANGELINA JOLIE

In the days that followed, Xian took me along to his business meetings. He seemed to enjoy my company as he went about his day or ate his lunch. I either talked too much or too little, both of which he liked. I followed how the seeds of money are sown and cultivated, how the economy's terrain is allowed to lie fallow. We went to Las Vegas, an area to the north of Naples. Las Vegas: that's what we call it around here, for several reasons. Just like Las Vegas, Nevada, which is built in the middle of the desert, the urban agglomerations here seem to spring up out of nothing. And you have to cross a desert of roads to reach the place. Miles of tar, wide thoroughfares that whisk you away from here, propelling you toward the highway, to Rome, straight to the north. Roads built not for cars but for trucks, not to move people but clothes, shoes, purses. As you arrive from Naples, these towns appear out of nowhere, planted in the ground one after another. Lumps of cement. Tangles of streets. A web of roads on which the towns of Casavatore, Caivano, Sant'Antimo, Melito, Arzano, Piscinola, San Pietro a Patierno, Frattamaggiore, Frattaminore, Grumo Nevano, endlessly rotate. Places so indistinguishable they seem to be one giant metropolis, with the streets of one town running into another.

I must have heard the area around Foggia called *Califoggia* a hundred times, the southern part of Calabria referred to as *Calafrica* or *Saudi Calabria*, Sala Consilina *Sahara Consilina*, or an area of Secondigliano (which means "second mile") called *Terzo Mondo*, Third World. But this Las Vegas really is Las Vegas. For years, anyone who wanted to try his hand at business could do it here. Live the dream. Use his severance pay, savings, or a loan to open a factory. You'd bet on a company: if you won, you'd reap efficiency, productivity, speed, protection, and cheap labor. You'd win just the way you win by betting on red or black. If you lost, you'd be out of business in a few months. Las Vegas. No regulations, no administrative or economic planning. Shoes, clothes, and accessories were clandestinely forced onto the international market. The towns didn't boast of this precious production; the more silently, the more secretly the goods were manufactured, the more successful they were. For years this area produced the best in Italian fashion. And thus the best in the world. But they didn't have entrepreneurs' clubs or training centers; they had nothing but work, nothing but their sewing machines, small factories, wrapped packages, and shipped goods. Nothing but the endless repetition of production. Everything else was superfluous. Training took place at the workbench, and a company's quality was demonstrated by its success. No financing, no projects, no internships. In the marketplace it's all or nothing. Win or lose. A rise in salaries has meant better houses and fancy cars. Yet this is not wealth that can be considered collective. This is plundered wealth, taken by force from someone else and carried off to your own cave. People came from all over to invest in businesses making shirts, jackets, skirts, blazers, gloves, hats, purses, and wallets for Italian, German, and French companies. Las Vegas stopped requiring permits, contracts, or proper working conditions in the 1950s, and garages, stairwells, and storerooms were transformed into factories. But lately the Chinese competition has ruined the ones producing midrange-quality merchandise. There's no more room for workmanship. Either you do the best work the fastest or someone else will figure out how to do average work more quickly. A lot of people found themselves out of work. Factory owners were crushed by debt and usury. Many absconded.

One place in particular has been threatened by the disappearance of these midrange industries: Parco Verde in Caivano. Its breath cut short, its growth stunted, it has become the emblem of the outer edge of urban sprawl. Here the lights are always on, the houses full of people, the courtyards crowded, the cars parked. No one leaves. Some people arrive, but few stay. There's never a moment during the day when the apartment houses are empty, never that sense of stillness after everyone has gone off to work or school in the morning. There's always a crowd here, the incessant noise of people.

Parco Verde rises up just off the central axis of the city, the knife of tar that slices right through Naples. It seems more like a junk pile than a neighborhood, cement constructions with aluminum balconies swelling like carbuncles from every opening. It looks like one of those places designed by an architect who got his inspiration at the beach, as if he'd meant the buildings to look like sand castles, the kind made from pails of sand dumped upside down. Dull, featureless buildings. In one corner is a tiny chapel. You almost don't notice it, but that wasn't always the case. There used to be a big, white chapel, a full-scale mausoleum dedicated to a boy named Emanuele. Emanuele was killed on the job. A job that in some places is even worse than moonlighting in a factory. But it's a way to make a living. Emanuele did robberies. He always struck on Saturdays—every Saturday for a while. Always in the same place. Same time, same street, same day. Because Saturday was the day for his victims, the day for lovers. And Route 87 was where all the lovers in the area went. A shitty road of patched tar and mini-landfills. Every time I pass there and see the couples, I think you must have to really unleash a lot of passion to feel good in such a disgusting setting. It was here that Emanuele and his two friends hid, waiting for a car to park, for the lights to be switched off. They'd wait a few more minutes—to give them time to get undressed—and then, when the lovers were most vulnerable, they'd strike. They'd shatter the window with the butt of a pistol and stick the barrel under the man's nose. After cleaning out their victims, they'd head off for the weekend with dozens of robberies under their belts and 500 euros in their pockets: meager booty, but it felt like a fortune.

Then one night a patrol of carabinieri intercepts them. Emanuele and his accomplices are so reckless that they don't realize that constantly pulling the same moves in the same location is the best way to get arrested. A chase, the cars ram into each other, shots ring out. Then all is still. Emanuele is in the car, mortally wounded. He'd been holding a pistol and had pointed it at the carabinieri. So they kill him, eleven shots in just a few seconds. Firing eleven shots at point-blank means your gun is aimed and you're ready to shoot at the least provocation. Shoot to kill first, and think of it as self-defense later. The bullets had flown in like the wind, drawn to Emanuele's body as to a magnet. His friends stop the car and are about to flee, but give up as soon as they realize Emanuele is dead. They open the car doors, putting up no resistance to the fists in the face that are a prelude to every arrest. Emanuele is bent over himself, a fake pistol in his hand. A cap gun, the kind that used to be called a dog-chaser, good for keeping stray dogs out of the chicken coop. A toy wielded as if it were real; after all, Emanuele was a kid who acted like a grown man, with a frightened look that feigned ruthlessness, and a desire for pocket money that pretended to be a thirst for riches. Emanuele was fifteen years old. Everyone called him Manù. He had a lean, dark, angular face, the kind you picture when you imagine the last kid you'd want to hang out with. Emanuele came from a corner of the world where you don't win honor and respect merely for having pocket money, but for how you get it. Emanuele belonged to Parco Verde. And when you come from a place that brands you, no mistake or crime can cancel out the fact of your belonging. The Parco Verde families took up a collection and built a small mausoleum. Inside they placed an image of the Neapolitan Madonna dell'Arco and a photo of Emanuele smiling. Emanuele's chapel was one of the more than twenty the faithful had built in honor of every Madonna imaginable. But the mayor couldn't stand that this one was dedicated to a lowlife, so he sent in a bulldozer to knock it down. The cement building crumbled instantly, as if it were made out of modeling clay. Word spread quickly, and the youth of Parco Verde arrived on their Vespas and motorcycles. No one spoke. They all just stared at the man who was working the bulldozer levers. Under the weight of their stares, he stopped and pointed to the marshal as if to say that he was the one who'd given the order. A gesture to identify the object of their wrath and remove the target from his own chest. Frightened, besieged, he locked himself in. A second later the fighting began. He managed to flee in a police car as the kids began attacking the bulldozer with fists and feet. They emptied beer bottles and filled them with gas, tilting their motor scooters so the fuel dripped right out of the tanks into the bottles, and threw rocks at the windows of a nearby school. If Emanuele's chapel had to come down, then so did all the rest. Dishes, vases, and silverware flew from apartment windows. Firebombs were hurled at the police. Trash cans were lined up as barricades, and everything they could get their hands on was set on fire. Preparations for guerrilla warfare. There were hundreds of them, they'd be able to hold out a long time. The rebellion was spreading, and soon it would reach Naples proper.

But then someone arrived, from not too far away. The whole area was surrounded by police and carabinieri cars, but a black SUV had managed to get past the barricades. The driver gave a signal, someone opened the door, and a few of the rebels got in. In less than two hours everything was dismantled. Handkerchiefs came off faces, barricades of burning trash were extinguished. The clans had intervened, who knows which one. Parco Verde is a gold mine for Camorra laborers. Anyone who wants conscripts can round them up here: the bottom rung, unskilled workers who make even less than than the Nigerian or Albanian pushers. Everybody wants Parco Verde kids: the Casalesi clan, the Mallardos in Giuliano, the Crispano "tiger cubs." They become drug dealers on fixed pay, with no percentage on their sales, or drivers, or lookouts, defending territories miles from home. And to get the job they don't even ask to be reimbursed for gas. Trustworthy kids, scrupulous in their work. Some wind up on heroin, the drug of the truly wretched. Some save themselves, enlist in the army, and get deployed; some of the girls manage to get away and never set foot in the place again. Hardly any of the younger generation become clan members; they work for the clans without ever becoming Camorristi. The clans don't want them. They merely employ them, take advantage of the offering. These kids have no skills or commercial talent. A lot of them work as couriers, carrying backpacks filled with hashish to Rome. Motorcycle muscles flexed to the max, after an hour and a half they're already at the capital gates. They don't get anything for these trips, but after about twenty rounds they're given a present—a motorcycle. To them it's precious, beyond compare, an acquisition out of reach with any other job available around here. They've been delivering goods that invoice at ten times the cost of the motorcycle, but they don't know that, can't even begin to imagine it. If they get stopped at a roadblock, they'll get less than ten years. The clan won't cover their legal costs or guarantee assistance to their families. But there's the roar of the exhaust in their ears and Rome to reach.

A few of the barricades came down slowly, depending on the degree of pent-up anger. Then everything fizzled. The clans weren't afraid of the revolt. As far as they were concerned, Parco Verde could burn for days, the inhabitants could all kill each other. Except that the uproar meant no work, no reserves of cheap labor. Everything had to return to normal right away. Everyone had to get back to work, or at least be ready if they were needed. This game of revolt had to end.

• • •

I went to Emanuele's funeral. In certain spots on the globe, fifteen is merely a number. In this slum neighborhood, dying at fifteen is more like fulfilling a death sentence than being deprived of life. The church was filled with grim-faced kids, and every now and then they'd let out a cry. Outside, a small chorus was even chanting, "He's still with us, he'll always be with us . . ." the traditional chant of the soccer fanatics when some old glory retires his number. It was as if they were at the stadium, but the only chants were ones of rage. The plainclothesmen did their best to keep out of the aisles. Everyone had recognized them but there was no room for a skirmish. I'd spotted them right away; or rather they'd spotted me, not finding any trace of my face in their mental archives. As if attracted by my sullenness, one of them came up to me and said, "They're all doomed here. Drugs, stealing, dealing in stolen goods, holdups . . . some are even streetwalkers. Not one of them is clean. The more of them who die here, the better it is for everyone."

Words that deserve a punch or a head butt in the nose. But everyone was really thinking the same thing. And maybe it was even wise. I looked at them one by one, those kids who'll do life for stealing 200 euros—the dregs, stand-ins, pushers. Not one of them over twenty. Padre Mauro, the priest performing Emanuele's funeral, knew whom he was burying. He also knew the other kids were hardly the picture of innocence.

"This is not a hero who has died today . . ."

He didn't hold his hands open as priests do when they read the parables on Sunday, but instead clenched his fists. And there was no note of homily in his voice, which was strangely hoarse, as if he'd been talking too long. He spoke with anger—there was no light punishment for this creature, no delegating anything.

He seemed like one of those priests during the guerrilla uprisings in El Salvador, when they'd finally had enough of performing funerals for murder victims, when they stopped having pity and started shouting. But no one knew Romero here. Padre Mauro had unusual energy. "For all the responsibility we can assign to Emanuele, the fact remains that he was fifteen years old. At that age the sons of families born in other parts of Italy are going to the pool, taking dance lessons. It's not like that here. God the Father will take into consideration the fact that the mistake was made by a fifteen-year-old boy. If in the south of Italy fifteen means you're old enough to work, to decide to steal, to kill and be killed, it also means you're old enough to take responsibility for certain things."

He inhaled deeply the foul air inside the church. "But fifteen years are few enough that they let us see more clearly what's behind them, and they require us to apportion the responsibility. Fifteen is an age that knocks at the conscience of those who merely play at legality, work, and responsibility. An age that doesn't knock gently, but claws with its nails."

The priest finished the homily. No one was completely sure what he really meant or who was to blame. The kids got all riled up. Four men carried the casket out of the church, but all of a sudden it lifted off their shoulders and floated above the crowd, swaying on a sea of hands, like a rock star who catapults from the stage into his fans. A bunch of motorcyclists pulled up around the hearse waiting to take Manù to the cemetery. They revved their engines and clamped down on the brakes: a chorus of burnouts for Emanuele's last race. Their tires squealing and mufflers howling, it was as if they wanted to escort him all the way to the hereafter. Thick smoke and the stench of gas filled the air, permeating everyone's clothes. I went in to the sacristy; I wanted to talk to the priest who'd uttered such fiery words. A woman got there before me. She wanted to tell him that the boy had gone looking for trouble, that his family hadn't taught him anything.

Then she confessed proudly, "My grandchildren would never have committed robbery, even though they're unemployed . . . But what did that boy learn?" she continued nervously. "Anything?"

. The priest looked at the floor. He was wearing a tracksuit. He didn't try to respond, didn't even look her in the face. He just kept staring at his sneakers as he whispered, "The fact is that the only thing you learn here is how to die." -

"Excuse me, Padre?"

"Nothing, signora, nothing."

But not everyone is underground here. Not everyone has ended up in the quagmire of defeat. At least not yet. Some successful factories are still strong enough to compete with the Chinese because they work for big designer names. By delivering speed and quality—extremely high quality—they still hold the monopoly on beauty for top-level garments. "Made in Italy" is made here. Caivano, Sant' Antimo, Arzano, and all across Las Vegas, Campania. "The face of Italy in the world" wears fabric draped over the bare head of the Naples suburbs. The brand names don't dare risk sending everything East, contracting out to Asia. Factories here are crowded into stairwells, on the ground floors of row houses, in sheds on the outskirts of these outlying towns. Lined up one behind the other, staring at the back of the person in front of them, the workers sew cloth, cut leather, and assemble shoes. A garment worker puts in about ten hours a day, bringing home from 500 to 900 euros a month. Overtime usually pays well, as much as 15 euros an hour more than the regular wage. Factories rarely have more than ten employees. There's almost always a television or radio so the workers can listen to music, maybe even hum along. But during crunch times the only noise is the march of needles. More than half the employees are women; they're skilled workers, born staring at a sewing machine. Officially these factories don't exist, and neither do the employees. If the same work were done legally, prices would go up and there'd be no more market—which means the work would disappear from Italy. The businessmen around here know this logic by heart. There's usually no rancor or resentment between factory workers and owners; class conflict here is as soft as a soggy cookie. Often the owner is a former worker, and he puts in the same hours as his employees, in the same room, at the same bench. When he makes a mistake, he pays for it out of his own pocket, in mortgages or loans. His authority is paternalistic. You have to fight for a day off or a few cents' raise. There's no contract, no bureaucracy. It's all head to head, and any concessions or benefits are individually negotiated. The owner and his family live above the factory. His daughters often babysit his employees' children, and his mother becomes their de facto grandmother, so that workers' and owner's children grow up together. This communal existence acts out the horizontal dream of post-Fordism:* workers and managers eat together, socialize with each other, and are made to feel they're all part of the same community.

No one acts ashamed here. They know they're doing top-quality work, and that they're being paid a pittance. But you can't have one without the other. You work to get what you need and you do it as best you can, so that no one will find any reason to fire you. No safety net, just cause, permission, or vacation days. It's up to you to negotiate your rights, to plead for time off. But there's nothing to complain about. Everything is just as it should be. Here there's only a body, a skill, a machine, and a salary. No one knows the exact number of clandestine workers in these parts, or how many workers with contracts are nevertheless forced to sign a monthly pay slip for sums they never receive.

---

*Post-Fordism is a mode of production that favors more flexible manufacturing practices and less hierarchical social dynamics than those developed in the assembly-line methods of Henry Ford's factories.—Trans.

• • •

Xian was supposed to take part in an auction. We went to an elementary-school classroom, but there were no children and no teacher, just sheets of construction paper with big letters tacked to the walls. About twenty company reps were milling around. Xian was the only foreigner. He only greeted two people, and without excessive familiarity. A car pulled into the school courtyard, and three people entered the room: two men and a woman. The woman was wearing a leather skirt and high-heeled patent-leather shoes. Everyone rose to greet her. They took their places and the auction began. One of the men drew three vertical lines on the blackboard and wrote as the woman dictated. In the first column:

"800"

This was the number of garments to produce. The woman listed the types of fabric and the quality of the articles. A businessman from Sant' Antimo went over to the window, turning his back to the rest of us, and offered his prices and times:

"Forty euros apiece in two months."

His proposal was written on the board:

"800 / 40 / 2"

The other businessmen didn't look worried. He hadn't dared enter the realm of the impossible, which evidently was to their liking. But not to the buyers'. So the bidding continued.

The auctions the big Italian brands hold in this area are strange. No one wins the contract and no one loses. The game consists in entering or not entering the race. Someone throws out an offer, stating his time and price. If his conditions are accepted, he won't be the only winner, however. His offer is like a head start the others can try to follow. When the brokers accept a bid, the other contractors decide if they want in; whoever agrees gets the fabric. The cloth is sent directly to the port of Naples, where the contractors go and pick it up. But only one of them will be paid for the completed work: the one who delivers first, and with top-quality merchandise. The other players are free to keep the fabric, but they don't get a cent. The fashion houses make so much money that the fabric isn't a loss worth considering. If a contractor takes advantage of the system to have free materials but repeatedly fails to deliver, he's excluded from future auctions. In this way the brokers are guaranteed speed: if someone falls behind, someone else will take his place. There's no relief from the rhythms of high fashion.

To the joy of the woman behind the desk, another hand went up. A well-dressed contractor, elegant.

"Twenty euros in twenty-five days."

In the end the bid was accepted. Nine of the twenty contractors signed on as well. But not Xian. He wouldn't have been able to coordinate quality and speed in such a short time and at such low prices. When the auction was over, the woman wrote up a list of the contractors' names and phone numbers and the addresses of their factories. The winner invited everyone to his house for lunch. His factory was on the ground floor, he and his wife lived on the second, his son on the third. "I'm applying for a permit to add another floor. My other son is getting married," he declared proudly. As we climbed the stairs, he continued to tell us about his family, which, like his villa, was under construction.

"Don't ever put men in charge of the female workers, it only causes problems. I've got two sons, and both of them married employees. Put the fags in charge. Make the fags manage the shifts and inspect the work, like in the old days . . ."

The workers, men and women, came up to toast the new contract. They faced a grueling schedule: first shift from 6 a.m. to 9 p.m., with an hour's break to eat, second shift from 9 p.m. to 6 a.m. The women were wearing makeup and earrings, and aprons to protect their clothes from the glue, dust, and machine grease. Like Superman, who takes off his shirt and reveals his blue costume underneath, they were ready to go out to dinner as soon as they removed their aprons.

The men were sloppier, in sweatshirts and work pants. After the toast one of the guests took the owner aside, along with the others who had agreed to the auction price. They weren't hiding, but simply respecting the ancient custom of not discussing money at table. Xian explained to me in great detail that the guest—the very image of a bank teller—was discussing interest rates. But he was not from a bank. Italian brands pay only when the work is completed. Or rather, only after it has been accepted. Everything—salaries, production costs, even shipping—is paid in advance by the manufacturers. The clans loan money to the factories in their territories. The Di Lauros in Arzano, the Verdes in Sant' Antimo, the Cennamos in Crispano, and so on. The Camorra offers low rates, 2 to 4 percent. No one should have an easier time obtaining bank credit than these companies, who produce for the Italian fashion world, for the market of markets. But they're phantom operations, and bank directors don't meet with ghosts. Camorra liquidity is also the only way for factory employees to obtain a mortgage. Thus in towns where more than 40 percent of the residents support themselves by moonlighting, six out of ten families still manage to buy a home. Even the contractors who don't satisfy the requirements of the designer labels manage to find a buyer. They sell the garments to the clans to be put on the fake-goods market. All the runway fashions, all the glitz for the most elegant premieres, comes from here. The Las Vegas towns and Casarano, Tricase, Taviano, and Melissano in Capo di Leuca, the lower Salento region, are the principal centers for black-market fashion. It all comes from here, from this hole. All merchandise has obscure origins. This is the law of capitalism. But to observe the hole, to see it in front of you, well, it causes a strange sensation. An anxious heaviness. Like the truth weighing on your stomach.

One of the winning contractor's workers was particularly skilled: Pasquale. A lanky figure, tall, slim, and a bit hunchbacked; his frame curved behind his neck onto his shoulders, a bit like a hook. The stylists sent designs directly to him, articles intended for his hands only. His salary didn't fluctuate, but his tasks varied, and he somehow conveyed an air of satisfaction. I liked him immediately, the moment I caught sight of his big nose. Pasquale had the face of an old man, though he was still young. A face that was constantly buried in fabric, fingertips that ran along seams. Pasquale was one of the only workers who could buy fabric direct. Some brand-name houses even trusted him to order materials directly from China and inspect the quality himself. Which is why he and Xian knew each other. They'd met at the port. One day we all had lunch together there. When we finished eating, we said goodbye to Pasquale, and Xian and I got in the car and headed toward Vesuvius. Volcanoes are usually depicted in dark colors, but Vesuvius is green; from a distance, it's a vast mantle of moss. But before we got to the turnoff for the towns around Vesuvius, the car pulled into the courtyard of a building. Pasquale was there waiting for us. I had no idea why. Pasquale got out of his car and climbed straight into the trunk of Xian's. I wanted an explanation:

"What's going on? Why's he getting in the trunk?"

"Don't worry. Now we'll go to Terzigno, to the factory."

A sort of Minotaur figure got in behind the wheel. He'd been in Pasquale's car and seemed to know exactly what to do. He put the engine in reverse, backed out the gate, and, before pulling out into the street, produced a pistol. A semiautomatic. He racked a round and stuck it between his legs. I didn't breathe, but the Minotaur, catching sight of me in the rearview mirror, realized I was staring at him anxiously.

"They tried to do us in once."

"Who?"

I tried to get him to explain it all from the beginning.

"The ones who don't want the Chinese learning to work in high fashion. The ones who just want fabric from China, nothing else."

I didn't understand. I just didn't understand. Xian intervened, in his usual soothing way.

"Pasquale's helping us learn. Learn to work the quality garments they don't trust us with yet. We're learning how to make clothes from him."

After Xian's explanation, the Minotaur attempted to justify the pistol:

"So . . . one of them popped up there once, right there, see, in the middle of the piazza, and fired on our car. Hit the motor and windshield wipers. If they'd wanted to, they could've bumped us off. But it was just a warning. If they try it again though, this time I'm ready."

The Minotaur explained that the best technique when driving is to keep the pistol between your thighs. Putting it on the dashboard slows you down—you lose too much time grabbing it. The road to Terzigno is uphill, and I could smell the clutch burning. I was less afraid of a burst of submachine-gun fire than the recoil of the engine, which might make the pistol fire into the driver's scrotum. We arrived without a hitch. As soon as the car came to a stop, Xian went and opened the trunk. Pasquale got out, looking like a balled-up Kleenex trying to flatten itself out. He came over to me and said:

"It's the same story every time. Not even a fugitive hides like this . . . But it's better they don't see me in the car, or else . . ."

He sliced a finger across his neck. The factory was big, but not enormous. Xian had described it to me proudly. It belonged to him, but housed nine microfactories of nine Chinese entrepreneurs. It was like a chessboard inside: each factory had a square, with its own workers and benches. Xian had given each company the same amount of space as the factories in Las Vegas, and the contracts were auctioned off using the same method. He'd decided not to let children into the work zone and had organized the shifts as in Italian factories. What's more, when they did work for other companies, they didn't ask for cash up front. In short, Xian was becoming a serious player in the Italian fashion business.

Chinese factories in China were competing with Chinese factories in Italy. As a result Prato, Rome, and the Chinatowns of half of Italy were suffering terribly; they'd experienced such a quick boom that the collapse felt even more sudden. There was only one way for the Chinese factories in Italy to save themselves: they had to become experts of high fashion, capable of doing top-quality work. They had to learn from the Italians, from the Las Vegas factory owners, to go from being junk manufacturers to the brands' trusted suppliers in southern Italy. They had to take the place of the Italian underground factories, appropriate their logic, workspaces, and language. They had to do the same work, but for a little less money and in a little less time.

Pasquale took some fabric out of a suitcase: a dress he was supposed to cut and sew in his factory. He did it here instead, on a table in front of a camera, his image projected onto a sheet hanging behind him. As he talked, a girl with a microphone translated into Chinese. This was his fifth lesson.

"You must take great care with the seams. The seam has to be light but not nonexistent."

The Chinese triangle: San Giuseppe Vesuviano, Terzigno, Ottaviano. The hub of the Chinese clothing business. Everything that's happening in the Chinese communities of Italy happened first in Terzigno. The first production cycles, the first quality manufacturing, as well as the first murders. This is where Wang Dingjm was killed. A forty-year-old immigrant who'd driven down from Rome for a party some other Chinese were throwing. They invited him, then shot him in the head. Wang was a snakehead—a scout—tied to the criminal cartels in Beijing that organize the clandestine entry of Chinese into Italy. Trafficking in humans, the snakeheads often clash with their clients. They promise a certain quantity and then they don't deliver. Just as a drug dealer is killed when he keeps back a part of his earnings, a snakehead is killed when he cheats on his goods, on human beings. But it's not just Mafiosi who die. On one of the factory doors was the photo of a young girl. Pretty face, pink cheeks, eyes so dark they seemed painted. It was hung exactly where one would tradition-ally expect the yellow face of Mao, but this was a picture of Zhang Xiangbi, a pregnant girl who had been killed a few years earlier. She used to work here. A mechanic from these parts had fancied her; she used to walk past his garage, and liking what he saw, he decided that was reason enough to have her. The Chinese work like dogs, they slither like snakes, they're quieter than deaf-mutes, they're not al-lowed any means of resistance or free will. Such is the axiom every-one—or almost everyone—bears in mind. But Zhang had resisted. She tried to escape when the mechanic came near her, but she couldn't report him. She was Chinese, and every sign of visibility was denied her. The next time the man didn't take no for an answer. He beat and kicked her until she fainted, then slit her throat and threw her body in a deep well, where it remained for days, bloated with wa-ter. Pasquale knew this story and was devastated by it. Every time he went to give a lesson, he made sure to go over to Zhang's brother and ask how he was, see if he needed anything. But he always got the same response: "Nothing, thanks."

Pasquale and I became close. He was like a prophet when he spoke about fabric and was overly fastidious in clothing stores; it was impos-sible even to go for a stroll with him because he'd plant himself in front of every shop window and criticize the cut of a jacket or feel ashamed for the tailor who'd designed such a skirt. He could predict the longevity of a particular style of pants, jacket, or dress, and the ex-act number of washings before the fabric would start to sag. Pasquale initiated me into the complicated world of textiles. I even started going to his home. His family—his wife and three children—made me happy. They were always busy without ever being frenetic. That evening the smaller children were running around the house barefoot as usual, but without making a racket. Pasquale had turned on the television and was flipping channels, but all of a sudden he froze. He squinted at the screen, as if he were nearsighted, though he could see perfectly well. No one was talking, but the silence became more intense. His wife, Luisa, must have sensed something because she went over to the television and clasped her hand over her mouth, as if she'd just witnessed something terrible and were holding back a scream. On TV Angelina Jolie was treading the red carpet at the Oscars, dressed in a gorgeous garment. One of those custom-made outfits that Italian designers fall over each other to offer to the stars. An outfit that Pasquale had made in an underground factory in Arzano. All they'd said to him was "This one's going to America." Pasquale had worked on hundreds of outfits going to America, but that white suit was something else. He still remembered all the measurements. The cut of the neck, the circumference of the wrists. And the pants. He'd run his hands inside the legs and could still picture the naked body that every tailor forms in his mind—not an erotic figure but one defined by the curves of muscles, the ceramics of bones. A body to dress, a meditation of muscle, bone, and bearing. Pasquale still remembered the day he'd gone to the port to pick up the fabric. They'd commissioned three suits from him, without saying anything else. They knew whom they were for, but no one had told Pasquale.

In Japan the tailor of the bride to the heir to the throne had had a state reception given in his honor. A Berlin newspaper had dedicated six pages to the tailor of Germany's first woman chancellor, pages that spoke of craftsmanship, imagination, and elegance. Pasquale was filled with rage, a rage that it's impossible to express. And yet satisfaction is a right, and merit deserves recognition. Deep in his gut he knew he'd done a superb job and he wanted to be able to say so. He knew he deserved something more. But no one had said a word to him. He'd discovered it by accident, by mistake. His rage was an end in itself, justified but pointless. He couldn't tell anyone, couldn't even whisper as he sat looking at the newspaper the next morning. He

couldn't say, "I made that suit." No one would have believed that Angelina Jolie would go to the Academy Awards wearing an outfit made
in Arzano, by Pasquale. The best and the worst. Millions of dollars
and 600 euros a month. Neither Angelina Jolie nor the designer could
have known. When everything possible has been done, when talent,
skill, ability, and commitment are fused in a single act, when all this
isn't enough to change anything, then you just want to lie down,
stretch out on nothing, in nothing. To vanish slowly, let the minutes
wash over you, sink into them as if they were quicksand. To do nothing but breathe. Besides, nothing will change things, not even an outfit for Angelina Jolie at the Oscars.

Pasquale left the house without even bothering to shut the door.
Luisa knew where he was going; she knew he was headed to Secondigliano and whom he was going to see. She threw herself on the
couch and buried her face in a pillow like a child. I don't know why,
but when Luisa started to cry, it made me think of a poem by Vittorio
Bodini. Lines that tell of the strategies southern Italian peasants used
to keep from becoming soldiers, to avoid going off to fill the trenches
of World War I in defense of borders they knew nothing of.

> At the time of the other war peasants and smugglers
> put tobacco leaves under their arms
> to make themselves ill.
> The artificial fevers, the supposed malaria
> that made their bodies tremble and their teeth rattle
> were their verdict
> on governments and history.

That's how Luisa's weeping seemed to me—a verdict on government and history. Not a lament for a satisfaction that went uncele-
brated. It seemed to me an amended chapter of Marx's *Capital*, a
paragraph added to Adam Smith's *The Wealth of Nations*, a new sentence in John Maynard Keynes's *General Theory of Employment, Inter-*

est and Money, a note in Max Weber's *The Protestant Ethic and the Spirit of Capitalism*. A page added or removed, a forgotten page that never got written or that perhaps was written many times over but never recorded on paper. Not a desperate act but an analysis. Severe, detailed, precise, reasoned. I imagined Pasquale in the street, stomping his feet as if knocking snow from his boots. Like a child who is surprised to discover that life has to be so painful. He'd managed up till then. Managed to hold himself back, to do his job, to want to do it. And do it better than anyone else. But the minute he saw that outfit, saw that body moving inside the very fabric he'd caressed, he felt alone, all alone. Because when you know something only within the confines of your own flesh and blood, it's as if you don't really know it. And when work is only about staying afloat, surviving, when it's merely an end in itself, it becomes the worst kind of loneliness.

I saw Pasquale two months later. They'd put him on truck detail. He hauled all sorts of stuff—legal and illegal—for the Licciardi family businesses. Or at least that's what they said. The best tailor in the world was driving trucks for the Camorra, back and forth between Secondigliano and Lago di Garda. He asked me to lunch and gave me a ride in his enormous vehicle. His hands were red, his knuckles split. As with every truck driver who grips a steering wheel for hours, his hands freeze up and his circulation is bad. His expression was troubled; he'd chosen the job out of spite, out of spite for his destiny, a kick in the ass of his life. But you can't tolerate things indefinitely, even if walking away means you're worse off. During lunch he got up to go say hello to some of his accomplices, leaving his wallet on the table. A folded-up page from a newspaper fell out. I opened it. It was a photograph, a cover shot of Angelina Jolie dressed in white. She was wearing the suit Pasquale had made, the jacket caressing her bare skin. You need talent to dress skin without hiding it; the fabric has to follow the body, has to be designed to trace its movements.

I'm sure that every once in a while, when he's alone, maybe when he's finished eating, when the children have fallen asleep on the couch, worn-out from playing, while his wife is talking on the phone with her mother before starting on the dishes, right at that moment Pasquale opens his wallet and stares at that newspaper photo. And I'm sure that he's happy as he looks at the masterpiece he created with his own hands. A rabid happiness. But no one will ever know.

THE SYSTEM

The huge international clothing market, the vast archipelago of Italian elegance, is fed by the System. With its companies, men, and products, the System has reached every corner of the globe. *System*—a term everyone here understands, but that still needs decoding elsewhere, an obscure reference for anyone unfamiliar with the power dynamics of the criminal economy. *Camorra* is a nonexistent word, a term of contempt used by narcs and judges, journalists and scriptwriters; it's a generic indication, a scholarly term, relegated to history—a name that makes Camorristi smile. The word clan members use is *System*—"I belong to the Secondigliano System"—an eloquent term, a mechanism rather than a structure. The criminal organization coincides directly with the economy, and the dialectic of commerce is the framework of the clans.

The Secondigliano System has gained control of the entire clothing manufacturing chain, and the real production zone and business center is the outskirts of Naples. Everything that is impossible to do elsewhere because of the inflexibility of contracts, laws, and copyrights is feasible here, just north of the city. Structured around the entrepreneurial power of the clans, the area produces astronomical capital, amounts unimaginable for any legal industrial conglomeration. The interrelated textile, leatherworking, and shoe manufacturing activities set up by the clans produce garments and accessories identical to those of the principal Italian fashion houses.

The workforce in clan operations is highly skilled, with decades of experience under Italy's and Europe's most important designers. The same hands that once worked under the table for the big labels now work for the clans. Not only is the workmanship perfect, but the materials are exactly the same, either bought directly on the Chinese market or sent by the designer labels to the underground factories participating in the auctions. Which means that the clothes made by the clans aren't the typical counterfeit goods, cheap imitations, or copies passed off as the real thing, but rather a sort of false-true. All that's missing is the final step: the brand name, the official authorization of the motherhouse. But the clans usurp that authorization without bothering to ask anybody's permission. Besides, what clients anywhere in the world are really interested in is quality and design. And the clans provide just that—brand as well as quality—so there really is no difference. The Secondigliano clans have acquired entire retail chains, thus spreading their commercial network across the globe and dominating the international clothing market. They also provide distribution to outlet stores. Products of slightly inferior quality have yet another venue: African street vendors and market stalls. Nothing goes unused. From factory to store, from retailer to distributor, hundreds of companies and thousands of employees are elbowing each other to get in on the garment business run by the Secondigliano clans.

Everything is coordinated and managed by the Directory. I hear the term constantly—every time bar talk turns to business, or in the usual complaints about not having work: "It's the Directory that wanted it that way." "The Directory better get busy and start doing things on a bigger scale." They sound like fragments from a discussion in postrevolutionary France, when the collective governing body was

Napoléon's Directoire. "Directory" is the name the magistrates at the Naples DDA—the District Anti-Mafia Directorate—gave to the economic, financial, and operative structure of a group of businessmen and Camorra family bosses in north Naples. A structure with a purely economic role. The Directory, and not the hit men or firing squads, represents the real power of the organization.

The clans affiliated with the Secondigliano Alliance—the Licciardi, Contini, Mallardo, Lo Russo, Bocchetti, Stabile, Prestieri, and Bosti families, as well as the more autonomous Sarno and Di Lauro families—make up the Directory, whose territory includes Secondigliano, Scampia, Piscinola, Chiaiano, Miano, San Pietro a Patierno, as well as Giugliano and Ponticelli. As the Directory's federal structure offered greater autonomy to the clans, the more organic structure of the Alliance ultimately crumbled. The Directory's production board included businessmen from Casoria, Arzano, and Melito, who ran companies such as Valent, Vip Moda, Vocos, and Vitec, makers of imitation Valentino, Ferré, Versace, and Armani sold all over the world. A 2004 inquiry, coordinated by Naples DDA prosecutor Filippo Beatrice, uncovered the Camorra's vast economic empire. It all started with a small detail, one of those little things that could have passed unnoticed: a clothing store in Chemnitz, Germany, hired a Secondigliano boss. A rather unusual choice. It turned out he actually owned the store, which was registered under a false name. From this lead, followed by wiretaps and state witnesses, the Naples DDA reconstructed each link in the Secondigliano clans' production and commercial chain.

They set up shop everywhere. In Germany they had stores and warehouses in Hamburg, Dortmund, and Frankfurt, and in Berlin there were two Laudano shops. In Spain they were in Barcelona and Madrid; in Brussels; in Vienna; and in Portugal in Oporto and Boavista. They had a jacket shop in London and stores in Dublin, Amsterdam, Finland, Denmark, Sarajevo, and Belgrade. The Secondigliano clans also crossed the Atlantic, investing in Canada, the United States, even in South America. The American network was immense; millions of jeans were sold in shops in New York, Miami Beach, New Jersey, and Chicago, and they virtually monopolized the market in Florida. American retailers and shopping-center owners wanted to deal exclusively with Secondigliano brokers; haute couture garments from big-name designers at reasonable prices meant that crowds of customers would flock to their shopping centers and malls. The names on the labels were perfect.

A matrix for printing Versace's signature Medusa's head was found in a lab on the outskirts of Naples. In Secondigliano word spread that the American market was dominated by Directory clothes, making it easier for young people eager to go to America and become salespeople. They were inspired by the success of Vip Moda, whose jeans filled Texas stores, where they were passed off as Valentino.

Business spread to the southern hemisphere as well. A boutique in Five Dock, New South Wales, became one of Australia's hottest addresses for elegant clothing, and there were also shops and warehouses in Sydney. The Secondigliano clans dominated the clothing market in Brazil—in Rio de Janeiro and São Paulo. They had plans to open a store for American and European tourists in Cuba, and they'd been investing in Saudi Arabia and North Africa for a while. The distribution mechanism the Directory had put in place was based on warehouses—that's how they're referred to in the wiretappings—veritable clearing stations for people and merchandise, depots for every kind of clothing. The warehouses were the center of a commercial hub, the place where agents picked up the merchandise to be distributed to the clans' stores or other retailers. The concept was old, that of the *magliari*, the Neapolitan traveling salesmen; after the Second World War they invaded half the planet, eating up the miles lugging their bags stuffed with socks, shirts, and jackets. Applying their age-old mercantile experience on a larger scale, the *magliari* became full-fledged commercial agents who could sell anywhere and every-where, from neighborhood markets to malls, from parking lots to gas stations. The best of them made a qualitative leap, selling large lots of clothing directly to retailers. According to investigations, some businessmen organized the distribution of fakes, offering logistical support to the sales reps, the *magliari*. They paid travel and hotel expenses in advance, provided vans and cars, and guaranteed legal assistance in the case of arrest or confiscation of merchandise. And of course they pocketed the earnings. A business in which each family invoiced approximately 300 million euros annually.

The Italian labels started to protest against the Secondigliano cartels' large fake market only after the DDA uncovered the entire operation. Before that, they had no plans for a negative publicity campaign, never filed charges, or divulged to the press the harmful workings of the illegal production. It is difficult to comprehend why the brands never took a stand against the clans, but there are probably many reasons. Denouncing them would have meant forgoing once and for all their cheap labor sources in Campania and Puglia. The clans would have closed down access to the clothing factories around Naples and hindered relations with factories in Eastern Europe and Asia. And given the vast number of shopping centers operated directly by the clans, denouncing them would have jeopardized thousands of retail sales contacts. In many places the families handle transportation and agents, so fingering them would have meant a sudden rise in distribution costs. Besides, the clans weren't ruining the brands' image, but simply taking advantage of their advertising and symbolic charisma. The garments they turned out were not inferior and didn't disgrace the brands' quality or design image. Not only did the clans not create any symbolic competition with the designer labels, they actually helped promote products whose market price made them prohibitive to the general public. In short, the clans were promoting the brand. If hardly anyone wears a label's clothes, if they're seen only on live mannequins on the runway, the market slowly dies and the prestige of the name declines. What's more, the Neapolitan factories produced counterfeit garments in sizes that the designer labels, for the sake of their image, do not make. But the clans certainly weren't going to trouble themselves about image when there was a profit to be made. Through the false-true business and income from drug trafficking, the Secondigliano clans acquired stores and shopping centers where genuine articles were increasingly mixed in with the fakes, thus erasing any distinction. In a way the System sustained the legal fashion empire in the moment when prices rose sharply; it actually took advantage of this crisis and continued to promote the "Made in Italy" concept throughout the world, earning exponential sums.

The Secondigliano clans realized that their vast international distribution and sales network was their greatest asset, even stronger than drug trafficking. Narcotics and clothing often moved along the same routes. The System's entrepreneurial energies were also invested in technology, however. Investigations in 2004 revealed that the clans use their commercial networks to import Chinese high-tech products for European distribution. Europe had the form—the brand, the fame, and the advertising—and China the content—the actual product, cheap labor, and inexpensive materials. The System brought the two together, winning out all around. Aware that the economy was on the brink, the clans targeted Chinese industrial zones already manufacturing for big Western companies; in this they followed the pattern of businesses that first invested in southern Italy's urban sprawl and then gradually shifted to China. They got the idea of ordering batches of high-tech products to resell on the European market, obviously with a fake brand name that would increase desirability. But they were cautious; as with a batch of cocaine, they first tested the quality of the products the Chinese factories sold them. After confirming their market validity, they launched one of the most prosperous intercontinental dealings in criminal history. Digital cameras, video cameras, and power tools: drills, grinders, pneumatic hammers, planes, and sanders, all marketed as Bosch, Hammer, or Hilti. When the Secondigliano boss Paolo Di Lauro started doing business with China, he was ten years ahead of the initiative of Confindustria, the Italian Manufacturers' Association, to improve business ties with Asia. The Di Lauro clan sold thousands of Canons and Hitachis on the East European market. Thanks to Camorra imports, items that were once the prerogative of the upper-middle class were now accessible to a broader public. To guarantee a stronger entry into the market, the clans offered practically the identical product, slapping the brand name on at the end.

The Di Lauro and Contini clans' investment in China, which was the focus of a 2004 Naples DDA inquiry, demonstrates the entrepreneurial farsightedness of the bosses. The era of big business was finished and the criminal conglomerates had crumbled as a result. The Nuova Camorra Organizzata or New Organized Camorra, established by Raffaele Cutolo in the 1980s, had been a sort of enormous company, a centralized conglomerate. It was followed by La Nuova Famiglia or New Family, which Carmine Alfieri and Antonio Bardellino operated as a federal structure of economically autonomous families united by common interests. But this too proved unwieldy.

The flexibility of today's economy has permitted small groups of manager bosses operating in hundreds of enterprises in well-defined sectors to control the social and financial arenas. There is now a horizontal structure—much more flexible than Cosa Nostra, and much more permeable to new alliances than the Calabrian 'Ndrangheta—that draws constantly on new clans, and adopts new strategies in entering cutting-edge markets. Dozens of police operations in recent years have revealed that both the Sicilian Mafia and the 'Ndrangheta needed to go through the Neapolitan clans to purchase big drug lots. The Naples and Campania cartels were supplying cocaine and heroin at good prices, so buying from them often proved easier and more economical than buying directly from South American and Albanian dealers.

The restructuring of the clans notwithstanding, the Camorra is the most solid criminal organization in Europe in terms of membership. For every Sicilian Mafioso there are five Camorristi, eight for every 'Ndranghetista. Three to four times as many members as the other organizations. The constant spotlight on Cosa Nostra and the obsessive attention to Mafia bombs have provided the perfect media distraction for the Camorra, which has remained practically unknown. With the post-Fordist restructuring, the Naples clans have stopped giving handouts to the masses, and the rise in petty crime in the city can be explained by this curtailing of stipends. Camorra groups no longer need to maintain widespread military-style control—or at least not always—because their principal business activities now take place outside Naples.

Investigations conducted by the Naples anti-Mafia prosecutor reveal that the Camorra's flexible, federalist structure has completely transformed the fabric of the families: instead of diplomatic alliances and stable pacts, clans now operate more like business committees. The Camorra's flexibility reflects its need to move capital, set up and liquidate companies, circulate money, and invest quickly in real estate without geographic restrictions or heavy dependence on political mediation. The clans no longer need to organize in large bodies. These days a group of people can decide to band together, rob, smash store windows, and steal without risking being killed or taken over by the clan. The gangs rampaging around Naples are not composed exclusively of individuals who commit crimes to pad their wallets, buy fancy cars, or live in luxury. They know that by joining forces and increasing the degree and amount of violence, they can often improve their economic capacity, becoming interlocutors for the clans. The Camorra is made up of groups that suck like voracious lice, thus hindering all economic development, and others that operate as instant innovators, pushing their businesses to new heights of development and trade. Caught between these two opposing yet complementary movements, the skin of the city is lacerated and torn. In Naples cruelty is the most complex and affordable strategy for becoming a successful businessman. The air of the city smells like war, you can breathe it through every pore; it has the rancid odor of sweat, and the streets have become open-air gyms for training to ransack, plunder, and steal, for exercising the gymnastics of power, and the spinning of economic growth.

In the urban outskirts the System has expanded, rising like bread dough. Local and regional governments thought they could oppose the System by not doing business with the clans. But that wasn't enough. They underrated the power of the families and neglected the phenomenon, considering it an aspect of urban blight. As a result Campania is now the Italian region with the highest number of cities under observation for Camorra infiltration. A total of seventy-one municipal administrations have been dissolved since 1991. An extraordinary number, far surpassing that in the other regions of Italy: forty-four in Sicily, thirty-four in Calabria, seven in Puglia. In the province of Naples alone, town councils have been dissolved in Pozzuoli, Quarto, Marano, Melito, Portici, Ottaviano, San Giuseppe Vesuviano, San Gennaro Vesuviano, Terzigno, Calandrino, Sant' Antimo, Tufino, Crispano, Casamarciano, Nola, Liveri, Boscoreale, Poggiomarino, Pompei, Ercolano, Pimonte, Casola di Napoli, Sant' Antonio Abate, Santa Maria la Carità, Torre Annunziata, Torre del Greco, Volla, Brusciano, Acerra, Casoria, Pomigliano d' Arco, and Frattamaggiore. Only nine of the ninety-two municipalities in the province of Naples have never had external commissioners, inquiries, or monitoring. Clan businesses have determined zoning regulations, infiltrated local sanitation services, purchased land immediately prior to its being declared suitable for building and then subcontracted the construction of shopping centers, and imposed patron saints' days festivities that depend on their multiservice companies, from catering to cleaning, from transportation to trash collection.

Never in the economy of a region has there been such a widespread, crushing presence of criminality as in Campania in the last ten years. Unlike the Sicilian Mafia groups, the Camorra clans don't need politicians; it's the politicians who need the System. In Campania a deliberate strategy leaves the political structures that are most visible, those under media scrutiny, formally immune to connivances and contiguities. But in the countryside, in the towns where the clans need armed protection and cover for fugitives, and where their economic maneuvers are more exposed, alliances between politicians and Camorra families are tighter. Camorra clans rise to power through their commercial empires. And that allows them to control everything else.

The business-criminal transformation of the suburbs of Secondigliano and Scampia was crafted by the Licciardi family, whose center of operations at Masseria Cardone is practically impregnable. The boss Gennaro Licciardi, known as 'a scigna—la scimmia, the monkey—for his striking resemblance to a gorilla or an orangutan, initiated the metamorphosis. In the late 1980s Licciardi was the Secondigliano lieutenant to Liugi Giuliano, the boss of Forcella, an area in the heart of Naples. The outskirts were considered an awful place—a territory without stores or shopping centers, on the margins of every kind of wealth, where not even the leeches could extort enough cuts to feed themselves on. But Licciardi realized the area could become a hub for drug sales, a free port for transportation, and a collection point for cheap labor. A place that would soon be sprouting the scaffolding of new construction as the city expanded. Gennaro Licciardi did not succeed in fully implementing his strategy. He died at thirty-eight, in prison, of an incredibly banal umbilical hernia—a pathetic end for a boss. Especially because he'd once been involved in a brawl with members of the two big Camorra fronts, the Nuova Camorra Organizzata and the Nuova Famiglia, while awaiting a hearing in the Naples courthouse lockup. He was stabbed sixteen times, all over his body. But he'd come out alive.

The Licciardi family transformed what was merely a reservoir of cheap labor into a machine for the narcotics trade: an international criminal business. Thousands of people were co-opted, enrolled, or crushed by the System. Clothes and drugs. Business investments before all else. After the death of Gennaro the monkey, his brothers Pietro and Vincenzo took over the militant side of the clan, but it was Maria, known as *'a piccerella—la piccoletta* or the little one—who wielded the economic power.

After the fall of the Berlin wall, Pietro Licciardi transferred the majority of his own investments, legal and illegal, to Prague and Brno. Criminal activity in the Czech Republic was completely controlled by the Secondigliano clan, which applied the logic of the productive outskirts and set out to capture the German market. Pietro Licciardi had a manager's profile, and his business associates called him "the Roman emperor" because of his authoritarian attitude and arrogant belief that the entire world was an extension of Secondigliano. He'd opened a clothing store in China—a commercial pied-à-terre in Taiwan—to take advantage of cheap labor and move in on the internal Chinese market. He was arrested in Prague in June 1999. Licciardi was a ruthless fighter, accused of ordering the bomb that was placed on Via Cristallini in the Sanità neighborhood in 1998 during the conflicts between the outlying and center-city clans. A bomb to punish the entire neighborhood, not merely the clan leaders. When the car exploded, metal and glass went flying like bullets, hitting thirteen people. But there wasn't sufficient proof to convict him and he was acquitted. The Licciardi clan's primary commercial activities in Italy were in the garment and retail industry, centered around Castelnuovo del Garda in the Veneto. Not far from there, in Portogruaro, Pietro Licciardi's brother-in-law Vincenzo Pernice was arrested, along with some clan supporters, including Renato Peluso, who lived in Castelnuovo del Garda. As a fugitive Pietro Licciardi was harbored by Veneto retailers and businessmen tied to the clan—not clan members in the full sense of the term, but accomplices intimately involved in the business-criminal organization. In addition to possessing a remarkable talent for business, the Licciardis also had a military squadron. Subsequent to Pietro's and Maria's arrests, the clan is run by Vincenzo Licciardi, the fugitive boss who coordinates both military and economic activities.

The Licciardi clan has always been particularly vindictive. In 1991 they brutally avenged the death of Gennaro Licciardi's nephew, Vincenzo Esposito. Heir to the ruling family in Secondigliano, Vincenzo was known as *il principino*, the little prince. He was twenty-one when he was killed in Monterosa, a neighborhood run by the Prestieris, one of the families in the Alliance. He'd gone there on his motorcycle to demand an explanation for the violent treatment some of his friends had received. With his helmet on, he was "mistaken" for a killer and shot. The Licciardis accused the Di Lauros, close allies of the Prestieris, of supplying the killers for the hit. According to the *pentito* or "penitent" Luigi Giuliano, it was Di Lauro himself who orchestrated the little prince's murder because he'd been meddling too much in certain affairs. Whatever the motive, Licciardi power was so unassailable that the clans involved were required to purge those potentially responsible for Esposito's death. They instigated a slaughter that in days left fourteen people dead for their direct or indirect involvement in the murder of the young heir.

The System also transformed classic extortion and usury practices. Aware that shopkeepers needed cash and banks were becoming increasingly rigid, the clans situated themselves between suppliers and retailers. Retailers who must purchase their own merchandise can either pay in cash or with drafts, but if they pay in cash things cost half to two-thirds less, so both retailer and supplier prefer this method. The clans have become hidden financiers, offering cash at 10 percent interest on average. In this way a corporate relationship is automatically established among the buyer, the seller, and the clan. The proceeds are split fifty-fifty, but if a retailer runs into debt, higher and higher percentages flow into the clan's coffers, and the retailer is eventually reduced to a straw man on a monthly salary. Unlike banks, which seize everything when someone falls into debt, the clans continue to utilize their assets by letting the experienced individuals who've lost their property continue to work. According to a *pentito* in the 2004 DDA investigation, 50 percent of the shops in Naples alone are actually run by the Camorra.

Only beggar clans inept at business and desperate to survive still practice the kind of monthly extortions seen in Nanni Loy's film *Mi manda Picone*, or the door-to-door rounds at Christmas, Easter, and on August 15. Everything has changed. The Nuvoletta clan of Marano, on the northern outskirts of Naples, set up a more efficient extortion racket based on reciprocal advantage and the taxing of supplies. Giuseppe Gala, known as Showman, had become one of the most valued reps in the food business. He was much in demand, representing Bauli and Von Holten, and through Vip Alimentari he became the exclusive Parmalat rep in Marano clan territory. He boasted of his talent in a wiretapped conversation submitted to the Naples DDA judges in the fall of 2003: "I've burned them all, we're the strongest on the market."

The companies Peppe Gala handled were, in fact, guaranteed representation throughout his territory as well as a high number of orders. And retailers and supermarkets were more than happy to deal with him since he could pressure suppliers into offering bigger discounts. Being a System man, Showman also controlled transportation, which meant he could ensure favorable prices and prompt delivery.

Products "adopted" by the clans are not imposed through intimidation but rather by means of advantageous pricing. The concerns Gala represented declared they had been victims of the Camorra racket and had had to submit to the diktat of the clans. Yet data from Confcommercio—the Italian business confederation—reveals that from 1998 to 2003 the companies that turned to Gala experienced a 40 to 80 percent increase in annual sales. Gala's financial strategies even resolved the clans' problems of ready cash. He went so far as to impose a surcharge on *panettone*, the ubiquitous Christmas cake, to give year-end bonuses to the families of imprisoned Nuvoletta clan members. Success was fatal to Showman, however. According to state witnesses, he tried to become the exclusive agent for the drug market as well. The Nuvoletta family wouldn't hear of it. In January 2003 he was found dead in his car; he'd been burned alive.

The Nuvolettas are the only family outside Sicily that sits in the cupola, the high command of Cosa Nostra. Not simply allies or affiliates, they are one of the most powerful groups in the bosom of the Mafia, with structural ties to the Corleones. So powerful—according to *pentito* Giovanni Brusca—that when in the late 1990s the Sicilians decided to plant bombs all over Italy, they asked the Marano clan for advice and cooperation. The Nuvolettas thought the idea was crazy, a strategy that had more to do with political favors than military results. They refused to participate in the attacks or provide logistical support, a refusal expressed without any hint of reprisal. Totò Riina personally implored the boss Angelo Nuvoletta to intervene and corrupt the judges in his first mass trial, but here too the Marano clan refused to help the military wing of the Corleone family. During the feuds within La Nuova Famiglia, after their victory over Cutolo, the Nuvolettas sent for Giovanni Brusca, the boss of San Giovanni Jato and the murderer of Judge Giovanni Falcone.* They wanted Brusca to elimi-

---

*Falcone, who was killed on May 23, 1992, was an important anti-Mafia magistrate and one of the major figures in the 1986–87 Maxi Trial, in which 360 Mafiosi were convicted. Falcone and his wife, Francesca Morvillo—also a magistrate—and three policemen were killed when a roadside bomb exploded as they drove from the airport to Palermo.—Trans.

nate five people in Campania and dissolve two of them in acid. They called him the way you'd call a plumber. He disclosed to the judges the technique for dissolving Luigi and Vittorio Vastarella:

> We gave instructions for the purchase of a hundred liters of hydrochloric acid, and we also needed two-hundred-liter metal containers, the kind normally used for storing olive oil, with the top part cut off. In our experience, each container takes fifty liters of acid, and seeing as how the suppression of two people was anticipated, we had them prepare two.

The Nuvolettas, in cooperation with the Nettuno and Polverino subclans, also altered narcotraffic investment strategies, creating a popular shareholding system for cocaine. A 2004 Naples DDA investigation revealed that the clan was allowing everyone to participate in the acquisition of cocaine via intermediaries. Retirees, workers, and small businessmen would hand over money to agents, who then invested it in drug lots. If you invested your pension of 600 euros in cocaine, you'd double your money in a month. The only guarantee was the middleman's word, but the investment proved regularly advantageous. The profit far outweighed the risk, especially compared with what one would have made in bank interest. The only disadvantage was organizational: small investors were often required to stash pats of cocaine—a way to distribute the supply and make it practically impossible to sequester. By involving the lower-middle class, who were far removed from criminal activity but tired of trusting the banks with their assets, the Camorra clans increased the amount of capital available for investment. The Nuvoletta-Polverino group also metamorphosed retail distribution, making barbers and tanning centers the new cocaine retailers. They used straw men to reinvest narcotraffic profits in apartments, hotels, stock in service companies, private schools, even art galleries.

The person accused of handling the majority of Nuvoletta assets was Pietro Nocera. One of the most powerful managers in the area, he preferred to travel by Ferrari or private jet. In 2005 the Naples Court ordered the seizure of properties and companies worth more than 30 million euros, a mere 5 percent of his economic empire. Salvatore Speranza, who turned state's witness, disclosed that Nocera administered all the Nuvoletta clan money and was responsible for "the organization's investments in lands and the building trade in general." The Nuvolettas invest in Emilia Romagna, Veneto, Marche, and Lazio through Enea, a production and labor cooperative that Nocera managed even in hiding. Enea obtained public contracts for millions of euros in Bologna, Reggio Emilia, Modena, Venice, Ascoli Piceno, and Frosinone, invoicing extraordinary amounts. Nuvoletta business spread to Spain years ago. Nocera went to Tenerife to argue with a clan leader over construction costs for an imposing building complex. Nocera accused him of spending too much on expensive materials. I only ever saw the complex on the Internet: an eloquent website, an enormous complex of swimming pools and cement that the Nuvolettas built to get in on the tourism industry in Spain.

Paolo Di Lauro is a product of the Marano school; he began his criminal career as a Nuvoletta lieutenant. But he gradually took his distance and in the 1990s became the right-hand man of Michele D'Alessandro, the boss of Castellammare, representing him when he went into hiding. Di Lauro's plan was to coordinate the open-air drug markets using the same logic with which he'd managed store chains and jacket factories. Di Lauro realized that, after Gennaro Licciardi's death in prison, northern Naples could become the largest open-air drug market Italy or Europe had ever seen, and completely controlled by his men. Paolo Di Lauro had always acted silently and was more skilled at finances than fighting; he never openly invaded other bosses' territories and never allowed himself to be traced in inquiries or searches.

Among the first to disclose the organization's flowchart was the

Camorra informant Gaetano Conte. An informant with a particularly interesting story: a carabiniere who served as Francesco Cossiga's bodyguard in Rome. The qualities that led to his escorting the president of the Italian Republic also promoted him to friendship with Di Lauro. After being involved in clan extortions and drug trafficking, Conte decided to collaborate with the authorities, offering a wealth of information and details only a carabiniere would know how to provide.

Paolo Di Lauro is known as *Ciruzzo 'o milionario*, Ciruzzo the millionaire. A ridiculous nickname, but such labels have a precise logic, a calibrated sedimentation. I've always heard System people called by their nicknames, to the point where first and last names are often diluted or forgotten. No one chooses his own nickname; it emerges suddenly out of somewhere, for some reason, and someone picks up on it. Camorra nicknames are determined by destiny. Paolo Di Lauro was rebaptized *Ciruzzo 'o milionario* by Luigi Giuliano: one evening the boss watched Di Lauro take his place at the poker table as dozens of hundred-thousand-lire bills fell out of his pockets. "Who's this," Giuliano exclaimed, "*Ciruzzo 'o milionario?*" A name born on a drunken evening, a flash, the perfect wisecrack.

The anthology of nicknames is infinite. The Nuova Famiglia boss Carmine Alfieri got his name *'o 'ntufato*, the angry one, thanks to the dissatisfied sneer he wears constantly. Then there are ancestral nicknames that stick to the heirs; Mario Fabbrocino, the Vesuvius-area boss who colonized Argentina with Camorra money, is known as *'o graunar*—the coal merchant—because his ancestors sold coal. Other nicknames spring from Camorristi passions, such as Nicola *'o wrangler* Luongo for his fixation with Wrangler four-wheel drives, the System men's vehicle of choice. A whole series of nicknames are based on physical traits, such as Giovanni Birra *'a mazza*—club or bat—for his long, thin body; Costantino *capaianca* Iacomino for his premature *capelli bianchi* or white hair; Ciro Mazzarella *'o scellone* or angel, for his pronounced shoulder blades that look like an angel's wings; Nicola 'o mussuto Pianese for his skin so white it looks like dried cod; Rosario Privato mignolino or pinky finger; Dario De Simone 'o nano, the dwarf. There are inexplicable nicknames such as that of Antonio di Fraia 'u urpacchiello, which means a riding crop made from a dried donkey's penis. Then there's Carmine Di Girolamo, known as 'o sbirro or the narc for his ability to involve policemen and carabinieri in his operations. For some unknown reason Ciro Monteriso is known as 'o mago, the wizard. Pasquale Gallo of Torre Annunziata is 'o bellillo, or bello for his sweet face. Others are old family names: the Lo Russos are i capitoni or eels, the Mallardos are the Carlantoni, the Belfortes are the Mazzacane—dog killers—and the Piccolos the Quaqquaroni. Vincenzo Mazzarella is 'o pazzo, the crazy one, and Antonio Di Biasi is pavesino for his habit of munching on pavesino biscuits while out doing a job. Domenico Russo, boss of the Quartieri Spagnoli area in Naples, is called Mimì dei cani, Little Domenico of the dogs, because as a kid he sold puppies along Via Toledo. As for Antonio Carlo D'Onofrio, known as Carlucciello 'o mangiavatt'—Little Charles the cat eater—legend has it that he learned to shoot using stray cats as targets. Gennaro Di Chiara, who bolted violently anytime someone touched his face, earned the name file scupierto or live wire. There are also nicknames based on untranslatable onomatopoeic expressions such as that of Agostino Tardi, known as picc pocc, Domenico di Ronza scipp scipp, or the De Simone family, known as quaglia quaglia, the Aversanos, known as zig zag, Raffaele Giuliano 'o zuì, and Antonio Bifone zuzù.

All it took for Antonio Di Vicino to become lemon was to order the same drink several times. Vincenzo Benitozzi's round face earned him the name Cicciobello or fat boy, and Gennaro Lauro became 'o diciassette, perhaps because his street number was 17. And Giovanni Aprea was punt 'e curtiello—puntare il coltello or point the knife—because his grandfather played the role of an old Camorrista who teaches the boys to use a knife in Pasquale Squitieri's 1974 film I guappi.

A well-calibrated nickname, such as Francesco Schiavone's famous, ferocious *Sandokan*, can make or break the media fortune of a boss. He earned it for his resemblance to Kabir Bedi, the star of the Italian television series *Sandokan, the Tiger of Malaysia*, based on Emilio Salgari's novel. Or Pasquale Tavoletta, known as Zorro for his resemblance to the actor in the TV series. Or Luigi Giuliano, *'o re*—the king—also known as Lovigino because in intimate moments his American lovers would whisper, "I love Luigino." His brother Carmine is *'o lione*, the lion. Francesco Verde's alias is *'o negus*, a title of Ethiopian emperors, in honor of his stateliness and longevity as boss. Mario Schiavone is called *Menelek* after the famous Ethiopian emperor who opposed Italian troops, and Vincenzo Carobene is *Gheddafi* for his uncanny resemblance to the son of the Libyan general. The boss Francesco Bidognetti is known as *Cicciotto di Mezzanotte*, because anyone who got in his way would see midnight—the end—even at dawn, but some claim it was because he worked his way up through the ranks by protecting prostitutes. His whole clan came to be known as the Midnight clan.

Nearly every boss has a nickname, an unequivocally unique, identifying feature. A nickname for a boss is like stigmata for a saint, the mark of membership in the System. Anybody can call himself Francesco Schiavone, but there's only one Sandokan. Anybody can be named Carmine Alfieri, but only one turns around when he hears *'o 'ntufato*. Anyone can call himself Francesco Verde, but only one answers to the name *'o negus*. Anyone can be listed as Paolo Di Lauro at the registrar's office, but there's only one *Ciruzzo 'o milionario*.

Ciruzzo had decided to organize his affairs quietly, with low intensity but extensive force. For a long time he remained a boss unknown even to the police. The only time he was summoned by the authorities before he went into hiding was for an incident involving his son Nunzio, who assaulted a professor who'd dared to reprimand him. Paolo Di Lauro was in direct contact with South American cartels and created vast distribution networks through his alliance with Albanian cartels. Narcotraffic follows precise routes these days. Cocaine heads from South America to Spain, where it's either picked up or sent overland to Albania. Heroin, on the other hand, comes from Afghanistan, traveling through Bulgaria, Kosovo, and Albania. Hashish and marijuana cross the Mediterranean from North Africa by way of the Turks and Albanians. Di Lauro had direct contact with every point of entry into the drug market, and by following a painstaking strategy he became a successful entrepreneur in both leather and narcotics. In 1989 he founded the famous Confezioni Valent di Paolo Di Lauro & Co. Scheduled by statute to terminate activity in 2002, the company was sequestered in November 2001 by the Court of Naples. Valent had been awarded numerous contracts for cash-and-carry operations throughout Italy, and its corporate potential was enormous, ranging from furniture to fabrics, from meatpacking to mineral water. Valent supplied meals to public and private institutions and oversaw the butchering of all kinds of meats. Its stated objective was to construct hotels, restaurants, entertainment chains, and anything "appropriate for leisure." According to the statute, "The company may acquire lands and contract or subcontract buildings, shopping centers, or housing." The City of Naples granted its commercial licence in 1993, and the company was administered by Paolo Di Lauro's son Cosimo. For reasons connected to the clan, Paolo Di Lauro exited the scene in 1996, passing his shares to his wife, Luisa. The Di Lauro dynasty is built on self-denial. Luisa Di Lauro produced ten children; like the great dames of Italian industry, she increased the number of offspring to keep pace with the family business. Cosimo, Vincenzo, Ciro, Marco, Nunzio, and Salvatore are all clan members; the rest are still minors. Paolo Di Lauro had a predilection for investments in France, with shops in Nice, on rue de Charenton 129 in Paris, and 22 quai Perrache in Lyon. He wanted Italian fashion in France to be shaped by his stores and transported by his trucks; he wanted the power of Scampia to be smelled on the Champs-Élysées.

But in Secondigliano the great Di Lauro company was beginning to show signs of strain. Its many branches had grown hurriedly and autonomously, and the air was thickening in the drug marketplaces. In Scampia, on the other hand, there was the hope that everything would be resolved like the last time, when a solution had been found over a drink. A special drink, consumed while Di Lauro's son Domenico was lying at death's door in the hospital after a serious road accident. Domenico was a troubled boy. The children of bosses often fall into a sort of delirium of omnipotence, believing that entire cities and their inhabitants are at their disposal. According to police investigations, in October 2003 Domenico, together with his bodyguard and a group of friends, attacked the town of Casoria, smashing windows, garages, and cars, burning trash bins, splattering doors with spray paint, and melting plastic doorbells with cigarette lighters. Damage his father knew to pay for in silence, with the diplomacy of families who have to make up for the disasters of their scions without compromising their own authority. Domenico was rounding a curve on his motorcycle when he lost control and crashed. He died of his injuries after a few days in a coma. This tragic episode led to a meeting of the leaders, a punishment as well as an amnesty. Everyone in Scampia knows the story. It may not be true, but it has become legendary and is important for understanding how conflicts are resolved within the Camorra.

Legend has it that Paolo Di Lauro's dauphin, Gennaro Marino, known as McKay, went to comfort the boss in the hospital where Domenico lay dying. Di Lauro accepted his solace and then took him aside and offered him a drink: he pissed in a glass and handed it to McKay. Word had reached the boss's ears of certain behavior on the part of his favorite, things he simply could not condone. McKay had made some economic decisions without consulting Di Lauro, and sums of money had been withdrawn without his knowledge. The boss was aware of his dauphin's desire for autonomy, but he longed to pardon him, to consider it an excess of exuberance on the part of someone who is too good at what he does. Legend has it that McKay drank it all, every last drop. A big gulp of piss resolved the first schism to occur within the leadership of the Di Lauro clan. A transient truce, one that no kidney could have drained dry later on.

THE SECONDIGLIANO WAR

McKay and Angioletto had made up their minds. They'd decided to form their own group and wanted to make it official. All the old guard had agreed, and they'd made it clear they weren't trying to start a conflict. They wanted to become competitors, fair competitors, on the open market. Side by side, but independent. And so—according to the *pentito* Pietro Esposito—they sent a message to Cosimo Di Lauro, the cartel's regent. They wanted to meet with his father, Paolo, the top man, the boss, the association's number one. To talk to him in person, tell him they didn't agree with his reorganization decisions, remind him that they had children of their own now. They wanted to look him in the eye. Enough of this passing word from mouth to mouth, of messages sticky from the saliva of too many tongues—cell phones were out of the question because they could reveal his hiding place. Genny McKay wanted to meet with Paolo Di Lauro, the boss who was responsible for his rise in the business.

Cosimo formally accepts the request for a meeting; it's a matter of assembling all the top brass of the organization: bosses, underbosses, and area capos. It's impossible to say no. But Cosimo's already got it all figured out, or so it seems. He's got a clear idea of where he's taking things and knows how to organize his defense. And so—according to investigations and state witnesses—Cosimo doesn't send his underlings. He doesn't send Giovanni *cavallaro* Cortese, the horse dealer, the official spokesman, the one who'd always handled the Di Lauro family's relations with the outside world. Cosimo sends his brothers. Marco and Ciro case the meeting place, check it out, see which way the wind is blowing, but without letting anyone know they're there. No bodyguards, just a quick drive by. But not too quick. They note the prepared exit routes and the sentries in position, all without attracting attention. Then they report back to Cosimo, give him the details. He takes it all in. The meeting is a setup, a trap, a way to kill Paolo and whoever comes with him and to ratify a new era in the running of the cartel. Then again, you don't divide up an empire with a handshake. You have to cut it with a knife. That's what they say, what all the investigations and informants say.

Cosimo, the son Paolo put in charge of the narcotics trade, the one to whom he'd given the greatest responsibility, has to decide. It will be war. But he doesn't declare it openly. He keeps it all in his head—he doesn't want to alarm his rivals. He watches and waits to see what they'll do. He knows they'll attack him soon, knows he needs to be prepared for their claws in his flesh, but he also needs to play for time, to come up with a precise, infallible, winning strategy. To figure out whom he can count on, what forces he can control. Who is with him and who's against him. Secondigliano isn't big enough for both of them.

The Di Lauros make excuses for their father's absence: he's on the run, a wanted man for over ten years, and the police investigations make it difficult for him to move about. A missed appointment is nothing serious if you're one of the thirty most dangerous fugitives in Italy. After decades of smooth operations, the biggest narcotraffic holding company nationally and internationally is about to face a lethal crisis.

The Di Lauro clan has always been a well-organized business, structured along the lines of a multilevel company. According to the Naples anti-Mafia prosecutor's office, the first tier is made up of clan leaders Rosario Pariante, Raffaele Abbinante, Enrico D'Avanzo, and Arcangelo Valentino; they act as promoters and financiers, controlling the peddling and drug-trafficking activities through their direct affiliates. The second tier, which includes Gennaro Marino, Lucio De Lucia, and Pasquale Gargiulo, actually handle the drugs, do the purchasing and packaging, and manage relations with the pushers, who are guaranteed legal defense in case of arrest. The third level is composed of open-air drug-market capos; they have direct contact with the pushers, coordinate lookouts and escape routes, and secure the storehouses and places where the drugs are cut. The fourth level, the pushers, is the most exposed. Every level has its own sublevels that report exclusively to their leader rather than to the entire structure. This setup brings in profits of 500 percent on initial investments.

The Di Lauro business model has always reminded me of the mathematical concept of fractals, which textbooks explain using a bunch of bananas: each individual banana is actually a bunch of bananas, and in turn each of those bananas is a bunch of bananas, and so on to infinity. The Di Lauro clan invoices 500,000 euros a day through narcotraffic alone. Pushers, storehouse operators, and couriers often aren't part of the organization but simply salaried workers. Drug peddling is an enormous activity employing thousands of individuals, but they don't know who their boss is. They have a general idea of which Camorra family they work for, but that's all. If someone gets arrested and decides to talk, his knowledge of the organization is limited to a small, well-defined area; he'd be incapable of revealing the entire flowchart, the vast circumnavigation of the organization's economic and military power.

The whole economic and financial structure is backed by a military set up: a team of ferocious hit men with a vast network of flank support. A legion of killers—including Emanuele D' Ambra, Ugo *ugariello* De Lucia, Nando *'o schizzato* Emolo, Antonio *'o tavano* Ferrara, Salvatore Tamburino, Salvatore Petriccione, Umberto La Monica, and Antonio Mennetta—are flanked by neighborhood capos Gennaro Aruta, Ciro Saggese, Fulvio Montanino, Antonio Galeota, Constantino Sorrentino, and Giuseppe Prezioso, Cosimo's personal bodyguard. An outfit at least three hundred strong, all on monthly salary. A complex structure, meticulously planned and organized. A large fleet of cars and motorcycles always ready for emergencies. A secret armory and a group of factories ready to destroy weapons immediately after they're used. A supply of inconspicuous tracksuits and motorcycle helmets, also to be destroyed afterward. Even a logistical network that immediately after the hit gets the killers to a shooting range that records their entrance time; that's how they construct an alibi and confound the findings in the event of a stub, a test that detects gunpowder residue. The stub is every killer's worst fear: gunpowder traces can't be removed and are the most damning evidence. The idea isn't so much to conceal an action, a murder, or an investment, but simply to render it unprovable in court. A flawless company, everything in perfect working order, or almost.

I'd been going to Secondigliano for a while. Ever since Pasquale quit working as a tailor, he'd been keeping me up-to-date on how the wind was blowing there. It was shifting fast, as fast as the flow of money.

I'd cruise around on my Vespa. The thing I like most about Secondigliano and Scampia is the light. The big, wide streets are airier than the tangle of the old city center, and I could imagine the countryside still alive under the asphalt and massive buildings. After all, space is preserved in Scampia's very name, which in a defunct Neapolitan dialect means "open land." A place where weeds grow. Where the infamous *Vele*, or Sails, a monstrous public housing project, sprouted in the 1960s. The rotten symbol of architectural delirium, or perhaps merely a cement utopia powerless to oppose the narcotraffic machine that feeds on this part of the world. Chronic unemployment and a total absence of social development planning have transformed the area into a narcotics warehouse, a laboratory for turning drug money into a vibrant, legal economy. Scampia and Secondigliano pump oxygen from illegal markets into legitimate businesses. In 1989 the Camorra Observatory, a Camorra-watch organization, noted in one of its publications that the northern outskirts of Naples had one of the highest ratios of drug pushers to inhabitants in all of Italy. This ratio is now the highest in Europe and one of the top five in the world.

Over time my face got to be known in the area. For the clan sentries or lookouts, familiarity is a neutral value. In a territory that's constantly under visual surveillance, there are negative values—the police, carabinieri, infiltrators from rival families—and positive ones: buyers. Anything else is considered neutral, useless. If you're put in this category, it means you don't exist. Open-air drug markets have always fascinated me; their impeccable organization contradicts any idea of absolute degradation. They run like clockwork, the people like gears, each move setting off another. It's bewitching to watch. Salaries are paid out weekly, 100 euros for the lookouts, 500 for the market coordinator and cashier, 800 for the pushers, and 1,000 for the people who run the storehouses and hide drugs in their homes. Shifts run from 3 p.m. to midnight and from midnight to 4 a.m.; it's too hard to deal in the morning, too many police around. Everyone gets a day off, and if you show up late, your pay is docked, 50 euros for every hour you miss.

Via Baku is always hopping. Clients arrive, pay, collect the goods, and leave. At times a line of cars actually forms behind the pusher. Especially on Saturday evenings, when pushers are pulled in from other areas. Via Baku brings in half a million euros a month; the narcotics squad reports that on average four hundred doses each of marijuana and cocaine are sold here every day. When the police show up, the pushers know exactly which houses to go to and where to stash the goods. A car or *motorino* usually pulls in front of the police car to slow it down, thus giving the lookouts time to pick up the pushers and whisk them away on their motorcycles. The lookouts are unarmed and usually have a clean record, so even if they're pulled over, there's little risk of indictment. If the pushers are arrested, reserves are called in, usually addicts or regular users willing to help out in emergencies. For every pusher who's arrested, another takes his place. Business is business, even in times of trouble.

Via Dante also brings in astronomical sums. It's a thriving market, one of the newest Di Lauro setups, and the pushers are all young kids. Then there's Viale della Resistenza, an old heroin market that also deals in kobret and cocaine. Here the marketplace coordinators actually have a headquarters furnished with maps and speakerphones where they organize the defense of their territory. Lookouts on cell phones keep them informed as to what is happening, permitting them to follow the movements of police and clients in real time.

One of the Di Lauro innovations is customer protection. Before the clan took over, only the pushers were protected from arrest and identification, whereas buyers could be stopped, identified, and taken down to headquarters. But Di Lauro provided lookouts for their customers as well—safe access for everyone. Nothing but the best for the casual consumer, a mainstay of the Secondigliano drug trade. In the Berlingieri neighborhood you can call ahead and they'll have your order ready for you. The same holds for Via Ghisleri, Parco Ises, the whole Don Guanella neighborhood, the H section of Via Labriola, and the Sette Palazzi quarter. In areas that have been transformed into profitable markets, the streets are guarded and the residents develop a survival instinct of selective vision, of deciding in advance what to see and what to block out as too horrendous. They live in an enormous supermarket, where every imaginable kind of drug is available. No substance gets introduced on the European market without first passing through Secondigliano. If the drugs were only for the inhabitants of Naples and Campania, the statistics would be unbelievably absurd. At least two coke addicts and one heroin addict to every family. And that's not even considering hashish, marijuana, kobret, and light drugs. Pills—what some people still call ecstasy, but there are actually 179 varieties—are huge sellers in Secondigliano, where they're called X files or tokens or candies. There's enormous profit in pills. They cost 1 euro to produce, are sold in bulk at 3 to 5 euros, and then resold in Milan, Rome, or other parts of Naples for 50 to 60 euros apiece. In Scampia they go for 15.

Secondigliano moved beyond the confines of the traditional drug market and identified cocaine as the new frontier. Thanks to the clans' new economic policies, what was once an elite substance is now well within everyone's reach, with various grades of quality to satisfy every need. According to the analyst group Abele, 90 percent of cocaine users are workers or students. No longer just for getting high, coke is now consumed at all times of the day: to relax after working overtime, to find the energy to do something that resembles a human activity and not simply to combat exhaustion; to drive a truck at night; to keep at it for hours in front of the computer; to carry on without stopping, to work for weeks without any sort of break. A solvent for fatigue, an anesthetic for pain, a prosthesis for happiness. No longer merely for stupefaction, drugs are a resource now. To satisfy this new desire, dealing had to become flexible and free of criminal rigidities. The supply and sale of drugs had to be liberalized. The Di Lauro clan was the first to make the leap in Naples. Italian criminal cartels traditionally prefer to sell large lots. But Di Lauro decided to sell medium lots to promote small drug-dealing businesses that would attract new clients. Autonomous businesses, free to do what they want with the goods, set their own prices, advertise how and where they choose. Anyone can access the market, for any amount, without needing to go through clan mediators. Cosa Nostra and 'Ndrangheta have extensive drug businesses, but you have to know the chain of command, and to deal through them you have to be introduced by clan members or affiliates. They insist on knowing where you'll be peddling, what the distribution will be. But not the Secondigliano System. Here the rule is laissez-faire, laissez-passer. Total and absolute liberalism. Let the market regulate itself. And so in no time Secondigliano attracted everyone eager to set up a small drug business among friends, anyone wanting to buy at 15 and sell at 100 to pay for a vacation, a master's degree, or a mortgage. The total liberalization of the market caused prices to drop.

Except for certain open-air markets, retail drug sales may eventually disappear. Now there are the so-called circles: the doctors' circle, the pilots' circle, circles for journalists and government employees. The lower-middle class is the perfect fit for an informal and hyperliberal distribution system. A friendly exchange, more like a Tupperware party, far removed from any criminal structures. Ideal for eliminating excessive moral responsibility. No pusher in a silk acetate tracksuit planted for days on end in the corner of the marketplace, protected by lookouts. Nothing but the products and the money, just enough space for commercial exchange. Italian police records reveal that one in three arrests is of a first-time offender. According to the Superior Health Institute, cocaine consumption has soared to historical highs, rising 80 percent from 1999 to 2002. The number of addicts who turn to SERT, the Italian services for substance abusers, doubles every year. The market expansion is immense. Genetically modified cultivation, which permits four harvests a year, has eliminated supply problems, and the absence of a single dominant organization favors free enterprise. I read in a newspaper that the singer Robbie Williams, who has had his problems with cocaine, was fond of saying, "Cocaine is God's way of letting you know you have too much money." These words came back to me when I heard some kids in the Case Celesti neighborhood singing the praises of product and place: "If Case Celesti cocaine exists, it means that God doesn't place any value on money."

Case Celesti—the name comes from the pale blue color the houses once had—an area which runs along Via Limitone d'Arzano, is one of Europe's finest cocaine markets. This wasn't always the case. According to investigations, it was Gennaro Marino McKay who made the place so profitable. He's the clan's point man in the area. And that's not all. Paolo Di Lauro likes the way he runs things so he gave him franchising rights on the local market. McKay operates independently; all he has to do is pay a monthly fee to the clan. Gennaro and his brother Gaetano are known as the McKays because their father resembled Zeb Macahan, which Italians pronounce as McKay, in the TV series *How the West Was Won*. And so the whole family became McKay. Gaetano has no hands. He lost them in 1991 in the war against the Pucas, an old Cutolo clan family, when a grenade he was holding went off. Now he has two stiff wooden prostheses that are painted black. Gaetano McKay always has a companion, a sort of majordomo who acts as his hands. But when Gaetano has to sign something, he jams a pen in his prosthesis and fixes it on the paper; contorting his neck and wrists, he somehow manages to produce a signature that is only slightly crooked.

According to the Naples anti-Mafia prosecutor's office, Genny McKay's operations store as well as peddle drugs. Suppliers' prices are tightly linked to their ability to stockpile, and the cement jungle and hundred thousand inhabitants of Secondigliano are a valuable asset. The mass of people with homes and daily lives forms a great wall around the drug depots. The Case Celesti marketplace is responsible for a decrease in cocaine prices. Normally they start at 50 to 60 euros a gram and can go as high as 100 or 200 euros. Here prices have dropped to the 25 to 50 range, but the quality remains high. It emerges from the DDA reports that Genny McKay is one of the most talented Italians in the cocaine business, dominating a market of unparalleled, exponential growth. Open-air drug markets could have been established in Posillipo, Parioli, or Brera—posh neighborhoods of Naples, Rome, and Milan—but instead they were established in Secondigliano. Labor costs in any other place would have been far too high. Here the serious lack of work and the impossibility of finding a way to earn a living—other than emigrating—make for low salaries, very low. It's no mystery, really, and there's no need to appeal to the sociology of poverty or a metaphysics of the ghetto. An area where dozens of clans are operating, with profit levels comparable only to a maneuver in high finance—just one family's activity invoices 300 million euros annually—cannot be a ghetto. The work is meticulous and the chain of production is extremely expensive. A kilo of cocaine costs the producer 1,000 euros, but by the time it reaches the wholesaler, it's already worth 30,000. After the first cut 30 kilos become 150: a market value of approximately 15 million euros. With a larger cut, 30 kilos can be stretched to 200. The cut is essential: caffeine, glucose, mannitol, paracetamol, lidocaine, benzocaine, amphetamines—but in emergencies even talc and calcium for dogs are used. The cut determines the quality, and a bad cut attracts death, police, and arrests. A bad cut clogs the arteries of commerce.

The Secondigliano clans are ahead of everyone else in drug cutting, a precious advantage. Here there are the Visitors: heroin addicts, named after characters in a 1980s TV program who devour mice and have greenish, slimy scales under seemingly normal human skin. The Visitors are used as guinea pigs, human guinea pigs for testing to see if a cut is dangerous, what reactions it causes, how much to dilute the powder. When the lab needs lots of guinea pigs, they lower the prices. From 20 down to as low as 10 euros a hit. Word gets out and the Visitors come from as far away as the Marche and Lucania for a few hits. The heroin market is collapsing. The number of addicts is in decline, and the ones who are left are desperate. They stagger their way onto buses, on and off trains all night, catch rides, walk for miles. But the cheapest heroin on the Continent is worth the effort. The guys who do the cut for the clan assemble the Visitors, give them a free dose, and wait. In a phone call included in a March 2005 preventive detention order released by the Court of Naples, two individuals organize a test of a cut. First they set things up:

"Can you give me five doses . . . for allergy testing?"

They talk again a bit later:

"Did you try the machine?"

"Yes . . ."

They clearly mean the testing.

"Yes, *mamma mia, troppo bello*, we're number one, my friend, the others will be out of business."

They rejoice, glad the guinea pigs didn't die; on the contrary, they really enjoyed it. A good cut doubles sales, and if it's really high quality, it'll soon be in demand nationally, trouncing the competition.

Only after I read this telephone exchange did I understand a scene I'd witnessed a while earlier. I could not believe my eyes. I was in Miano, not far from Scampia, in a clearing near some storage hangars, where a dozen or so Visitors had been rounded up. I hadn't ended up there by chance; I believe that the way to truly understand, to get to the bottom of things, is to smell the hot breath of reality, to touch the nitty-gritty. I'm not convinced it's necessary to be there, to observe in order to know things, but being there is absolutely essential for things to know you. A well-dressed fellow—white suit, navy blue shirt, brand-new running shoes—unfolded a chamois cloth with a few syringes in it on the hood of the car. The Visitors elbowed their way forward; it looked like one of those scenes they show on the news when a truck full of flour arrives in Africa. Identical, always the same, year after year. But then a Visitor started yelling:

"No, I won't take it, not even if you give it to me . . . you want to kill us . . ."

All it took was one suspicious person and the others withdrew immediately. The fellow just waited; he didn't seem particularly eager to convince anyone. The air was full of dust from the Visitors' trampling around, and every now and then he'd spit out the grit that settled on his teeth. Two of the Visitors finally went up to him, a couple actually. They were trembling, really on the edge, in withdrawal. The veins in the guy's arms were shot, so he took off his shoes, but even the soles

of his feet were ruined. The girl picked up a syringe and held it between her teeth as she slowly opened his shirt, as if it had a hundred
buttons, then jabbed him in the throat. The syringe contained coke.
Once it's in the bloodstream it becomes clear pretty quickly if the cut
is good or if it's off, too heavy, or poor quality. After a bit he started to
sway, frothing lightly at the corners of his mouth. He fell to the
ground, jerked around and then stretched out flat, closed his eyes,
and went stiff. The man in the white suit started calling on his cell.

"He looks dead to me . . . Okay, okay, I'll try giving him a massage . . ."

He began pounding the Visitor's chest with his boot, lifting his
knee and dropping his leg violently: a cardiac massage with his foot.
Next to him the girl was blithering something, the words hanging on
her lips: "You're doing it wrong, you're doing it wrong. You're hurting
him . . ." With all the strength of a wet noodle she tried to push him
away from her boyfriend's body. But the man was disgusted, almost
frightened by her and the Visitors in general:

"Don't touch me . . . you're disgusting . . . don't you dare come
near me . . . don't touch me or I'll shoot!"

He went on kicking the guy's chest, and then, resting his foot on
his sternum, he made another call:

"He's a goner . . . Oh yeah, the Kleenex . . . hang on, let me see . . ."

He took a Kleenex out of his pocket, moistened it, and spread it
over the guy's lips. Even the faintest breath would make a hole, indi-
cating that he was still alive. A precaution to keep from touching the
body. He phoned one last time:

"He's dead. We have to make it lighter."

The man got back in his car. The driver, meanwhile, had been
bouncing up and down the whole time, dancing in his seat to some
silent music; I couldn't hear a sound even though he acted as if it
were playing full blast. Within a few minutes everyone moved away
and started wandering around in that patch of dust. The guy was still
stretched out on the ground, his girlfriend whimpering beside him.

Even her crying stuck to her lips, as if the only form of vocal expression the heroin allowed was a hoarse moan.

I couldn't understand why, but the girl got up, dropped her pants, squatted right over his face, and pissed. The Kleenex stuck to his mouth and nose. After a bit he regained his senses, and wiped his face with his hands, like when you come up from underwater. This Lazarus of Miano, resurrected by who knows what substances in her urine, slowly got up. I swear that if I hadn't been so stunned, I would have cried out, "Miracle!" Instead I paced back and forth, which is what I always do when I don't understand or don't know what to do. I nervously occupy space. My moving around must have attracted attention, since the Visitors came nearer and started yelling at me. They thought I was connected to the guy with the syringes. They kept shouting, "You . . . you . . . you wanted to kill him."

They hovered around me, but scattered as soon as I quickened my pace. They followed me though, hurling disgusting objects they'd picked up from the ground. I hadn't done anything, but if you're not an addict, you must be a pusher. Suddenly a truck appeared. Dozens of them had been pulling out of the warehouses all morning. It stopped near me and a voice called my name. It was Pasquale. He opened the door and had me jump in. Not a guardian angel who saves his favorite charge—more like two rats running in the same sewer, pulling each other by the tail.

Pasquale looked at me with the severity of a father who'd foreseen everything. That sarcastic smile said it all; no need to waste time scolding me. I stared at his hands instead. Even redder, more chapped, knuckles cracked, palms anemic. Fingers accustomed to silk and velvet have trouble adjusting to ten hours at the steering wheel. Pasquale was talking, but I couldn't get the Visitors out of my head. Monkeys. Less than monkeys. Guinea pigs, testing the cut of a drug that will be distributed all over Europe—the clans can't take the chance it might kill someone. Human guinea pigs, so that people in Rome, Naples, Abruzzo, Lucania, and Bologna won't end up dead, blood dripping from their nose and foaming at the mouth. A dead Visitor in Secondigliano is only one more wretch whose demise will go uninvestigated. It's already a lot if he's picked up off the ground, his face wiped clean of vomit and piss, and buried. Elsewhere there'd be an autopsy, an investigation, conjectures about his death. Here there's just one word: overdose.

Pasquale took the road that links the northern suburbs of Naples. Sheds, warehouses, rubbish dumps, rusting junk strewn around, trash tossed everywhere. No industrial complexes here. There's the stink of factory smoke but no factories. Houses scattered along streets, piazzas defined by the presence of a bar. A confused and complicated desert. Pasquale realized I wasn't listening so he braked suddenly. Without coming to a full stop, just a little whiplash—just enough to shake me up. Then he looked at me and said, "Things are going to get rough in Secondigliano . . . 'a vicchiarella is in Spain with everybody's money. You've got to quit coming around here. I can feel the tension everywhere. Even the asphalt would peel off the ground if it could get out of here."

I decided to follow what was going to happen in Secondigliano. The more Pasquale insisted it would be dangerous, the more I became convinced that it was impossible not to try to understand the elements of the disaster. And understanding meant being part of it somehow. I had no choice; as far as I'm concerned, it's the only way to understand things. Neutrality and objective distance are places I've never been able to find. Raffaele Amato—'a vicchiarella, the old woman—a second-tier clan executive in charge of the Spanish drug markets, had fled to Barcelona with the Di Lauro cash box. At least that's what was being said. In truth he had failed to turn his quota over to the clan, a way of demonstrating that he no longer felt the least obligation to the people who wanted to keep him on a salary. The schism was official. For the moment it involved only Spain, which had always been controlled by the clans: Andalusia by the Casalesi of Caserta, the islands by the Nuvolettas of Marano, and Barcelona by the "secessionists." That's the name the first crime reporters on the story gave to the Di Lauro men who broke away. But everyone in Secondigliano calls them the Spaniards. With their leader in Spain, they took the lead not only in peddling but in narcotraffic as well, Madrid being a crucial junction for cocaine coming from Colombia and Peru. According to investigations, Amato's men had long employed a brilliant stratagem for moving huge amounts of drugs: garbage trucks. Trash on the top, drugs underneath. An infallible method for escaping controls. No one would stop a garbage truck in the middle of the night.

According to the inquiries, Cosimo Di Lauro sensed that his managers were turning less and less capital over to the clan. Profit was supposed to be reinvested in wagers, the investments that managers make when purchasing drug lots with Di Lauro capital. *Wager:* the term comes from the irregular, hyperliberal cocaine and pill trade, in which there is no measure or certainty. So one bets, like in Russian roulette. If you wager 100,000 euros and things go well, fourteen days later you've got 300,000. Whenever I come across such exponential figures, I remember what Giovanni Falcone told a group of students: "In order to understand how prosperous the drug trade is, consider that a thousand lire invested in drugs on the first of September become a hundred million by the first of August of the following year." His example was recorded in hundreds of school notebooks.

The sums Di Lauro's managers turned over remained astronomical, but progressively smaller. Over the long term this sort of practice would strengthen some and weaken others, and eventually—as soon as a group gathered enough organizational and military force—they'd give Paolo Di Lauro the shove. Not just some stiff competition, but the big shove, the one you don't get up from, a shove with lead in it. So Cosimo ordered everyone be put on salary. He wanted them all to depend on him. The decision ran counter to those his father had always made, but it was necessary to protect his business, his authority, his family. No more loose ties, with everyone free to decide how much to invest, what type and quality of drugs to put on the market. No more liberty and autonomy within a multilevel corporation. Salaried employees. Some were saying 50,000 euros a month. An extraordinary amount, but a salary nevertheless. A subordinate role. The end of the entrepreneurial dream, replaced by a manager's job. And the administrative revolution didn't end there. Informants testify that Cosimo also imposed a generational turnover. Immediate rejuvenation of the top management, so no executives over thirty. The market doesn't make concessions for the appreciation of human assets. It doesn't make concessions for anything. You have to hustle to win. Every bond, be it affection, law, rights, love, emotion, or religion, is a concession to the competition, a stumbling block to success. There's room for all that, but economic victory and control come first. Old bosses used to be listened to out of respect, even when they proposed outdated ideas or gave ineffective orders; their decisions counted precisely because of their age. And age was what posed the biggest threat to the leadership of Paolo Di Lauro's offspring.

So now they were all on the same level; no appealing to a mythical past, previous experience, or respect owed. Everyone had to get by on the strength of his proposals, management abilities, or charisma. The Secondigliano commandos began unleashing their force before the secession occurred. But it was already brewing. One of their first objectives was Ferdinando Bizzarro, also known as *bacchetella* or Uncle Fester, after the bald, slippery little character on *The Addams Family*. Bizzarro was the *ras* of Melito. *Ras* is a term for someone with a great deal of authority but who is still subject to the higher power of the boss. Bizzarro was no longer performing diligently as a Di Lauro area capo. He wanted to manage his own money, to make pivotal, and not merely administrative, decisions. This wasn't a classic revolt; he merely wanted to be promoted, to become an autonomous partner. But he promoted himself. The Melito clans are ferocious; they run underground factories that make high-quality shoes for half the world and generate cash for loan-sharking. Underground factory owners almost always support the politician who will guarantee the least amount of business regulation, or the regional capo who gets him elected. The Secondigliano clans have never been slaves to politicians and have never wanted to establish programmatic pacts, but in this region it's essential to have friends.

The very person who had been Bizzarro's political point man became his angel of death. The clan asked Alfredo Cicala, a former mayor of Melito and local leader of the center-left political party La Margherita, for help with Bizzarro. According to the Naples DDA investigations, Cicala provided precise information about Bizzarro's whereabouts. If one reads the wiretaps, it doesn't seem as if they were planning a murder, but simply rotating leaders. In the end, it's really the same thing. Business has to go on, and Bizzarro's decision to be autonomous threatened to cause problems. It had to be done, by whatever means. When Bizzarro's mother died, Di Lauro's affiliates considered going to the funeral and shooting at everyone and everything. Taking out Bizzarro, his son, his cousins. Everyone. They were ready. But Bizzarro and his son didn't show. Detailed plans for an ambush continued, however. The clan even faxed information and orders to its affiliates:

"There's no one left from Secondigliano, he's sent them all away . . . he only goes out on Tuesday and Saturday, with four cars . . . you're not to move for any reason. Uncle Fester sent a message saying that for Easter he wants 250 euros a store and isn't afraid of anyone. They're going to torture Siviero this week."

A strategy orchestrated by fax. An appointment to torture marked on the calendar, just like an invoice, an order, or an airplane reservation. As are the reports on the traitor's activities: Bizzarro has four escort cars and is extorting 250 euros a month. Siviero, Bizzarro's faithful driver, is to be tortured, perhaps so he'll spill the routes his boss is planning to take in the future. But the catalog of hypotheses for killing Bizzarro doesn't end here. They consider going to his son's house, where they "won't spare anyone." And then a phone call: a killer heard that Bizzarro had stuck his nose out, and appeared in public to demonstrate his power and safety. The killer moans about losing such a perfect opportunity:

"Damn it, Madonna, we're missing out here, he's been in the piazza all morning."

Nothing is hidden. Everything seems clear, obvious, woven into the fabric of the everyday. But the former mayor of Melito divulges the name of the hotel where Bizzarro holes up with his lover, where he goes to release tension and sperm. You can get used to everything: to living with the lights off so no one knows you're home, to being escorted by four cars, to not making or receiving phone calls, to skipping your own mother's funeral. But not to be able to see your lover—no. That would feel like a mockery, the end of all your power.

On April 26, 2004, Bizzarro is at the Hotel Villa Giulia, on the fourth floor. In bed with his lover. The commandos arrive wearing police bibs. The concierge doesn't even ask the supposed officers to show their badges before giving them the magnetic key. They pound on the door. Bizzarro is still in his underwear. They hear him approach and start shooting. Two bursts of fire penetrate the door and his body. Lead and splinters hammer into his flesh. More shots demolish the door, and they finish him off with a bullet to the head. It's clear now how the slaughter will unfold. Bizzarro was the first. Or one of the first. Or at least the first test of the Di Lauro clan's strength, of their ability to attack whoever dares break the alliance or violate the business agreement. The secessionists' strategy hasn't completely taken shape yet, it's not immediately comprehensible. You can breathe the tension in the air, but it's as if they're still waiting for something. Clarity—a declaration of war—comes on October 20, 2004, a few months after Bizzarro's murder: Fulvio Montanino and Claudio Salerno are killed, shot fourteen times. According to investigations, they operated open-air drug markets and were extremely loyal to Cosimo. Since the idea of ensnaring and eliminating Cosimo and his father came to nothing, their killing marks the beginning of hostilities. The conflict is unleashed. Faced with dead bodies, there's nothing else to do but fight. All the leaders decide to rebel against Di Lauro's sons: Rosario Pariante, Raffaele Abbinante, as well as the new managers Raffaele Amato, Gennaro Marino McKay, Arcangelo Abate, and Giacomo Migliaccio. The De Lucias, Giovanni Cortese, Enrico D'Avanzo, and a large—very large—group of supporters remain loyal to Di Lauro. Young men who are promised promotions, booty, and economic and social advancement within the clan. Paolo Di Lauro's sons Cosimo, Marco, and Ciro assume the leadership. It's highly likely that Cosimo realized he was risking imprisonment or his life. Arrests and economic crises. But you have to choose: either wait to be slowly defeated by the rival clan growing in your own bosom, or try to save your business—or at least your hide. Economic defeat means immediate physical defeat as well.

This is war. No one knows how it will be fought, but everyone knows for sure it will be long and terrible. The most ruthless war that southern Italy has seen in the last ten years. The Di Lauros have fewer men, are much weaker, and far less organized. They had always reacted forcefully to the internal schisms arising from their liberalist management style, which some people misunderstood as autonomy, as permission to set up their own business. But in the Di Lauro clan, freedom is given; you cannot presume to own it. In 1992 the old ruling group resolved the schism sparked by Antonio Rocco, head of Mugnano, by entering the Fulmine bar armed with submachine guns and hand grenades. They killed five people. Rocco turned government witness to save his skin, and based on the information he provided, the state placed nearly two hundred of Di Lauro's targets under protection. But it didn't make any difference; the association's management was untarnished by Rocco's testimony.

But this time Cosimo Di Lauro's men start getting worried, as the December 7, 2004, provisional confinement order issued by the Court of Naples reveals. Two affiliates, Luigi Petrone and Salvatore Tamburino, talk on the phone about the declaration of war that came in the form of Montanino's and Salerno's murders.

Petrone: "They killed Fulvio."

Tamburino: "Ah . . ."

Petrone: "You understand?"

The battle strategy, which Tamburino claims is dictated by Cosimo Di Lauro, begins to take shape. Take them out one by one, kill them, even if you have to use bombs.

Tamburino: "Even bombs, you hear? Cosimino said so, he said, 'Now I'm going to take them out one by one . . . I'm going to kill them . . . real nasty, he said . . . all of them . . .'"

Petrone: "The important thing is that the people are behind it, that they 'work' . . ."

Tamburino: "Gino, there's millions of 'em here. They're kids, all of them . . . kids . . . now I'll show you what he's up to, that one . . ."

It's a new strategy. Bring in the kids, promote them to the rank of soldier, transform the well-oiled operation of drug dealing, investments, and territorial control into a fighting machine. Boys who work in delicatessens and butcher's shops, mechanics, waiters, and unemployed youth are to become the clan's new and unforeseen power. Montanino's death sets off a long and bloody attack and counterattack, deaths on top of deaths, one, two ambushes a day, clan supporters first, then relatives, houses burned, people beaten, suspicions flying.

Tamburino: "Cosimino's very cool, 'Eat, drink, and fuck' is what he said. What can we do . . . it happened, we have to move on."

Petrone: "But I don't feel like eating any more. I eat just to put something in my stomach . . ."

The order to fight mustn't seem desperate, though. It's essential to look like winners, for a business just as for an army. Whoever lets it be seen that he's in trouble, whoever escapes, disappears, or retreats, has already lost. Eat, drink, fuck. As if nothing had happened, as if nothing were happening. But Petrone and Tamburino are really scared; they don't know how many affiliates have gone over to the Spaniards and how many have remained on their side.

Tamburino: "And how do we know how many of them have thrown in their lot with the others . . . we don't know!"

Petrone: "Ah! How many of them have gone over? A whole bunch of them have stayed, Totore! I don't understand . . . these ones here . . . don't they like the Di Lauros?"

Tamburino: "If I were Cosimino, you know what I'd do? I'd start killing them all. If I had any doubts . . . all of them. I'd start taking them out . . . you understand!"

Kill them all. Every one of them. Even if you have doubts. Even if you don't know which side they're on, or if they're even involved. Shoot! They're slime, nothing but slime. In the face of war, danger, and defeat, allies and enemies are interchangeable. They're no longer individuals, but elements for testing and expressing your strength. Groups, alliances, and enemies will take shape afterward. But first the shooting has to start.

On October 30, 2004, Di Lauro's men show up at the home of Salvatore de Magistris: a man in his sixties married to the mother of Biagio Esposito, one of the secessionists. They want to know where Esposito's hiding. The Di Lauros have to get them all, before they organize, before they realize they're in the majority. They break de Magistris's arms and legs with a club and crush his nose. With each blow they ask for information on his wife's son. He doesn't answer, and every refusal provokes another blow. They kick him relentlessly. He has to confess. But he doesn't. Or maybe he really doesn't know where Esposito is hiding. He dies after a month of agony.

On November 2, Massimo Galdiero is killed in a parking lot. They were supposed to hit his brother Gennaro, allegedly a friend of Raffaele Amato's. On November 6, Antonio Landieri is killed on Via Labriola; to get him they fire on the whole group he's with, seriously wounding five others who were dealing in cocaine, apparently for Gennaro McKay. The Spaniards answer back. On November 9 they evade a series of roadblocks and leave a white Fiat Punto in Via Cupa Perrillo. It's the middle of the afternoon when the police find three bodies. Stefano Maisto, Mario Maisto, and Stefano Mauriello. One in the front, one in the back, one in the trunk: wherever they look they find a body. On November 20, Di Lauro's men slay Biagio Migliaccio. They go to the car dealership where he works. "This is a holdup," they say, then fire at his chest. His uncle Giacomo was the target. The Spaniards respond on the same day, killing Gennaro Emolo, father of one of Di Lauro's most loyal men, accused of being part of the military arm of the organization. Domenico Riccio and Salvatore Gagliardi, both close to Raffaele Abbinante, are in a tobacco shop on November 21 when the Di Lauros take them out. An hour later Francesco Tortora is slain. The killers travel by car instead of motorcycle. They drive up, shoot, pick up his body like a sack, and take it to the outskirts of Casavatore, where they set car and body on fire, solving two problems at once. At midnight on the twenty-second the carabinieri find a burned-out car. Another one.

I'd got hold of a radio that picked up the police frequencies in order to follow the feud, so I'd arrive on my Vespa more or less at the same time as the police squads. But that night I'd fallen asleep. The cadenced crackle and squawk of police headquarters had become a sort of melodic lullaby. This time it was a phone call in the middle of the night that alerted me to what had happened. When I arrived at the scene, I found a car completely gutted by fire. They'd doused it with gasoline, gallons of it everywhere. Gas on the front seats, gas on the backseats, on the tires and steering wheel. The flames had already died and the windows exploded when the firemen arrived. I don't exactly know why I rushed headlong to that carcass of a car. The stench was terrible, like burned plastic. A few people milling about, a policeman with a flashlight peering inside the metal frame. He sees a body, or something that looks like one. The firemen open the doors and remove the cadaver, disgust on their faces. A carabiniere feels sick and leans against the wall and vomits up the pasta and potatoes he'd eaten a few hours earlier. All that's left is a stiff black trunk, a blackened skull, legs flayed by the flames. They pick it up by the arms, lower it to the ground, and wait for the mortuary van.

death-catcher van circulates constantly. I see it driving around npia and Torre Annunziata. It collects bodies, accumulating cadavers of people who've been shot and killed. Campania has the highest murder rate in Italy, among the highest in the world. The mortuary van's tires are worn smooth; it would be enough to photograph the nibbled rims and the gray sidewalls to capture the symbol of this place. Wearing filthy lattice gloves that have been used a thousand times, the men get out of the van and go to work. They slide the cadaver into a bag, one of those black body bags usually used for dead soldiers. It looks like one of the figures that emerge from the ashes of Vesuvius when the archaeologists pour plaster into the void left by the body. By now throngs of people have gathered around the car, but they're all silent. As if no one were there. We barely even dare breathe. After the Camorra war started, many people stopped setting limits to what they could stand. And now they've come to see what else will happen. Every day they learn what more is possible, what else they have to endure. They learn, go home, and carry on. The carabinieri start taking photographs, and the van leaves with the dead body. I go to police headquarters. They'll have to say something about this death. The usual journalists and a few policemen are in the pressroom. After a while the comments start: "They're killing each other off, so much thé better!" "Look how you end up if you become a Camorrista." "You enjoyed earning all that money, so now enjoy being dead, you piece of shit." The usual remarks, only more disgusted and exasperated. As if the cadaver were present and everyone had something to fling in his face: this night that had been ruined, this war that never ends, the garrisons that sprout up on every corner of Naples. It takes the doctors a long time to identify the body. Someone supplies the name of a neighborhood capo who'd disappeared a few days before. One of the many, one of the bodies piled up in cold storage in Cardarelli Hospital, awaiting the worst name possible. But they announce it's not him.

Someone covers his mouth with his hands. The journalists swallow so hard their mouths go dry. The policemen shake their heads and stare at the tips of their shoes. The angry remarks are guiltily cut short. That body belonged to Gelsomina Verde, a twenty-two-year-old woman. She'd been kidnapped, tortured, and killed, a bullet in the back of the neck, fired from so close that it came out the front of her skull. Then they threw her in a car—her car—and set it on fire. Gelsomina had dated Gennaro Notturno, a young guy who had first decided to stay with the Di Lauros but then moved over to the Spaniards. She'd gone out with him for a few months, a while back. But someone had seen them embrace, maybe riding on a Vespa or sitting in a car together. Gennaro had been condemned to death, but he'd given them the slip; who knows where he'd disappeared to, maybe even some garage near where Gelsomina had been killed. He didn't feel the need to protect her because they weren't together anymore. But the clans have to strike, and the map of an individual is drawn through his acquaintances, relatives, even his possessions. A map on which messages can be written. The most terrible messages.

Punishment is necessary. If someone goes unpunished, it might legit-imize new betrayals or schisms. It's too big a risk. Strike, in the worst way possible. This is the order. The rest doesn't mean a thing. And so the Di Lauro loyalists find Gelsomina, use some excuse to meet her. They grab her, beat her bloody, torture her, ask her where Gennaro is. She doesn't answer. Maybe she doesn't know, or maybe she prefers to endure herself whatever they would have done to him. So they kill her. Maybe the Camorristi sent to do the job are high on cocaine, or maybe they need to stay straight to catch even the smallest detail. But their methods for eliminating every type of resistance, for negating every last breath of humanity, are well-known. Burning the body seemed to me like a way of erasing the traces of torture. The tor-mented body of a young woman would have provoked a dark rage throughout the neighborhood, and even though the clan can't claim to have people's consent, it doesn't want hostility either. So burn, burn everything. It's not her death that is so grievous, no more so than any other death during wartime. But it is unbearable to imagine how she died, how the torture was carried out. I breathe deeply and spit out the mucus in my chest in order to block those images.

Gelsomina Verde, or Mina, as she was called in the neighborhood. That's how the newspapers call her as well, when they start to fondle her with those guilty, day-after feelings. It would have been easy to not distinguish her flesh from the people who are killing each other. Or, had she still been alive, to keep on thinking of her as the girlfriend of a Camorrista, one of the many who go along for the money or the sense of importance it gives them. Just one more signora who enjoys the riches of her Camorra husband. But *Saracino*, or Saracen, as Gen-naro Notturno is called, has just started out. If he makes local capo and oversees the pushers, he could earn 1,000 or 2,000 euros a month. But it's a long road. Compensation for a murder is probably 2,500 euros. And if you have to strike camp because the carabinieri are about to nab you, the clan will pay for a month in northern Italy or abroad. Maybe Gennaro even dreamed of becoming boss, of ruling half of Naples and investing all over Europe.

If I stop and take a deep breath, I can easily imagine their meeting, even though I wouldn't recognize their faces. They probably met in a typical bar, one of those damned bars you find in the outskirts of southern cities, around which the existence of everyone, from kids to ninety-year-olds with cataracts, whirls. Or maybe they met in some discotheque. A stroll in Piazza Plebiscito, a kiss before going home. Then Saturdays together, going for pizza in the countryside, the bedroom door locked on Sundays after lunch when everyone else is nodding off, exhausted from all the eating. And on it goes. Just as it always does, for everyone, for Christ's sake. Then Gennaro joins the System. He'll have gone to some Camorra friend of his, gotten himself introduced, and started working for Di Lauro. I imagine Gelsomina probably knew and would have tried to find him something else to do. That's how it usually goes around here, the girls rushing around for their boyfriends. But maybe in the end she forgot about Gennaro's profession. After all, it was a job like any other. Driving a car, delivering a few packages, it all starts with the little things. With nothing. But it allows you to live, to work, and at times even makes you feel accomplished, appreciated, satisfied. And then their relationship ends.

Those few months were enough, though. Enough to associate Gelsomina with Gennaro. To mark her as traced by him, one of his affections. Even if their relationship was already over or had never really even begun. It doesn't matter. These are only conjectures, fantasies. What remains is that a girl was tortured and killed because they saw her while she caressed or kissed someone a few months earlier somewhere in Naples. It's almost impossible to believe. Gelsomina slaved a lot, like everyone around here. Often the young women and wives have to support their families because so many men suffer years of depression. Even the people who live in Secondigliano—the Third

World—have a psyche. Being out of work for years changes you, and it kills you to be treated like shit by your superiors, with no contract, no respect, and no money. Or you become a beast. And then you're really on the edge, near the end. So Gelsomina worked, just like everyone else who holds down at least three jobs to hoard up enough money, half of which she gave to her family. She also did volunteer work, assisting the elderly, something the newspapers outdid themselves in praising, as if they were competing to bring her back to life.

In war it's impossible to maintain amorous ties or relationships, anything that could become an element of weakness. The emotional earthquake that occurs in the lives of the young men who become clan affiliates can be heard in the phone calls the carabinieri intercept, such as that between Francesco Venosa and his girlfriend Anna, transcribed in the holding order issued by the Naples anti-Mafia prosecutor's office in February 2006. The last call before the number is changed, before Francesco flees to Lazio. First he sends an SMS to his brother, warning him not to go out on the street because he's under fire:

"Hi bro luv u. dont go out for any reason. ok?"

Then Francesco has to tell his girlfriend he has to go away, explain that the life of a System man is complicated:

"I'm eighteen now . . . these guys don't kid around . . . they throw you away . . . kill you, Anna!"

But Anna is obstinate. She would like to become a carabiniere, to change her life and make Francesco change his. He doesn't disapprove in the least of Anna's professional aspirations, but thinks he's already too old to turn his life around.

Francesco: "I told you, I'm happy for you . . . But my life's different . . . And I'm not about to change my life."

Anna: "Oh, bravo, that's great . . . Fine, stay just the way you are!"

Francesco: "Anna, Anna . . . don't be like this . . ."

Anna: "But you're eighteen, you can easily change . . . Why have you given up already? I don't know . . ."

Francesco: "I'm not changing my life, not for anything in the world."

Anna: "Right, because you're fine the way you are."

Francesco: "No, Anna, I'm not fine like this, but for the moment we're down, and we have to regain the respect we lost . . . Before when we walked around the neighborhood, people didn't dare to look us in the face . . . now they all hold their heads high."

For Francesco, a Spaniard, the most serious insult is that no one is in awe of their power. They've suffered so many losses that everyone in the neighborhood sees them as a group of worthless killers, failed Camorristi. This is intolerable. He has to react, even at the price of his life. Anna tries to stop him, to make him feel he's not already condemned.

Anna: "You don't have to throw yourself into that mess, you can live just fine . . ."

Francesco: "No, I don't want to change my life . . ."

This young secessionist is terrified that the Di Lauros will go after her, but he reassures her by telling her he's had lots of girls so no one will associate the two of them. But then the romantic in him makes him confess she's the only one: "I used to go with thirty women in the neighborhood—but now I'm only with you . . ."

Anna, girl that she is, seems to forget all fears of retaliation and only thinks about the last words Francesco has said: "I'd like to believe you."

The war goes on. On November 24, 2004, they shoot Salvatore Abbinante in the face. He's the nephew of Raffaele Abbinante, a Spaniard, one of the leaders, a Marano man. Nuvoletta territory. To become players on the Secondigliano market, the Maranos transferred lots of their members with their families to the Monterosa neighborhood, and the alleged leader of this group of Mafiosi planted in the heart of Secondigliano is Raffaele Abbinante. He was one of the most charismatic figures in Spain, where he was in command of the Costa del Sol region. In 1997, 2,500 kilos of hashish, 1,020 ecstasy pills, and 1,500 kilos of cocaine were seized in a huge operation. The authorities proved that the Neapolitan cartels of the Abbinantes and Nuvolettas were managing nearly all the synthetic-drug traffic in Spain and Italy. After Salvatore Abbinante's murder it was feared that the Nuvolettas would intervene, that Cosa Nostra would have something to say about the Secondigliano feud. But nothing happened, or at least nothing violent. The Nuvolettas opened their borders to the secessionists on the run; this was the criticism that the Cosa Nostra men in Campania leveled at Cosimo's war. On November 25 the Di Lauros killed Antonio Esposito in his grocery store. When I got to the scene, his body was still lying amid the bottles of water and cartons of milk. Two men lifted him by his jacket and feet and placed him in a metal coffin. After the mortuary van left, a woman appeared in the store. She began picking the cartons up off the floor, cleaning the blood splatters from the glass of the cold-cuts counter. The carabinieri let her be. The ballistic traces, fingerprints, and clues had already been gathered, the information already futilely recorded in the ledger. The woman worked all night long putting the shop back in order, as if fixing up the place could cancel out what had happened, as if returning the milk cartons to the shelf and straightening up the snacks could relegate the weight of death to those few minutes in which the ambush occurred, to those few minutes only.

Meanwhile in Scampia a rumor spreads that Cosimo Di Lauro is offering 150,000 euros in exchange for essential information on the whereabouts of Gennaro Marino McKay. A big bounty, but not that big, not for an economic empire such as the Secondigliano System—

a shrewd desire not to overvalue the enemy. But no one takes the bait. The police get there first. All the secessionist leaders still in the area are gathered on the thirteenth floor of a building on Via Fratelli Cervi. As a precaution they've lined the landing in armor plating and installed metal-reinforced doors and a cage that seals off the head of the stairs. The police surround the building. What had been designed to protect the Spaniards against eventual enemy attacks now condemns them to sit there, unable to do anything, as the grinder cuts through the metal grating and the steel doors are knocked down. Waiting to be arrested, they throw a backpack with a submachine gun, some pistols, and hand grenades out the window. As it falls, the machine gun lets off a round. A shot grazes the neck of a policeman, just caressing his nape. He's so nervous he jumps, breaks out in a sweat, and suffers an anxiety attack. Dying from a bouncing bullet spit from a machine gun hurled from the thirteenth floor is a scenario one doesn't even consider. Nearly delirious, he begins talking to himself, insulting everyone, muttering names, and waving his hands around as if he were trying to shoo mosquitoes from his face:

"They squealed. They weren't able to get in there, so they squealed and sent us in instead . . . We're being double-crossed, we're saving these guys' lives. Let's leave them here, let them slit each other's throats, let them cut everybody's throats, what the fuck do we care?"

His colleagues signal for me to get out of there. That night in the house on Via Fratelli Cervi they arrest Arcangelo Abete and his sister Anna, Massimiliano Cafasso, Ciro Mauriello, Mina Verde's exboyfriend Gennaro Notturno, and Raffaele Notturno. But the real scoop is Gennaro Marino McKay, the secessionist leader. The Marinos were the feud's primary targets. They'd set fire to Gennaro's properties—a restaurant, Orchidea, on Via Diacono in Secondigliano, a bakery on Corso Secondigliano, and a pizzeria on Via Pietro Nenni in Arzano—and his house, a Russian dacha on Via Limitone d'Arzano. In his territory of reinforced concrete, crumbling streets, obstructed manholes, and sporadic street lighting, the boss of Case Celesti had torn a corner off and turned it into a mountain retreat. He'd built a villa out of precious woods and planted Libyan palms—the most expensive kind—on the grounds. Someone said that he'd gone to Russia for business and had fallen in love with the dacha where he'd been a guest. At that time nothing and no one could prevent Gennaro Marino from building a dacha in the heart of Secondigliano: a symbol of the power of his business, and a promise of success for his boys, who, if they knew how to act, might one day have such luxury, even in the outskirts of Naples, even on the darkest shore of the Mediterranean. Now all that remains of the dacha is a cement skeleton and carbonized wood beams. The carabinieri flushed Gennaro's brother Gaetano out of a room at La Certosa, a luxury hotel in Massa Lubrense. So as not to risk his skin, he'd holed himself up in a room by the sea, an unusual way of removing himself from the conflict. When the carabinieri arrived, the majordomo, the man who acted as Gaetano's hands, looked them in the eye and said, "You've ruined my vacation."

But the Spaniards' arrest doesn't stem the hemorrhage. Giuseppe Bencivenga is killed on November 27. On November 28 they shoot Massimo de Felice, and on December 5 it's Enrico Mazzarella's turn.

The tension creates a kind of screen between people. In war you can't let your gaze be distracted. Every face, every single face, has to tell you something. You need to decipher it, fix it with your eyes. Silently. You have to know which shop to enter, be certain of every word you utter. Before you decide to go for a walk with someone, you need to know who he is. You have to be more than certain, eliminate every possibility he's a pawn on the chessboard of the conflict. To stroll next to him and speak to him means to share the field. In war the attention threshold of all the senses is multiplied; it's as if you perceive things more acutely, see into things more deeply, smell things more intensely. Even though all such cunning is for naught when the decision is made to kill. When they strike, they don't worry about whom to save and whom to condemn. In a wiretapped call, Rosario Fusco, allegedly a Di Lauro territory capo, is notably tense even though he's trying to sound convincing to his son:

"You can't go with anyone, that much is clear, just like I wrote you: listen to your daddy, you want to go out, you want to go take a walk with a girl, fine, but you just can't hang around any boys, because we don't know who they're with or who they belong to. And if they have to do something to him and you're next to him, they'll hit you too. You understand what the problem is now, your daddy's telling you . . ."

The problem is that no one can afford to think he's not involved. It's not enough to assume that the way you live your life will protect you from every danger. It's no longer enough to say, "They're killing each other." During a Camorra conflict even the most solid construction is at risk, like a sand fence washed away by the undertow. People try to go unnoticed, to reduce to a minimum their presence in the world. Anonymous colors, little makeup, but that's not all. The asthma sufferer locks himself up in his house because he can't run, but then he finds an excuse to go out, invents a reason, because holing yourself up in your house could seem like an admission of guilt, of who knows what—and is certainly a confession of fear. Women stop wearing high heels—too hard to run in them. In a war that is not officially declared, not recognized by governments, and not recorded by reporters, the fear also goes unspoken. It hides under your skin, making you feel bloated, as after a huge meal or a night of cheap wine. A fear that doesn't explode in newspapers or on billboards. There are no invasions, no skies darkened with planes. It's a war you feel inside. Almost like a phobia. You don't know if you should show your fear or hide it. You can't decide if you're exaggerating or underestimating. There are no sirens to warn you, but the most discordant information gets through. They say the Camorra war is fought among gangs, that they kill off each other. But no one knows where the border is between who's them and who's not. The cara-

binieri jeeps, the police roadblocks, and the helicopters flying over-
head at all hours don't comfort you, but seem almost to shrink the
battlefield. They are not reassuring. They subtract space, surround
you, restrict the area of the struggle even further. You feel trapped,
shoulder to shoulder, and the heat of the person next to you becomes
unbearable.

I would ride my Vespa through this pall of tension. In Secondigliano,
I'd be frisked at least ten times a day. If I'd had so much as a Swiss
Army knife on me, they would have made me swallow it. First the police would stop me, then the carabinieri, sometimes the financial police as well, and then the Di Lauro and Spanish sentinels. All with the
same simple authority, the same mechanical gestures and identical
phrases. The law enforcement officers would look at my driver's license, then search me, while the sentinels would search me first and
then ask lots of questions, listening for the slightest accent, scanning
for lies. During the heat of the conflict the sentinels searched everyone, poked their heads into every car, cataloging your face, checking if
you were armed. The *motorini* would arrive first, piercing your very
soul, then the motorcycles, and finally the cars on your tail.

Medics filed complaints: before they could assist someone—
anyone, not just those with gunshot wounds, but even the little old
lady with a fractured femur or a heart attack victim—they had to get
out of the ambulance, submit to a search, and let a sentinel check if
it really was an ambulance or a vehicle for hiding weapons, killers, or
escapees. The Red Cross is not recognized during Camorra wars, and
no clan has signed the Geneva conventions. Even the unmarked cars
the carabinieri use are vulnerable. When some plainclothes officers
were mistaken for rivals, shots ripped into their car, wounding a few
of the men. A couple of days later a boy showed up at the barracks,
carrying a small suitcase with his underwear in it; he knew exactly
what to do during an arrest. He confessed everything immediately,

perhaps because the punishment he would have received for shooting at the carabinieri would have been far worse than jail. Or more likely, the clan, promising to give him his due and pay his legal expenses, made him turn himself in so as to avoid triggering any private feuds between men in uniform and Camorristi. Once inside the barracks the boy unhesitatingly declared, "I thought they were Spaniards so I fired."

On December 7, I am awakened again by a phone call in the middle of the night. A photographer friend was calling to inform me of the blitz. Not any blitz, but *the* blitz, the one that local and national politicians had been demanding in response to the feud.

Secondigliano is surrounded by a thousand officers. A large area whose nickname, Terzo Mondo, says it all, as does the graffiti near the entrance to the main street: "Third World, do not enter." It's a huge media operation, and Scampia, Miano, Piscinola, San Pietro a Patierno, and Secondigliano will soon be invaded by journalists and television crews. After twenty years of silence the Camorra suddenly lives again. But the lack of steady attention means that the tools of analysis are old, ancient, as if a brain that had gone into hibernation twenty years ago was just now waking up. As if it were still dealing with the Camorra of Raffaele Cutolo and the logic of the Mafia that blew up highways to kill judges. Today everything has changed except for the eyes of the observers, no matter how experienced. Among those arrested is Ciro Di Lauro, one of the boss's sons. Some say he's the clan's accountant. The carabinieri break down the door, search everyone, and aim their rifles at kids' faces. All I manage to see is an officer shouting at a boy who is pointing a knife at him.

"Drop it! Drop it! Now! Now! Drop it!"

The boy drops the knife. The officer kicks it away, and as it bounces off the baseboard, the blade folds into the handle. It's plastic, a Ninja Turtle knife. Meanwhile the other officers are frisking, photographing, searching everywhere. Dozens of blockhouses are knocked down. Reinforced concrete walls are gutted, revealing drug stashes under stairwells. Gates closing off entire portions of streets are toppled, exposing drug warehouses.

Hundreds of women pour onto the streets, setting trash bins on fire and throwing things at the police cars. Their sons, nephews, neighbors are being arrested. Their employers. Yet it's not just a criminal solidarity that I sense on their faces, in their angry words, or their hips, swathed in sweatpants so tight that they seem about to explode. The drug market provides a means of support for most Secondigliano residents, but it is minimal. The only ones who get rich, who reap exponential advantages, are the clan businessmen. All the rest, those who work selling, storing, hiding, or protecting get nothing but ordinary salaries, though they risk arrest and months or years in prison. The women's faces wear masks of rage. A rage that tastes of gastric acid. A rage that is both a defense of their territory and an accusation against those who have always considered it nonexistent, lost, a place to forget.

This gigantic deployment of law and order seems staged, arriving all of a sudden, and only after countless deaths, only after a local girl has been tortured and burned. To the women here it reeks of mockery. The police and bulldozers haven't come to change things, but merely to help out whoever now needs to make arrests or knock down walls. As if all of a sudden someone changed the categories of interpretation and were now declaring that their lives are all wrong. The women know perfectly well everything is wrong here; they didn't need helicopters and armored vehicles to remind them, but up till then this error was their principal form of life, their mode of survival. What's more, after this eruption that will only complicate their lives, no one will really make any effort to improve things. And so those women jealously guard the oblivion of their isolation and their mistaken lives, chasing away those who have suddenly become aware of the dark.

The journalists lie in wait in their cars. They're careful not to get under the carabinieri's boots, and only start covering the blitz after it's all over. At the end of the operation fifty-three people are in handcuffs. The youngest is nineteen. They've all grown up in the Naples Renaissance, in the new political dimension of the late 1990s, which was supposed to alter people's destiny. They all know what to do as the carabinieri handcuff them and load them into the prison vans: call this or that lawyer and wait till the clan stipend is delivered to their homes on the twenty-eighth of the month along with the boxes of pasta for their wives and mothers. The men with adolescent sons at home are the most worried, wondering what role their boys will be assigned now. But they have no say in the matter.

After the blitz the war knows no truce. On December 18 Pasquale Galasso, namesake of one of the most powerful bosses of the 1990s, is bumped off behind the counter of a bar. On December 20 Vincenzo Iorio is killed in a pizzeria. On the twenty-fourth they kill Giuseppe Pezzella, thirty-four years old. He tries to take cover in a bar, but they unload a whole magazine into him. Then a pause for Christmas. The guns of war fall silent. They reorganize, try to establish some rules, devise strategies in this most disorderly of conflicts. On December 27 Emanuele Leone is killed with a bullet to the head. He was twenty-one years old. On December 30 the Spaniards murder Antonio Scafuro, twenty-six, and hit his son in the leg. He was related to the Di Lauro area capo in Casavatore.

The most complicated thing was to understand. Understand how it was possible for the Di Lauros to wage a war and win. To strike and disappear. To shield themselves among the people, get lost in the neighborhoods. Lotto T, Vele, Parco Postale, Case Celesti, Case dei Puffi, and Terzo Mondo are a jungle, a rain forest of reinforced concrete where it's easy to disappear, blend in with the crowd, turn into phantoms. The Di Lauros had lost all their top management and area capos, but they'd still managed to trigger a ruthless war without suf-fering serious losses. It was as if a government, toppled by a coup and without a president, decided that the way to preserve its power and protect its interests was to arm schoolboys and draft mailmen, civil servants, and office clerks, to grant them access to the new power center instead of relegating them to the rank and file.

A bug planted in the car of Ugo De Lucia, the Di Lauro loyalist and alleged murderer of Gelsomina Verde, picks up a conversation that is filed in a December 2004 injunction:

"I'm not making a move without orders, that's the way I am!"

The perfect soldier displays his total obedience to Cosimo. Then he comments about an episode in which someone was wounded.

"I would've killed him, I wouldn't have just shot him in the leg, if I'd been there, his brain would be pulp, you know! . . . Let's use my neighborhood, it's tranquil there, we'll be able to work . . ."

Ugariello, as he is known in his neighborhood, would never have merely wounded. He would have killed.

"I say now it's up to us, let's all get together . . . all of us in one place . . . five in one house . . . five in another . . . and five in another and you send for us only when you need us to go blow someone's brains out!"

Ugariello proposes they form hit squads, or trawlers, as Camorristi call them, men who hole up in safe houses and never leave their hid-ing places except to strike. But Petrone, his interlocutor, isn't as re-laxed:

"Yeah, but if one of these bastards ends up finding some hidden trawler somewhere, if they spot us and trail us, they'll smash our heads . . . let's at least do in a few of them before we die, you know what I mean? At least let me eliminate four or five of them!"

Petrone's ideal would be to murder the ones who don't know they've been found out:

"The simplest thing is when they're comrades, you get them in your car and then you take them out."

• • •

The Di Lauros win because they are less predictable when they strike, and because they already foresee their destiny. But before the end they have to inflict as many losses as possible on the enemy. A kamikaze logic, no explosions. The only strategy that offers any chance of winning when you're in the minority. They start hitting right away, even before the trawlers are formed.

On January 2 they kill Crescenzo Marino, the McKays' father. He hangs facedown in his Smart, the most expensive model, an unusual automotive choice for a sixty-year-old man. Maybe he thought it would fool the lookouts. A single shot right in the center of his forehead. The merest trickle of blood runs down his face. Maybe he thought it wouldn't be dangerous to go out just for a few minutes, just for a second. But it was. On the same day the Spaniards bump off Salvatore Barra in a bar in Casavatore. It's the day that Carlo Azeglio Ciampi, the president of the Italian Republic, arrives in Naples to ask the city to react, to offer institutional words of courage and express the support of the state. Three ambushes occur during the hours of his visit.

On January 5 they shoot Carmela Attrice in the face. She is the mother of the secessionist Francesco Barone 'o russo—the Russian— whom investigations identified as being close to the McKays. She no longer leaves her house, so they use a kid as bait. He rings the bell. She knows him, knows who he is, so she doesn't think there's any danger. Still in her pajamas, she goes downstairs, opens the door, and someone sticks the barrel of a gun in her face. Blood and brains pour out of her head as from a broken egg.

When I arrived at the scene in Case Celesti, the body hadn't yet been covered with a sheet. People were walking in her blood, leaving footprints everywhere. I swallowed hard, trying to calm my stomach. Carmela Attrice hadn't run away even though they'd warned her. She knew her son was a Spaniard, but the Camorra war is full of uncertainty. Nothing is defined, nothing is clear. Things become real only when they happen. In the dynamics of power, of absolute power, nothing exists other than what is concrete. And so fleeing, staying, escaping, and informing are choices that seem too suspended, too uncertain, and every piece of advice always finds its opposite twin. Only a concrete occurrence can make you decide. But when it happens, all you can do is accept the decision.

When you die on the street, you're surrounded by a tremendous racket. It's not true that you die alone. Unfamiliar faces right in front of your nose, people touching your legs and arms to see if you're already dead or if it's worth calling an ambulance. All the faces of the seriously wounded, all the expressions of the dying, seem to share the same fear. And the same shame. It may seem strange, but the instant before death is marked by a sense of humiliation. *Lo scuorno* is what they call it here. A bit like being naked in public—that's how it feels when you're mortally wounded in the street. I've never gotten used to seeing murder victims. The nurses and policemen are calm, impassive, going through the motions they've learned by heart, no matter whom they're dealing with. "We've got calluses on our hearts and leather lining our stomachs," a young mortuary van driver once said to me. When you get there before the ambulance does, it's hard to take your eyes off the victim, even if you wish you'd never seen him. I've never understood that this is how you die. The first time I saw someone who'd been killed, I must have been about thirteen. It is still vivid in my mind. I woke up feeling embarrassed: poking out from my pajamas was the clear sign of an unwanted erection. That classic morning erection, impossible to disguise. I remember it because on my way to school I ran smack into a dead body in the same situation. Five of us, our backpacks filled with books, were walking to school when we came across an Alfetta riddled with bullets. My friends were terribly curious and rushed over to see. Feet sticking up on the seat. The most daring kid asked a carabiniere why the feet were where the head should have been. The officer didn't hesitate to respond, as if he hadn't realized how old his interlocutor was.

"The spray turned him upside down."

I was only a boy, but I knew that "spray" meant machine-gun fire. The Camorrista had taken so many blows that his body had flipped. Head down and feet in the air. When the carabinieri opened the door, the corpse fell to the ground like a melting icicle. We watched undisturbed, without anyone telling us this was no sight for children. Without any moral hand covering our eyes. The dead man had an erection. It was obvious under his tight-fitting jeans. And it shocked me. I stared at it for a long time. For days I wondered how it could have happened, what he'd been thinking about, what he'd been doing before dying. My afternoons were spent trying to imagine what was in his head before he was killed. It tormented me until I finally got up the courage to ask for an explanation. I was told that an erection is a common reaction in male murder victims. As soon as Linda, one of the girls in our group, saw the dead body slide out from behind the steering wheel, she started to cry and hid behind two of the boys. A strangled cry. A young plainclothes officer grabbed the cadaver by the hair and spit in his face. Then he turned to us and said:

"No, what are you crying for? This guy was a real shit. Nothing happened, everything's okay. Nothing happened. Don't cry."

Ever since then, I've had trouble believing those scenarios of forensic police who wear gloves and tread softly, careful not to displace any powder or shells. When I get to a body before the ambulance does and gaze on the final moments of life of someone who realizes he's dying, I always think of *Heart of Darkness*, the scene when the woman who loved Kurtz asks Marlow what his last words were. And Marlow lies. He says Kurtz asked about her, when in reality he didn't utter any sweet words or precious thoughts, but simply repeated, "The horror." We like to think that a person's last words convey his ultimate, most important, most essential thoughts. That he dies articulating the reason life was worth living for. But it's not like that. When you die, nothing comes out except fear. Everyone, or almost everyone, repeats the same thing, a simple, banal, urgent sentence: "I don't want to die." Their faces are superimposed on Kurtz's and express the torment, disgust, and refusal to end so horrendously, in the worst of all possible worlds. The horror.

After seeing dozens of murder victims, soiled with their own blood as it mixes with filth, as they exhale nauseating odors, as they are looked at with curiosity or professional indifference, shunned like hazardous waste or discussed with agitated cries, I have arrived at just one certainty, a thought so elementary that it approaches idiocy: death is revolting.

In Secondigliano everyone, down to the little kids, has a perfectly clear idea of how you die and the best way to go. I was about to leave the scene of Carmela Attrice's murder when I overheard two boys talking. Their tone was extremely serious.

"I want to die like the signora. In the head, bang bang and it's all over."

"But in your face? They hit her in the face, that's the worst!"

"No, it's not, and besides, it's only an instant. Front or back, but in the head for sure!"

Curious, I butted into their conversation, asking questions and trying to have my say:

"Isn't it better to be hit in the chest? One shot in the heart and it's all over."

But the boy understood the dynamics of pain far better than I did. He explained in great detail and with professional expertise the impact of bullets.

"No, in the chest it hurts a whole lot and it takes you ten minutes to die. Your lungs have to fill with blood, and the bullet is like a fiery needle that pierces and twists inside you. It hurts to get hit in the arm or leg too. But in the chest it's like a wicked snakebite that won't go away. The head's better, because you won't piss yourself or shit in your pants. No flailing around on the ground for half an hour."

He had seen. And much more than just one dead body. Getting hit in the head saves you from trembling in fear, pissing your pants, or having the stench of your guts ooze out of the holes in your stomach. I asked him more about the details of death and killing. Every conceivable question except the only one I should have asked: why was a fourteen-year-old thinking so much about death? But it didn't occur to me, not even for a second. The boy introduced himself by his nickname: Pikachu, one of the Pokémon figures. His blond hair and stocky figure had earned him the name. Pikachu pointed out some individuals in the crowd that had formed around the body of the dead woman. He lowered his voice:

"See those guys, they're the ones that killed Pupetta."

Carmela Attrice had been known as Pupetta. I tried to look them straight in the face. They seemed worked up, palpitating, moving their heads and shoulders to get a better look as the police covered the body. They'd killed her with their faces unmasked and had gone to sit nearby, under the statue of Padre Pio; as soon as a crowd started to form around the body, they'd come back to see. They were caught a few days later. Retail drug dealers made over into soldiers, trained to ambush a harmless woman, killed in her pajamas and slippers. This was their baptism of fire. The youngest was sixteen, the oldest twenty-eight, the alleged assassin twenty-two. When they were arrested, one of them, catching sight of the flashbulbs and video cameras, started to laugh and wink at the journalists. They also arrested the alleged bait, the sixteen-year-old who had rung the bell so that the woman would come downstairs. Sixteen, the same age as Carmela Attrice's daughter, who realized what had happened as soon as she heard the shots and went out onto the balcony and started to cry. The investigators also claimed that the executioners had returned to the scene of the crime. They were too curious; it was like starring in your own movie. First as actor and then as spectator, but in the same film. It must be true that you don't have a precise memory of your actions when you shoot because those boys went back, eager to see what they'd done and what sort of face the victim had. I asked Pikachu if the guys were a Di Lauro trawler, or if they at least wanted to form one. He laughed.

"A trawler! Don't they wish! They're just little pissers, but I saw a real trawler."

I didn't know if Pikachu was bullshitting me or if he'd merely pieced together what was being said around Scampia, but his story was credible. He was pedantic, precise to the point of eliminating any doubt. He was pleased to see my stunned expression as he talked. Pikachu told me he used to have a dog named Careca, like the Brazilian forward who plays for Napoli, the Italian champions. This dog liked to go out onto the apartment landing. One day he smelled someone in the apartment opposite, which is usually empty, so he started scratching at the door. A few seconds later a burst of gunfire exploded from behind the door and hit him full on. Pikachu told the story complete with sound effects:

"Rat-tat-tat-tat . . . Careca dies instantly—and the door—bang—slams open real quick."

Pikachu sat on the ground, planted his feet against a low wall, and made as if he were cradling a machine gun, imitating the sentinel that had killed his dog. The sentinel who's always sitting behind the door, a pillow behind his back and his feet braced on either side. An uncomfortable position, to keep you from falling asleep, but above all because shooting from below is a sure way to eliminate whoever is on the other side of the door without getting hit yourself. Pikachu told me that as a way of apology for killing his dog, they gave his family some money and invited him into the apartment. An apartment in which an entire trawler was hiding. He remembered everything, the rooms bare except for beds, a table, and a television.

Pikachu spoke quickly, gesticulating wildly to describe the men's positions and movements. They were nervous, tense, one of them with "pineapples" around his neck. Pineapples are the hand grenades the killers wear. Pikachu said a basket full of them was near a window. The Camorra has always had a certain fondness for grenades. Clan arsenals everywhere are filled with hand grenades and antitank bombs from Eastern Europe. Pikachu said that the men spent hours playing PlayStation, so he'd challenged and beat them all. Because he always won, they promised him that "one of these days they'd take me with them to shoot for real."

One of the popular neighborhood legends has it that Ugo De Lucia was obsessed with *Winning Eleven*, PlayStation's most famous soccer video game. According to informants, in four days he not only committed three murders, but also played an entire soccer championship.

The *pentito* Pietro Esposito, known as Kojak, recounts something that seems more than just legend. He'd gone to a house where Ugo De Lucia was stretched out on the bed in front of the television and commenting on the news:

"We've done two more pieces! And they've done one piece in Terzo Mondo."

The television was the best way to follow the war in real time without having to make compromising calls. From this point of view, the media attention the war had brought to Scampia was a strategic advantage for the fighters. But what struck me even more was the word *piece*—the new term for a homicide. Even Pikachu used it; he'd talk about the pieces done by the Di Lauros and the pieces done by the secessionists. The expression *to do a piece* came from contract labor or piecework. Killing a human being became the equivalent of manufacturing something, it didn't matter what. A piece.

Pikachu and I went for a walk and he told me about the boys in the clan, the real strength of the Di Lauros. I asked him where they hung out, and he offered to take me to a pizzeria where they'd go in the evening; he wanted me to see that he knew them all. First we picked up a friend of Pikachu's, one of the boys who'd been part of the System for a while. Pikachu worshipped him and described him as a sort of boss; the System kids looked up to him because he'd been given the task of providing food for the fugitives and even doing the shopping for the Di Lauro family, or so he claimed. He was called Tonino Kit Kat because he was known to devour masses of candy bars. Kit Kat assumed the attitude of a little boss, but I let him see I was skeptical. He got fed up answering my questions, so he lifted his sweater. His entire torso was speckled with round bruises: violet circles with yellow and greenish clots of crushed capillaries in the centers.

"What have you done?"

"The vest."

"What vest?"

"The bulletproof vest."

"The vest doesn't give you those bruises, does it?"

"No, but these eggplants are the hits I took."

The bruises—eggplants—were the fruit of the bullets that the jacket had stopped an inch before they penetrated flesh. To train the boys not to be afraid of weapons, they make them put on a vest and then fire at them. Faced with a weapon, a vest alone isn't enough to convince you not to flee. A vest is not a vaccine against fear. The only way to anesthetize every fear is to show how the weapons can be neutralized. The boys told me that they were taken out to the countryside beyond Secondigliano. They'd put the vests on under their T-shirts, and then, one by one, half a clip would be unloaded at them. "When you're hit, you fall on the ground, you can't breathe, you gasp for air, but you can't inhale. You just can't do it. It's like you've been punched in the chest, you feel like you're dying . . . but then you get back up.

That's the important thing. After you've been hit, you get back up."
Kit Kat had been trained along with others to take the hit. He'd been
trained to die, or rather to almost die.

The clans enlist the boys as soon as they're capable of being loyal.
Twelve to seventeen years old. Lots of them are sons or brothers of
clan affiliates, while others come from families without steady in-
comes. This is the Neapolitan Camorra clans' new army, recruited
via well-structured clan affiliations, drawn from the old city center,
from the Sanità, Forcella, Secondigliano, San Gaetano, Quartieri
Spagnoli, and Pallonetto neighborhoods. A whole army of them. The
advantages for the clan are many: a boy earns half the salary of a low-
ranking adult, rarely has to support his parents, doesn't have the bur-
dens of a family or fixed hours, doesn't need to be paid punctually,
and above all, is willing to be on the streets at all times. There's
a whole range of jobs and responsibilities. They start with pushing
light drugs, hashish in particular. The boys position themselves in the
most crowded streets, and they're almost always issued a *motorino*.
They work their way up to cocaine, which they peddle at the univer-
sities, outside the nightclubs, in front of hotels, inside the subway stations. These baby pushers are fundamental to the flexible economy of
drug peddling because they attract less attention, do business between a soccer match and a *motorino* ride, and will often deliver directly to the client's home. The clan doesn't usually make them work
mornings; in fact, they continue to go to school, in part because
if they dropped out, they would be easier to identify. After the first
couple of months, the boy affiliates go about armed, both in self-
defense and as a way of asserting themselves. The weapons—
automatics and semiautomatics the boys learn to use in the garbage
dumps outside of town or in the city's underground caverns—are both
a promotion on the field and a promise of possibility, of rising to the
top of the clan.

When they prove themselves reliable and win the area capo's complete trust, they take on a role that goes well beyond that of pusher:

they become lookouts. Lookouts make sure that all the trucks unloading goods at the supermarkets, stores, and delicatessens on their assigned street are ones imposed by the clan, and they report when a shop is using a distributor other than the "preselected" one. The presence of lookouts is also essential at construction sites. Contracting firms often subcontract to Camorra companies, but at times the work is assigned to firms that are "not recommended." To discover if work is being given to "external" firms, the clans monitor the sites constantly, and in a way that is above suspicion. The boys observe, check, and report back to the area capo, who tells them what to do if a site steps out of line. These young affiliates behave like and have the responsibilities of adult Camorristi. They start their careers young and charge up through the ranks; their rise to positions of power is radically altering the genetic structure of the clans. Baby capos and boy bosses make for unpredictable and ruthless interlocutors; they follow a logic that keeps law officers and anti-Mafia investigators from understanding their dynamics. The faces are new and unfamiliar. Following Cosimo's reorganization, entire divisions of the drug market are run by fifteen- and sixteen-year-olds who give orders to forty- and fifty-year-olds without feeling the least bit embarrassed or inadequate. The car of one of these boys, Antonio Galeota Lanza, was bugged by the carabinieri. The stereo blasting, Antonio talks about his life as a pusher:

"Every Sunday evening I make eight or nine hundred euros, even if being a pusher means you deal with crack, cocaine, and five hundred years of jail."

The System boys now tend to try to obtain everything they want with "iron," as they call their pistols, and the desire for a cell phone or a stereo, a car or a *motorino*, easily transmutes into a killing. It's not unusual to hear baby soldiers at the checkout counter in a supermarket or shop say things like "I belong to the Secondigliano System" or "I belong to the Quartieri System." Magic words that allow the boys to walk off with whatever they want and in the face of which no shopkeeper would ever ask them to pay what they owe.

In Secondigliano this new structure of boys was militarized. Pikachu and Kit Kat took me to see Nello, a pizza chef in the area who was responsible for feeding the System boys when they'd finished their shifts. A group came into Nello's pizzeria just after I got there. They were awkward and ungainly, their sweaters puffed out from the bulletproof vests underneath. They'd left their *motorini* on the sidewalk and came in without saying hello to anyone. The way they walked, with their padded chests, made them look like football players. Boyish faces, thirteen to sixteen years old, a few with the first hints of a beard. Pikachu and Kit Kat had me sit with them, and no one seemed to mind. They were eating and, above all, drinking. Water, Coca-Cola, Fanta. An incredible thirst that they tried to quench even with the pizza; they asked for a bottle of olive oil and then poured large amounts on the pizzas, saying they were too dry. Everything dried up in their mouths, from their saliva to their words. I realized immediately that they were coming off a night shift as watch guards and had taken pills. They gave them MDMA pills—ecstasy—to keep them awake, to keep them from stopping to eat twice a day. After all, the German drugmaker Merck patented MDMA during World War I for soldiers in the trenches—those German soldiers referred to as *Menschenmaterial*, human material—to enable them to overcome hunger, cold, and terror. Later it was used by the Americans for espionage operations. And now these little soldiers received their dose of artificial courage and adulterated resistance. They cut slices of pizza and sucked them down; the sounds coming from the table were of old people slurping their soup. The boys resumed talking and kept ordering bottles of water. And then I did something that could have been met with violence, but I sensed I could get away with it, that these were kids I was looking at. Padded with plates of lead, but kids nevertheless. I put a tape recorder on the table and addressed them all in a loud voice, trying to catch each one's eye:

"*Forza*, go ahead and talk into this, say whatever you feel like."

This didn't strike anyone as strange, and no one suspected they were sitting with a narc or a journalist. Someone hurled a few insults at the recorder, then one boy, encouraged by some of my questions, recounted his career. It seemed as if he couldn't wait to tell it.

"First I worked in a bar. I made two hundred euros a month, two fifty with tips, but I didn't like the work. I wanted to work in the garage with my brother, but they didn't take me. In the System I get three hundred euros a week, but if I sell well, I also get a percentage on every brick of hashish and can make up to three hundred fifty, four hundred euros. I have to bust my ass, but in the end they always give me something more."

After a volley of belches that two of the kids wanted to record, the boy called Satore, a name halfway between Sasà and Totore, two diminutives for Salvatore, continued:

"Before I was out on the street, it annoyed me that I didn't have a *motorino* and had to get around on foot or take the bus. I like the work, everyone respects me, and I can do what I want. Now they gave me iron and I have to stay around here all the time, Terzo Mondo, Case dei Puffi. Always in the same place, back and forth. And I don't like it."

Satore smiled at me, then laughed loudly into the recorder:

"Let me out of here! Tell that to the boss!"

They'd been given iron—a pistol—and a limited territory in which to work. Kit Kat began to speak into the recorder, his lips touching the holes of the microphone, so that even his breath registered.

"I want to open a remodeling company or else a warehouse or a store. The System will have to give me the money to get set up, but then I'll worry about the rest, even who to marry. I want to get married, not to somebody from here, though, but a model, black or German."

Pikachu took a pack of cards from his pocket, and four of them started to play. The others got up and stretched, but no one removed his bulletproof vest. I kept asking Pikachu about the trawlers, but he was starting to get irritated at my insistence. He told me he'd been at a trawler house a few days before, but that they'd dismantled every-thing; the only thing left was their MP3 player with the music they listened to when they went to do pieces, which was now dangling from his neck. Inventing an excuse, I asked if I could borrow it for a few days. Pikachu laughed as if to say that he wasn't offended that I'd taken him for an idiot, for someone stupid enough to lend things. So I bought it. I coughed up 50 euros and he gave me the player. I imme-diately stuck the headphones in my ears; I wanted to know what trawler background music was. I was expecting rap, acid rock, heavy metal, but instead it was an endless round of Neapolitan neo-melodic music and pop. In America, killers pump themselves up on rap, but in Secondigliano they go off to kill with love songs in their ears.

Pikachu started shuffling and asked me if I wanted in, but I've always been hopeless at cards, so I got up from the table. The waiters at the pizzeria were the same age as the System boys, and they looked at them admiringly, lacking even the courage to serve them. The owner took care of them himself. To work as an errand boy, waiter, or on a construction site is considered a disgrace here. In addition to the usual, eternal reasons—no contract, no sick days or vacation, ten-hour shifts—there's no hope of bettering your situation. The System at least grants the illusion that commitment will be recognized, that it's possible to make a career. An affiliate will never be seen as an er-rand boy, and girls will never feel they are being courted by a failure. These padded boys, these ridiculous sentinels who looked like pup-pets of football players, didn't dream of being Al Capone but Flavio Briatore, not gunslingers but entrepreneurs with beautiful models on their arms; they wanted to become successful businessmen.

On January 19, 2005, the forty-five-year-old Pasquale Paladini is killed. Eight shots to the chest and head. A few hours later, Antonio

Auletta, age nineteen, is hit in the legs. But January 21 seems to be a turning point. Word spreads quickly, there's no need for a press office. Cosimo Di Lauro has been arrested. According to the Naples anti-Mafia prosecutor's office, Cosimo is the prince of the gang and the leader of the slaughter. According to state witnesses, he's the clan commander. Cosimo was hiding in a hole forty meters square and sleeping on a dilapidated bed. The heir to a criminal association that invoices 500,000 euros a day from narcotics alone, and who had a villa worth 5 million euros in the heart of one of the poorest regions of Italy, was reduced to hiding in a stinking little hole not far from his alleged palace.

A villa that rose out of nothing in Via Cupa dell'Arco, near the Di Lauro family home. An elegant, eighteenth-century farmhouse, restructured like a Pompeian villa, complete with impluvium, columns, plaster decorations, false ceilings, and grand staircases. No one knew it existed. No one knew the official owners. The carabinieri were investigating, but no one in the neighborhood had any doubts. It was for Cosimo. The carabinieri discovered the place by chance. After breaching the thick walls surrounding it, they came across some workers, who ran off as soon as they saw the uniforms. The war interrupted work on the villa, kept it from being filled with furniture and paintings fit for a prince, from becoming the heart of gold of the decaying body of the Secondigliano building industry.

When Cosimo hears the rumble of the carabinieri amphibians and the clatter of their rifles, he doesn't try to escape. He doesn't even arm himself. Instead he goes to the mirror, wets his comb, pulls his hair off his forehead, and ties it in a ponytail at his nape, letting the curly mane fall onto his neck. He is wearing a dark polo-neck sweater and a black raincoat. Dressed as a clown of crime, a warrior of the night, Cosimo Di Lauro descends the stairs, chest out. A few years earlier he took a disastrous spill on his motorcycle, and the legacy was a lame leg. But he's even thought about his limp; as he walks down the stairs he leans on the forearms of the carabinieri who escort him, so as not to reveal his handicap, and proceeds with a normal gait. The new military sovereigns of the Neapolitan criminal associations don't present themselves as neighborhood tough guys, don't have the crazy, wide-eyed look of Raffaele Cutolo, don't feel the need to pose as the Cosa Nostra boss Luciano Liggio or caricatures of Lucky Luciano and Al Capone. *The Matrix, The Crow,* and *Pulp Fiction* give a better idea of what they want and who they are. They are models everyone recognizes and that don't need too much mediation. Spectacle is superior to enigmatic codes of winking or the well-defined mythology of infamous crime neighborhoods. Cosimo looks straight at the cameras, lowers his chin, and sticks out his forehead. He didn't let himself be found out the way Giovanni Brusca did, wearing a pair of threadbare jeans and a shirt with spaghetti sauce stains; he's not frightened like Totò Riina, who was quickly loaded into a helicopter, or surprised with a sleepy look on his face like Giuseppe Misso, the Sanità neighborhood boss. Cosimo has been brought up in the world of show business, and he knows how to go onstage. He appears like a warrior who has stumbled for the first time. The expression on his face says this is the price he must pay for having so much courage and zeal. He acts as if he weren't being arrested, but simply moving headquarters. He knew the risk when he triggered the war, but he had no choice. It was war or death. He wants his arrest to seem like the proof of his victory, the symbol of his courage that disdains any form of self-defense as long as it preserves the family system.

The people in the neighborhood feel their stomachs churn. They set off a revolt, overturning cars and launching Molotov cocktails. This hysterical attack is not, as it may seem, to prevent the arrest, but rather to exorcise any act of revenge. To erase every trace of suspicion. To let Cosimo know that no one betrayed him, no one blabbed, that the hieroglyphics of his hiding place had not been deciphered with their help. The revolt is an elaborate rite of apology, a metaphysical chapel of atonement that the neighborhood people build from burned-out carabinieri cars, dumpsters used as barricades, and black smoke from fuming tires. If Cosimo suspects them, they won't even have time to pack their bags before the ax falls in yet another ruthless condemnation.

Just days after his arrest, Cosimo's haughty gaze stares out of the screen savers of the cell phones of dozens of kids in Torre Annunziata, Quarto, and Marano. Mere provocations, banal gestures of adolescent foolishness. Of course. But Cosimo knew. You have to act this way to be recognized as a capo, to touch people's hearts. You have to know how to work the TV screen and the newspaper, how to tie your ponytail. Cosimo clearly represents the new model of System entrepreneur, the image of the new bourgeoisie, liberated of every constraint, motivated by the absolute desire to dominate every corner of the market and to have a hand in everything. To let go of nothing. Choosing doesn't mean limiting your field of action, depriving yourself of all other options. Not for someone who thinks of life as a place where you risk losing everything so as to win it all. It means taking into account that you can be arrested, end badly, die. But it doesn't mean giving up. To want everything now, to have it as soon as possible. This is Cosimo Di Lauro's appeal, the power he symbolizes.

Everyone, even those who take special care of themselves, gets caught in the trap of retirement, finds out sooner or later he's been cuckolded, or ends up having a Polish nurse. Why should you die of depression looking for a job that will kill you, or end up working part-time answering phones? Become an entrepreneur. For real. One who deals in anything and does business even with nothing. Ernst Jünger would say that greatness consists in being exposed to the storm. The Camorra bosses would say the same thing. To be the center of every action, the center of power. To use everything as a means and themselves as the ends. Whoever says that it's amoral, that life can't exist without ethics, that the economy has limits and must obey certain rules, is merely someone who has never been in command, who's been defeated by the market. Ethics are the limit of the loser, the protection of the defeated, the moral justification for those who haven't managed to gamble everything and win it all. The law has fixed codes, but justice doesn't. Justice is something else, an abstract principle that involves everyone, that is tolerable depending on how it is interpreted to absolve or condemn every human being: guilty are the ministers and popes, the saints and heretics, the revolutionaries and reactionaries. Guilty, every one of them, of betrayal, murder, error. Guilty of growing old and dying. Guilty of becoming obsolete and defeated. Guilty, every one of them, in the eyes of the universal court of historical morals and absolved by the court of necessity. Justice and injustice, in reality, have only one significance. Victory or defeat, something done or endured. If someone offends you, treats you wrong, he is committing an injustice; if instead he treats you with goodwill, he does you justice. These are the terms of evaluation to use when observing the clans. These are the standards of judgment. They are enough. They have to be. This is the only real way to evaluate justice. The rest is just religion and confessional booths. This is the logic that shapes the economic imperative. It's not the Camorristi who pursue deals, but deals that pursue the Camorristi. The logic of criminal business, of the bosses, coincides with the most aggressive neoliberalism. The rules, dictated or imposed, are those of business, profit, and victory over all the competition. Anything else is worthless. Anything else doesn't exist. You pay with prison or your skin for the power to decide people's lives or deaths, promote a product, monopolize a slice of the economy, and invest in cutting-edge markets. To have power for ten years, a year, an hour—it doesn't matter for how long. What counts is to live, to truly command. To win in the market arena, to stare at the sun, as the Forcella boss Raffaele Giuliano did, challenging it from his prison cell, showing that he was not blinded even by that supreme light. Raffaele Giuliano, who ruthlessly spread hot pepper on a knife before stabbing the relative of an enemy, so as to make him feel excruciating, burning pain as the blade pierced his flesh, inch by inch. In prison he was feared not for his bloodthirsty punctiliousness, but for the challenge of his gaze, which looked directly into the sun. To know you are a businessman destined to end up dead or in jail and still feel the ruthless desire to dominate powerful and unlimited economic empires. The boss is arrested or killed, but the economic system he generated remains, and it continues to mutate, evolve, improve, and produce profits. The mentality of these samurai liberalists who know that you have to pay to have power—absolute power—was summed up in a letter a boy in juvenile detention wrote and gave to a priest. It was read during a conference. I still remember it by heart:

> Everyone I know is either dead or in jail. I want to become a boss. I want to have supermarkets, stores, factories, I want to have women. I want three cars, I want respect when I go into a store, I want to have warehouses all over the world. And then I want to die. I want to die like a man, like someone who truly commands. I want to be killed.

This is the new rhythm of criminal entrepreneurs, the new thrust of the economy: to dominate it at any cost. Power before all else. Economic victory is more precious than life itself. Than anyone's life, including your own.

They even started calling the System kids "the talking dead." In a wiretapped conversation included in the holding order issued by the anti-Mafia prosecutor's office in February 2006, a boy explains who the neighborhood capos in Secondigliano are:

"They're young kids, the talking dead, the living dead, the walking dead . . . they kill you without even thinking twice about it, but you're already as good as dead."

Boy capos, clan kamikazes who go to their death not for any religion but for money and power, at all costs, in defense of the only way of life worth living.

• • •

The body of Giulio Ruggiero is found on the evening of January 21, the same night in which Cosimo Di Lauro is arrested. A burned-out car, a cadaver in the driver's seat. Decapitated. The head is on the backseat. It hadn't been cut off with a hatchet, a clean blow, but with a metal grinder: the kind of circular saw welders use to polish soldering. The worst possible tool, and thus the most obvious choice. First cut the flesh, then chip away at the bones. They must have done the job right there because the ground was littered with flakes of flesh that looked like tripe. The investigations hadn't even begun, but everyone in the area seemed convinced it was a message. A symbol. Cosimo Di Lauro could not have been arrested without a tip-off. In everyone's mind, that headless body was a traitor. Only someone who has sold a capo can be ripped apart like that. The sentence is passed before the investigations even begin. It doesn't really matter if the sentence is correct or if it's chasing an illusion. I looked at that abandoned car and head in Via Hugo Pratt without getting off my Vespa. I could hear the talk of how they had burned the body and the severed head, filling the mouth with gasoline, placing a wick between its teeth, and setting it on fire so that the whole face would explode. I started my Vespa and drove off.

When I arrived on the scene on January 24, 2005, Attilio Romanò was lying dead on the floor. A horde of carabinieri were nervously pacing in front of the store where the ambush had taken place. Yet another one. An agitated youth comments as he passes, "A death a day, that's the refrain of Naples." He stops, doffs his hat to the dead he doesn't even see, and walks on. The killers had entered the shop with their pistols ready. It was clear that they weren't there to steal but to kill, to punish. Attilio had tried to hide behind the counter. He knew it wouldn't make a difference, but maybe he hoped to show he was unarmed, that he wasn't involved, that he hadn't done anything. Maybe he knew they were soldiers in the Camorra war the Di Lauros were waging. They shot him, emptying their magazines into him, and after the "service" they left the store—calmly, people say—as if they had just bought a cell phone instead of killing a human being. Attilio Romanò is on the floor. Blood everywhere. It seems as if his soul had drained out of the holes that riddled his body. When you see that much blood on the ground, you start touching yourself, checking if you've been wounded, if it's your own blood you're looking at. You develop a psychotic anxiety and try to make sure that you haven't been wounded somehow without realizing it. And still you can't believe that there could be so much blood in just one man. You're sure there's far less inside you. And when you've ascertained that it wasn't you who lost all that blood, you still feel empty. You become a hemorrhage yourself, you feel your legs go weak, fur on your tongue, your hands dissolve in that thick lake. You wish someone would look at the whites of your eyes to check if you're anemic. You want to ask for a blood transfusion, you wish you could eat a steak, if you could just get it down without vomiting. You have to shut your eyes and try not to breathe. The smell of congealed blood, like rusty iron, has already penetrated the plaster on the walls. You have to leave, go outside, get some air before they start throwing sawdust on the blood because the combination smells so terrible it will make you vomit for sure.

I couldn't truly understand why I had decided to show up yet again at a murder scene. But I was sure of one thing: it's not important to map out what has happened, to reconstruct the terrible drama that has unfolded. It's pointless to study the traces of the bullets, the chalk circles drawn around them, like a children's game of marbles. The thing to do instead is to try to understand if something remains. Maybe this is what I want to track down. I try to understand if anything human is left, if there is a path, a tunnel dug by the worm of existence that can lead to a solution, an answer that could give some sense of what is happening.

Attilio's body is still on the floor when his family arrives. Two women, maybe his mother and his wife, I don't know. They walk shoulder to shoulder, cling to each other as they approach. They're the only ones who are still hoping it is not as they know it to be. They understand perfectly well. But they wrap their arms around each other, support one another in the instant before they face the tragedy. And in those very seconds, in the steps that wives and mothers take toward crumpled cadavers, one senses the irrational, mad, and pointless faith in human longing. They hope, hope, hope, and hope some more that there has been a mistake, that the rumors are wrong, a misunderstanding on the part of the carabiniere official who had told them of the ambush and the killing. As if clinging stubbornly to their belief can actually alter the course of events. In that moment the blood pressure of hope is at its peak. But there's nothing to be done. The cries and weeping reveal reality's force of gravity. Attilio is on the floor. He worked in a phone store and, to make a little extra money, at a call center. He and his wife, Natalia, hadn't had children yet. They hadn't had time; maybe they didn't have the means; maybe they were waiting for the chance to raise them somewhere else. Their days were consumed by work, and when they were finally able to put a little something aside, Attilio had thought it a good idea to buy into the business where he met his death. But the other owner is a distant relative of Pariante, the boss of Bacoli, a Di Lauro colonel who turned against him. Attilio doesn't know or maybe he underestimates the danger; he trusts his partner, it's enough that he's someone who supports himself, someone who works hard, too hard. After all, around here you don't choose your lot, and a job seems like a privilege, something you hold on to once you've gotten it. You feel fortunate, as if a lucky star had shone on you, even if it means you're away from home thirteen hours a day, you get only half of Sunday off, and your 1,000 euros a month are hardly enough to cover your mortgage. No matter how you got the job, you have to be thankful and not ask too many questions—of yourself or of fate.

But someone has his doubts. And so the body of Attilio Romanò gets added to those of the Camorra soldiers killed in recent months. The bodies are the same, fallen in the same war, but the reasons for their deaths are different. The clans are the ones to decide who you are and what part you play in the game of risk. They decide independently of individuals' wills. When the armies take to the streets, it is impossible to move according to any other dynamic than their strategy; it is they who decide meaning, motives, causes. In that moment, the shop where Attilio worked represented an economy linked to the Spaniards, one that had to be destroyed.

Natalia, or Nata as Attilio called her, is stunned by the tragedy. They'd only been married for four months, but she is not consoled, the president of the Republic doesn't attend the funeral, there's no minister or mayor to hold her hand. Perhaps it's just as well: she is spared the institutional theater. But an unjust suspicion hovers over Attilio's death, a suspicion that is the silent approval of the rule of the Camorra. Yet another assent to the clans' activities. But the people who worked with Attila—the nickname they gave him because of his fierce desire to live—at the call center organize candlelight vigils and insist on marching even if other murders occur during the protests and blood still stains the streets. They demonstrate, light candles, clarify, remove all shame, cancel out all suspicion. Attila died on the job and had no ties to the Camorra.

In truth, after an ambush suspicion falls on everyone. The clan machine is too perfect. There are no mistakes, only punishments. And so it is the clan who is believed, not the relatives who don't understand, the colleagues who know him, or the life story of the individual. In this war, innocent individuals are crushed and cataloged as side effects or listed among the probably guilty.

On December 26, 2004, Dario Scherillo, a twenty-six-year-old, is riding his motorcycle when he's shot in the face and chest and left to die in a puddle of his blood, which soaks his shirt completely. An innocent man. But he was from Casavatore, a town that has been chewed up by the conflict. For him there is still silence and incomprehension. No epigraph, no plaque, no remembrance. "When someone is killed by the Camorra, you never know," an old man tells me as he crosses himself at the spot where Dario was killed. Not all blood is the same color. Dario's is reddish purple and seems to still be flowing. The piles of sawdust have a hard time absorbing it all. After a bit a car takes advantage of the space and parks on top of the stain. Everything comes to an end. Everything gets covered over. Dario was killed to send a message to the town, a message of flesh sealed in an envelope of blood. As in Bosnia, Algeria, Somalia, as in any confused internal war, when it's hard to understand which side you're on, it's enough to kill your neighbor, a dog, your friend, or your relative. The hint of kinship or physical resemblance is all it takes to become a target. It's enough to walk down a certain street to immediately acquire an identity of lead. What matters is to concentrate as much pain, tragedy, and terror as possible, and the only objective is to show absolute strength, uncontested control, and the impossibility of opposing the real and ruling power. To the point that you get used to thinking the way they do, like those who might take offense at a gesture or a phrase. To save your life, to avoid touching the high-voltage line of revenge, you have to be careful, wary, silent. As I was leaving, as they were taking away Attilio Romanò, I started to understand. To understand why there is not a moment in which my mother does not look at me with anxiety, unable to understand why I don't leave, run away, why I keep living in this hell. I tried to recall how many have fallen, how many have been killed since the day I was born.

You don't need to count the dead to understand the business of the Camorra. The dead are the least revealing element of the Camorra's real power, but they are the most visible trace, what sparks a gut reaction. I start counting: 100 deaths in 1979, 140 in 1980, 110 in 1981, 264 in 1982, 204 in 1983, 155 in 1984, 107 in 1986, 127 in

1987, 168 in 1988, 228 in 1989, 222 in 1990, 223 in 1991, 160 in 1992, 120 in 1993, 115 in 1994, 148 in 1995, 147 in 1996, 130 in 1997, 132 in 1998, 91 in 1999, 118 in 2000, 80 in 2001, 63 in 2002, 83 in 2003, 142 in 2004, 90 in 2005.

Since I was born, 3,600 deaths. The Camorra has killed more than the Sicilian Mafia, more than the 'Ndrangheta, more than the Russian Mafia, more than the Albanian families, more than the total number of deaths by the ETA in Spain and the IRA in Ireland, more than the Red Brigades, the NAR,* and all the massacres committed by the government in Italy. The Camorra has killed the most. Imagine a map of the world, the sort you see in newspapers such as *Le Monde Diplomatique*, which marks places of conflict around the globe with a little flame. Kurdistan, Sudan, Kosovo, East Timor. Your eye is drawn to the south of Italy, to the flesh that piles up with every war connected to the Camorra, the Mafia, the 'Ndrangheta, the Sacra Corona Unita in Puglia, and the Basilischi in Lucania. But there's no little flame, no sign of a conflict. This is the heart of Europe. This is where the majority of the country's economy takes shape. It doesn't much matter what the strategies for extraction are. What matters is that the cannon fodder remain mired in the outskirts, trapped in tangles of cement and trash, in the black-market factories and cocaine warehouses. And that no one notice them, that it all seem like a war among gangs, a beggars' war. Then you understand the way your friends who have emigrated, who have gone off to Milan or Padua, smile sarcastically at you, wondering whom you have become. They look at you from head to toe, try to size you up, figure out if you are a *chiachiello* or a *bbuono*. A failure or a Camorrista. You know which direction you chose at the fork in the road, which path you're on, and you don't see anything good at the end.

---

*The NAR, the Nuclei Armati Rivoluzionari or Armed Revolutionary Nuclei, was a neofascist terrorist organization active in Italy in the late 1970s.—Trans.

I went home, but I couldn't sit still. I went out again and started to run, faster and faster, my knees gyrating, my heels drumming my buttocks, my arms flailing like a puppet's. My heart was pounding, my tongue and teeth were drowning in saliva. I could feel the blood swelling the veins in my neck, flooding my chest, I was out of breath, inhaling all the air I could and then exhaling hard, like a bull. I started running again, my hands frozen, my face on fire, my eyes closed. I felt I had absorbed all the blood I had seen on the ground, that all the blood that had gushed out, as if from a broken faucet, was now pumping through my body.

I ran to the shore and climbed on the rocks. Haze mixed with the darkness so I couldn't even make out the lights of the ships crossing the gulf. The water rippled, the waves were beginning to pick up. It seemed as if they were reluctant to touch the mire of the battleground, but they didn't return to the distant maelstrom of the open sea. The waves were immobile, stubbornly resisting, impossibly fixed, clinging to their foamy crests, no longer sure where the sea ends.

Reporters start arriving a few weeks later. All of a sudden, the Camorra has come back to life in the region they believed hosted nothing but gangs and bag-snatchers. Within a few hours Secondigliano becomes the center of attention. Special correspondents, press photographers from the most important news agencies, even a permanent BBC garrison. Some kids have their picture taken next to a cameraman who's carrying a video camera with the CNN logo. "Just like the ones for Saddam," the kids in Scampia say with a giggle. The cameras make them feel they've been transported to the earth's center of gravity, and the media attention seems to grant these places a real existence for the first time. After twenty years of neglect, the Secondigliano massacre focuses attention on the Camorra. The war kills quickly, out of respect for the reporters. In less than a month dozens and dozens of victims are accumulated; it seems done on purpose so that every correspondent has his own death. Success all around. Flocks of interns are sent to get experience. Microphones and cameras sprout all over the place to interview drug dealers and capture the forbidding, angular profile of the Vele projects. A few interns even manage to interview some alleged pushers, shooting them from behind. Almost everyone gives some change to the heroin addicts who mumble their stories. Two young female reporters have their camera operator photograph them in front of a burned-out car. A souvenir from their first little war as reporters. A French journalist calls me to ask if he should wear a bulletproof vest to go photograph Cosimo Di Lauro's villa. Media crews drive around shooting, as if they were exploring a forest where everything has been transformed into a stage set. Other journalists travel with bodyguards. The worst way of reporting on Secondigliano is to be escorted by the police. These are not inaccessible areas; the strength of the local drug markets is that they guarantee complete accessibility to everyone. The journalists who go around with bodyguards will only be able to record what they can already find printed by any news agency. Like sitting in front of their office computers, except that they're moving.

More than a hundred reporters in less than two weeks. All of a sudden Europe's drug market exists. Even the police are swamped with requests; everyone wants to take part in an operation, see at least one pusher arrested, one house searched. Everyone wants to insert a few images of confiscated handcuffs and machine guns into their fifteen-minute broadcast. A lot of officers start liberating themselves of the hordes of reporters and budding investigative journalists by having them photograph plainclothes policemen who pose as pushers. A way to give them what they want without losing too much time. The worst possible story in the shortest possible time. The worst of the worst, the horror of horrors. Broadcast the tragedy, the blood and guts, the submachine-gun shots, the crushed skulls and burned flesh. The worst they tell is merely the waste of the worst. Many reporters think they have found the ghetto of Europe in Secondigliano, a place of total misery. But if they didn't run away, they would realize that they are looking at the pillars of the economy, the hidden mine, the darkness where the beating heart of the market gets its energy.

The television reporters made the most incredible proposals. Some asked me to wear a tiny video camera on my ear as I go about certain streets—"you know which ones"—following "you know who." They dreamed of making Scampia into a reality show, with footage of a homicide or drug deal. One scriptwriter handed me a story of blood and death, where the devil of the new century is conceived in Terzo Mondo. I got a free dinner every evening for a month from the television crews who presented me with absurd proposals, trying to gather information. During the feud a veritable industry of guides, official interpreters, informers, and Indian scouts grew up among the Camorra reserves in Secondigliano and Scampia. Many kids developed a special technique. They wandered over to the area where the reporters were gathered, pretending to be pushers or lookouts, and as soon as someone got up the courage to approach them, they announced their availability to talk, explain, be photographed. They stated their fees right away. Fifty euros for their story, 100 euros for a tour of an open-air drug market, 200 to go inside the house of one of the dealers who lives in the Vele projects.

To understand the cycle of gold you can't just look at the nugget or the mine. You have to start in Secondigliano and follow the tracks of the clans' empires. The Camorra wars put the towns ruled by the clans on the map: the Campania hinterland, the land of poverty, territories that some call the Italian Far West, where, according to one grim legend, there are more submachine guns than forks. But beyond the violence that erupts in particular moments, these areas produce an exponential wealth, of which they only see the distant shimmer. But none of this gets reported. Media coverage is only concerned with the aesthetics of the Neapolitan slums.

• • •

On January 29, Vincenzo De Gennaro is killed. On January 31, they kill Vittorio Bevilacqua in a delicatessen. On February 1, Giovanni Orabona, Giuseppe Pizzone, and Antonio Patrizio are slain. They use an ancient yet effective strategy: the killers pose as policemen. Giovanni Orabona was the twenty-three-year-old forward on the Real Casavatore soccer team. They were taking a walk when a car with a siren stopped them. Two men with police badges got out. The men didn't try to flee or put up resistance. They knew how to behave, so they let themselves be handcuffed and loaded into the car. But the car stopped suddenly and they were made to get out. The three men might not have understood right away, but everything became clear at the sight of the guns. It was an ambush. These were Spaniards, not policemen. Members of the rebel group. Two of the men were shot in the head as they knelt, dying instantly. The third, judging from the evidence at the scene, tried to escape, but, hands tied behind his back and only his head to help him balance, he fell, got up, and fell again. The killers caught him and stuck an automatic in his mouth. When his body was found, his teeth were broken. Instinctively he'd tried to bite the barrel, to break it off.

On February 27 word arrives from Barcelona that Raffaele Amato has been arrested. He'd been playing blackjack in a casino, trying to divest himself of some cash. The Di Lauros had only managed to hit his cousin Rosario, burning down his house. According to the accusations of the Neapolitan magistracy, Amato was the charismatic leader of the Spaniards. He'd grown up right on Via Cupa dell'Arco, the same street as Paolo Di Lauro and his family. Amato became an important manager when he started mediating narcotraffic and handling wager investments. According to *pentiti* and anti-Mafia investigations, he enjoyed unlimited credit with the international traffickers and imported tons of cocaine. When police in ski masks threw him face-down on the floor, it was not the first hiatus in his career. Raffaele Amato had been arrested in a hotel in Casandrino together with another lieutenant and a big Albanian trafficker who was aided by an interpreter par excellence, the nephew of a government minister.

On February 5, it's Angelo Romano's turn. On March 3, Davide Chiarolanza is killed in Melito. He knew his killers and might even have had an appointment with them. He was done in as he tried to flee to his car. But it is not the courts or the carabinieri and police who can put an end to the feud. The forces of law and order can slow things down by taking out Camorristi, but they are unable to stop the violence. While the press chases after the crime reports, tripping over interpretations and evaluations, a Neapolitan newspaper comes out with news of a pact between the Spaniards and the Di Lauros, a temporary peace mediated by the Licciardi clan. The other Secondigliano clans, as well as the other Camorra cartels, are eager for an agreement; they fear that the conflict will break the silence concerning their power. It is crucial that the legal universe return to ignoring the world of criminal accumulation. The pact is not written overnight by some charismatic boss in a jail cell, not circulated secretly, but published in an article by Simone Di Meo in the *Cronache di Napoli* on June 27, 2005. On the newsstands for all to read and understand. Here are the points of the published agreement:

1. The secessionists demand the restitution of the lodgings that were vacated between November and January in Scampia and Secondigliano. Circa eight hundred people were forced by the Di Lauro hit squad to leave their homes.
2. The Di Lauro monopoly on the drug market has been broken. There's no going back. The territory must be divided up fairly. The province to the secessionists, Naples to the Di Lauros.

3. The secessionists can make use of their own channels to import drugs; they are no longer required to depend on Di Lauro middlemen.

4. Private vendettas are separate from business; in other words, business is more important than personal matters. If in the future there is a vendetta connected to the feud, it will not reignite hostilities but will remain a private matter.

The boss of bosses of Secondigliano must have returned. He'd been sighted everywhere, from Puglia to Canada. The secret service has been working for months to nab him. Paolo Di Lauro leaves the most elusive of traces—invisible, like his power before the feud. It seems that he was operated on in a clinic in Marseille, the same one that treated the Cosa Nostra boss Bernardo Provenzano. He has returned to sign the peace pact or to limit damages. He's here, you can feel his presence; the wind has shifted. The boss who has been missing for ten years, the one who "had to come back, even if he has to run the risk of prison," as one affiliate stated over the phone. The phantom boss, whose face is a mystery even to his affiliates. One of them pleaded with the boss Maurizio Prestieri, "I beg you, let me see him, just for a second, just one second, one look and then I'll go."

Paolo Di Lauro is nabbed on Via Canonico Stornaiuolo on September 16, 2005. Hidden in the modest home of Fortunata Liguori, the woman of a low-ranking affiliate. An anonymous house, similar to the one where his son Cosimo had hid. It's easier to camouflage yourself in the cement forest; in a nondescript home you're not noticed, not talked about. The urban environment offers total absence, and hiding in the city provides greater anonymity than behind a trapdoor or in an underground hideout. Paolo Di Lauro was nearly arrested on his birthday. It was a challenge to return home to eat with his family when half of Europe's police were on his trail. But someone warned him in time. When the carabinieri entered the family villa, they found the table set and his place empty. But this time the ROS, the special operations unit of the carabinieri, are sure. The officers are agitated when they enter the house at 4 a.m. after a whole night of surveillance. The boss, on the other hand, doesn't react; in fact he soothes them.

"Come in . . . I am calm . . . There's no problem."

Twenty vehicles escort the car carrying Paolo Di Lauro, and four motorcycles ride ahead, making sure everything is under control. The motorcade speeds along, with the boss in the armored car. There are three possible routes to the barracks: to cross Via Capodimonte and then dart along Via Pessina and Piazza Dante; to block all access to Corso Secondigliano and get onto the beltway toward Vomero; or, if the situation looks extremely dangerous, to land a helicopter and take him by air. The motorcycles indicate a suspicious automobile along the route. Everyone is expecting an ambush, but it turns out to be a false alarm. The motorcade delivers Di Lauro to the barracks on Via Pastrengo, in the heart of Naples. The helicopter swoops down, kicking up dust and dirt from the flowerbed in the piazza, which whirls about along with plastic bags, Kleenex, and newspapers. A whirlwind of rubbish.

There's absolutely no danger. But it's necessary to trumpet his arrest, to show that they've managed to catch the uncatchable one, to arrest the boss. When the carousel of armored cars arrives at the barracks and the carabinieri see that the reporters are already gathered at the entrance, they straddle the car doors; sitting on them like saddles, they make a show of brandishing their pistols, wearing ski masks and carabinieri vests. After Giovanni Brusca's arrest, every policeman and carabiniere wants to be photographed in this pose: the reward for the long nights of waiting in position, the satisfaction of having captured one's prey, the PR astuteness of knowing it will make the front page of the newspaper. Paolo Di Lauro does not exhibit his son Cosimo's arrogance; leaving the barracks, he bends over, face to the ground, offering only his balding head to the cameras. Perhaps it's merely a form of self-protection. Being photographed from every angle by hundreds of lenses and filmed by dozens of video cameras would have showed his face to all of Italy, perhaps causing unsuspecting neighbors to report having seen him, having lived near him. Better not abet the investigations, better not reveal his secret ways. But some interpret his lowered head as a simple irritation at the flash of the cameras, the irritation at being reduced to a beast on display.

After a few days Paolo Di Lauro is brought to court, room 215. He takes his place amid a public made up of relatives. The only word the boss pronounces is "Present"; all the rest he articulates without speaking. Gestures, winks, and smiles are the mute syntax he uses to communicate with from his cage. Greetings, responses, reassurances. Paolo Di Lauro seems to be staring at me, but he is really catching the eye of the gray-haired man behind me. They look at each other for a few seconds, then the boss winks at him.

After learning of his arrest, many people apparently came to greet the boss whom they had been unable to meet for years because he was in hiding. Paolo Di Lauro is wearing jeans, a dark sweater, and Paciotti shoes, the brand worn by all the local clan managers. His jailers had removed his handcuffs, and he has a cage all to himself. The elite of all the northern Naples clans are brought in: Raffaele Abbinante, Enrico D'Avanzo, Giuseppe Criscuolo, Arcangelo Valentino, Maria Prestieri, Maurizio Prestieri, Salvatore Britti, and Vincenzo Di Lauro. The boss's men and ex-men are now divided between two cages, one for the Di Lauro faithful and one for the Spaniards. Prestieri is the most elegant, in a blue jacket and dark blue oxford shirt. He is the first to go up to the protective glass that separates them from the boss. They greet each other. Enrico D'Avanzo comes over as well, and they even manage to whisper something between the cracks in the bulletproof glass. Many of the managers hadn't seen him for years. His son Vincenzo hasn't seen him since 2002, when Vincenzo went into hiding in Chivasso in Piedmont, where he was arrested in 2004.

I never take my eyes off the boss. Every gesture, every expression is material to fill pages of interpretation, to establish new grammars of body language. A strange, silent dialogue unfolds between father and son. With his right index finger Vincenzo indicates the ring finger of his left hand, as if to ask his father, "Your wedding ring?" The boss passes his hands over the sides of his head, then mimes holding a steering wheel, as if he were driving. I can't decipher their gestures. The interpretation the newspapers give is that Vincenzo had asked his father why he wasn't wearing his wedding ring, and his father explained that the carabinieri had taken away all his gold. After all the gestures, facial expressions, fast-moving lips, winks, and hands on the bulletproof glass, Paolo Di Lauro just stares at his son and smiles. They kiss each other through the glass. At the end of the hearing the boss's lawyer asks that the two be permitted to embrace. The request is granted. Seven policemen guard them.

"You're pale," Vincenzo says, and his father looks him in the eye as he responds, "This face hasn't seen the sun for years and years."

When they are caught, fugitives are often at the end of their rope. Their constant flight demonstrates the impossibility of enjoying one's wealth, which brings the bosses even closer to their chiefs of staff, and this becomes the only true measure of their economic and social success. With the elaborate protection systems, the morbid and obsessive need to plan every step, spending most of their time holed up in a room regulating and coordinating their interests, fugitive bosses become prisoners of their own business. A woman in the courtroom recounts an episode from when Di Lauro was in hiding. She looks a bit like a professor, her hair more yellow than blond, with dark roots. Her voice is hoarse and heavy, and she seems almost sorry for his difficulties. She tells me about when Paolo Di Lauro still moved about Secondigliano, albeit with meticulous planning. He had five cars, all the same color, model, and license plate. When he had to go somewhere, he would send all five of them out, even though obviously he was in only one of them. All five cars were escorted, and none of his men knew for sure which one he was in. As each car left the villa, the men would line up behind to follow it. A sure way to avoid betrayal, even the simple betrayal of signaling that the boss was about to move. The woman recounts all this in a tone of profound commiseration for the suffering and solitude of a man who must always think he is about to be killed. After the tarantellas of gestures and embraces, after the greetings and winks of people who make up the most ferocious power structure of Naples, the bulletproof glass separating the boss from the other men is full of different sorts of signs: handprints, greasy smears, the shadow of lips.

Less than twenty-four hours after the boss's arrest, a Polish kid is found at the Arzano roundabout, trembling like a leaf as he struggles to throw an enormous bundle in the trash. He is smeared with blood and crippled with fear. The bundle is a body. A mangled, tortured, badly disfigured body; it seems impossible that a person could be treated that way. If he had been made to swallow a mine that then exploded in his stomach, it would have wreaked less destruction. The body belonged to Edoardo La Monica, though his features were no longer recognizable. Only his lips were still intact; the rest of his face was completely crushed. His body was riddled with holes and encrusted with blood. They had tied him up and tortured him with a spiked bat—slowly, for hours. Every blow cut new holes, piercing his flesh and breaking his bones as the nails sunk in and were then yanked out. They had cut off his ears, cropped his tongue, shattered his wrists, gouged out his eyes with a screwdriver—all while he was still alive, awake, conscious. Then to finish him off they smashed his face with a hammer and carved a cross on his lips with a knife. His body was supposed to end up in the trash so that it would be found rotting in a dump. The message inscribed on his flesh was perfectly clear to everyone. We cut off the ears with which you heard where the boss was hiding, shattered the wrists you extended to take the blood money, gouged out the eyes you saw with, cut out the tongue you talked with. We crushed the face you lost in the eyes of the System by doing what you did. Your lips are sealed with a cross, closed forever to the faith you betrayed. Edoardo La Monica had a clean record. But he had a loaded last name, belonging to one of the families that had turned Secondigliano into Camorra territory and a mine for business. The family with whom Paolo Di Lauro had taken his first steps. Edoardo La Monica's murder resembles that of Giulio Ruggiero. Both of them torn to pieces, meticulously tortured just hours after the arrest of a boss. Flayed, beaten, quartered, skinned. Homicides with such deliberate and bloody symbolism hadn't been seen for years, since the end of Cutolo's reign. Cutolo's favorite killer, Pasquale Barra 'o nimale—the animal—became famous for murdering Francis Turatello in prison by ripping his heart out with his bare hands and then biting into it. These rituals had died out, but the Secondigliano feud revived them, transforming every gesture, every inch of flesh, and every word into a means of communication in the war.

In a press conference the special operations carabinieri officers declared that Di Lauro's arrest came about after the clan member who purchased Di Lauro's favorite fish, the *pezzogna*, or blue-spotted bream was identified. The story seemed calculated to shatter Di Lauro's image: the supremely powerful boss who controls hundreds of sentinels, but who lets himself get nabbed because of his sin of gluttony. No one in Secondigliano buys the story of the *pezzogna* trail, not for a minute. Many figured that SISDE, Italy's domestic intelligence agency, had to be solely responsible. The forces of law and order confirmed that SISDE had indeed intervened, but its presence in Secondigliano was extremely difficult to perceive. In snippets of barroom chat I had picked up the hint of something that sounded awfully close to numerous reporters' hypotheses, namely that SISDE had put several people in the area on the payroll in exchange for information or lack of interference. Men drinking their espresso or cappuccino with a croissant would say things like:

"Since you take money from James Bond . . ."

Twice in those days I heard furtive or allusive mention of 007. The references were too insignificant or too ridiculous to allow me to draw any conclusions, but at the same time they were too anomalous to ignore.

The secret service's strategy may have been to identify and recruit those who were technically responsible for lookouts, getting them to station all the sentinels in other zones so that they would be unable to sound the alarm and allow the boss to flee. The family of Edoardo La Monica denies any possible involvement on his part, maintains that he had never been part of the System and was afraid of the clans and their business affairs. Maybe he paid for someone else in his family, but the surgical torture seems to have been intended specifically for him rather than to be delivered to someone else via his body.

One day I noticed a small group of people not far from where Edoardo La Monica's body had been found. One of the boys pointed to his ring finger, touched his head, and moved his lips without making a sound. Vincenzo Di Lauro's courtroom gestures came back to me in a flash: that strange sign, that asking his father about his wedding ring, his first question after not seeing him for years. The ring— anello—which in Neapolitan becomes aniello. A message referring to Aniello La Monica, the family patriarch, and the ring finger, which symbolizes faith or loyalty. Thus loyalty betrayed, as if he were signaling the root of the family that had betrayed him. The family responsible for his arrest. The person who had talked.

For years the La Monicas had been called the anielli in the neighborhood, just as the Gionta di Torre Annunziata family members were called valentini after the boss Valentino Gionta. According to the declarations of the pentito Antonio Ruocco and of Luigi Giuliano, Aniello La Monica had been eliminated by none other than his godson, Paolo

Di Lauro. It is true that the La Monica men are all in the ranks of the Di Lauro clan. But this atrocious killing could be the punishment, a more violent message than a simple burst of gunfire, the revenge for that death twenty years earlier—revenge is a dish best served cold. A long memory, very long. A memory shared by the Secondigliano clans that later rose to power and by the very territory they rule. But which rests on rumors, hypotheses, and suspicions, producing sensational arrests or tortured bodies, without, however, ever taking the shape of truth. A truth that must always be obstinately interpreted, like a hieroglyphic. One that is better left undeciphered.

Secondigliano returned to its regular economic rhythms. All the Spaniard and the Di Lauro managers were in prison. New neighborhood capos were emerging, new boy managers were taking their first steps up the chain of command. Over a few months the word *feud* fell out of use and was replaced by *Vietnam*.

"That one there . . . he was in Vietnam . . . so now he has to keep calm."

"After Vietnam everyone's afraid around here . . ."

"Is Vietnam over or not?"

Fragments of sentences that the new clan conscripts speak into their cell phones. Intercepted conversations that on February 8, 2006, led to the arrest of Salvatore Di Lauro, the eighteen-year-old son of the boss, who had a small army of baby drug dealers. The Spaniards had lost the battle, but it seems they managed to achieve their goal of becoming autonomous, with their own cartel run by young kids. The carabinieri intercepted an SMS that a girl sent to a young drug-market capo who had been arrested during the feud and who took up dealing as soon as he was released: "Good luck with your work and your return to the neighborhood, I'm excited for your victory, congratulations!"

The victory was a military one, the congratulations for having fought on the right side. The Di Lauros are in jail, but they saved the skin and the business of the family.

Things suddenly calmed down after the clan negotiations and arrests. I wandered about a Secondigliano that was exhausted, trampled, photographed, filmed, abused by too many people, a Secondigliano weary of it all. I stopped in front of the murals by Felice Pignataro with their sun faces and skulls combined with clowns. Murals that gave the cement some light and unexpected beauty. All of a sudden the sky exploded with fireworks and the air echoed with the obsessive trictrac of explosions. The news crews who were dismantling their posts after the boss's arrest came running to see what was going on. Precious material for their final broadcast: festivities involving two entire apartment buildings. They turned on their microphones and spotlights and called in to their editors to announce a special report on the Spaniards' celebrating Paolo Di Lauro's arrest. I went over to see what was happening, and a boy, pleased that I asked, told me, "It's for Peppino, he's come out of coma." Last year Peppino was on his way to work when his Ape, the three-wheeled vehicle he drove to the market, started to veer and then overturned. Neapolitan roads are water soluble; after two hours of rain the volcanic paving stones start to float and the tar dissolves as if it were mixed with salt. They brought a tractor from the countryside to recover the Ape from the escarpment where it had ended up. Peppino suffered severe cranial trauma. After a year in a coma he had revived, and a few months later he was allowed to go home. The neighborhood was celebrating his homecoming. They set off the first fireworks right as he was getting out of the car and settling into his wheelchair. Children had their picture taken caressing his shaven head. Peppino's mother protected him from kisses and embraces that were too much for his condition. The correspondents called their offices again and canceled the report; the .38-caliber serenade they hoped to film had faded into a party for a kid who had come out of a coma. They headed back to their hotels, but I continued on to Peppino's house, feeling like a merry draft dodger at a party that was too festive to miss. I toasted Peppino's health all night long with his neighbors, the party spilling onto the stairs and landings, apartment doors wide-open and tables laden with food, no worries as to whose homes they were. Completely drunk, I played courier on my Vespa, ferrying bottles of red wine and Coca-Cola from a late-night bar to Peppino's. That night Secondigliano was silent and exhausted, emptied of reporters and helicopters, without lookouts and sentinels. A silence that made you want to sleep, the way you do at the beach in the afternoon, stretched out on the sand with your arms under your head, not thinking of anything.

WOMEN

It was as if I had an indefinable odor on me. Like the smell that permeates your clothing when you go to one of those fried-food places. When you leave, the smell gradually becomes less noticeable, blending with the poison of car exhaust, but it's still there. You can take countless showers, soak for hours in heavily perfumed bath salts and oils, but you can't get rid of it. And not because—like the sweat of a rapist—it has penetrated your flesh, but because you realize it was already inside you. As if it were emanating from a dormant gland that all of a sudden started secreting, activated more by a sensation of truth than of fear. As if something in your body were able to tell when you are staring at the truth, perceiving it with all your senses, with no mediation. Not a recounted or reported or photographed truth, but a truth that exists and that gives itself to you: the realization of how things work, the path the present is taking. No way of thinking can attest to the truth of what you have seen. After you've stared a Camorra war in the face, your memory swells with too many images to recall individually, and they come flooding back all at once, confused and blending together. You can't trust your eyes. After a Camorra war there are no ruins of buildings, and the sawdust soon soaks up the blood. It's as if you were the only one to see or suffer, as if someone were ready to point a finger at you and say, "It's not true."

The aberration of a clan war—of assets that face off, investments that cut each other's throat, financial ventures that devour each other—will always find a reason for consolation, a significance that distances the danger, making the conflict seem far away when in reality it's taking place on your doorstep. And so you can file it all away in those pigeonholes of reason that you gradually construct for yourself. But not the odors. They can't be regimented. They linger, like the last trace of a patrimony of lost experience. They stuck in my nose—the odor of blood and sawdust, the aftershave the boy soldiers slap on their beardless cheeks, but above all the female smells, the heavy odor of deodorant, hairspray, and sweet perfume.

Women are always a part of clan power dynamics. It is no accident that the Secondigliano feud eliminated two women with a savagery usually reserved for bosses. And that hundreds of women poured into the streets to prevent pushers and sentinels from being arrested, setting trash bins on fire and yanking on the carabinieri's elbows. I saw the girls go running every time a video camera materialized; all smiles, they would throw themselves in front of the lenses, singing little ditties and asking to be interviewed, hovering around to see the logo on the camera so they could figure out which channel was filming them. You never know. Someone might see them and invite them to be on a show. Around here, opportunities don't happen; you have to rip them out with your teeth, buy them, or dig for them. They have to be here, somewhere, somehow. Nothing is left to chance. Not even finding a boyfriend is left to the casualness of an encounter or the fate of falling in love. Every conquest is a strategy. And the girls who don't develop a strategy risk committing dangerous frivolities, hands touching them all over and insistent tongues drilling through their clenched teeth. Tight jeans, clingy T-shirts: beauty as bait. In some places beauty is a trap, the most pleasing kind. But if you give in, pursue the pleasure of the moment, you don't know what you may find. The girl will be that much better if she can get herself courted by the best, and, once she has snared him, hold on to him, put up with him, hold her nose and swallow him. But keep him—all of him—for herself. Passing in front of a school once, I saw a girl getting off the back of a motorcycle. She moved slowly, giving everyone time to notice the bike, her helmet, motorcycle gloves, and pointy boots, which barely touched the ground. A janitor who had worked there for ages and had watched over generations of kids, went up to her and said, "France', *ma già fai ammore*? And with Angelo? You know he'll end up in Poggioreale, don't you?"

Around here *fa ammore* does not mean "to make love," but to go steady or be engaged. Angelo had recently entered the System, and it didn't look as if he was just doing little jobs, so the janitor concluded he'd soon end up at the Poggioreale jail. Francesca, instead of defending her boyfriend, had her answer ready: "And what's the problem as long as he gives me the monthly allowance? He really loves me."

The monthly allowance. This is her first success. If her boyfriend ends up in jail, she'll have earned herself a salary: the money the clans give to affiliates' families. If an affiliate has a serious girlfriend, the money goes to her, even though it's best to be pregnant, just to be sure. Not married necessarily—a baby is enough, even one that's on the way. If you're only engaged, there's a risk that some other girl he's been keeping on the side, someone you didn't know about, will come forward. In this case the neighborhood capo may decide to split the money between the two—a risky proposition because it generates a lot of tension between the girls' families—or he may make the affiliate decide which one to give it to. Most of the time it's decided to give it to his family instead, neatly resolving the dilemma. Matrimony and childbirth provide solid guarantees. To avoid leaving clues on people's bank records, the money is almost always hand-delivered by a "submarine"—so called because he slithers along the bottom of the streets without ever letting himself be seen. He always takes a different route to get to the same house, surfacing suddenly so that he won't be trailed—precautions against being blackmailed, robbed, or compromised. The submarine handles the stipends of the bottom-level members, whereas the managers deal directly with the treasurer, asking for the amount they need when they need it. Submarines are not part of the System and do not become affiliates, so they can't try to use their position to rise in the ranks. They are almost always retirees, bookkeepers or shop accountants who work for the clans to round out their pensions and to have a reason to get out of the house and not rot in front of the television. The submarine knocks on the twenty-eighth of every month, sets his plastic bags on the table, then extracts the envelope bearing the imprisoned or dead affiliate's name from the stack of them stuffed inside his jacket. He hands the envelope to the affiliate's wife or, if she's not there, the oldest child. He almost always brings some food as well: prosciutto, fruit, pasta, eggs, bread. The sounds of grocery bags rubbing against the wall and heavy step on the stairs announce his arrival. He always goes to the same shops, buying everything at once, then makes his rounds, weighed down like a mule. You can get an idea of how many prisoners' wives and Camorrista widows live on a particular street by how loaded down the submarine is.

Don Ciro was the only submarine I got to know. He lived in the old city center and delivered stipends for clans that had been drifting but were now on the upswing, given the prosperous climate. He worked for clans in the Quartieri Spagnoli and Forcella for a few years, then off and on for those in the Sanità neighborhood. Don Ciro was so good at finding houses, basement apartments, buildings with no street number, and homes carved out of corners of landings that at times the mailmen, who kept getting lost in the labyrinth of streets, would give him letters to deliver to his clients. Don Ciro's battered shoes—there was a bump from his big toe and the soles were worn through at the heels—were the emblem of the submarine, the symbol of the miles he'd covered on Naples's backstreets and hills, his journeys made longer by the paranoia of being followed or robbed. Don

Ciro's pants were clean but not pressed; he had lost his wife, and his new Moldavian companion was really too young to concern herself with such things. A timorous type, he always kept his eyes on the ground, even when talking with me. His mustache was stained yellow from nicotine, as were the index and middle fingers of his right hand. A submarine also delivers monthly allowances to men whose women have landed in jail. It's humiliating for them to receive their wife's money, so the submarine usually goes to her mother's house and has her distribute the money to the prisoner's family. In this way the submarine avoids the false reprimands, shouts on the stairway, and theatrics of the man who kicks him out of the house, never failing, however, to first collect the envelope. The submarine hears all sorts of complaints from affiliates' wives—the rent increase, the high utilities bill, kids who are failing school or want to go to college. He listens to every request, every bit of gossip about the other wives who have more money because their husbands were more clever in climbing the ranks of the clan. As the women complain, the submarine just keeps repeating, "I know, I know." He lets them vent, and in the end he offers two types of response: "It's not up to me" or "I just bring the money, I'm not the one who decides." The wives know perfectly well that the submarine doesn't make any decisions, but they hope that if they keep pouring out their complaints to him, sooner or later something will come out of his mouth in front of some neighborhood capo, who might decide to increase her allowance or grant bigger favors. Don Ciro was so used to saying "I know, I know" that he would chant it whenever I spoke with him, no matter what the topic of conversation. He had delivered money to hundreds of Camorra families and could have charted generations of wives and girlfriends as well as men whose women were in jail. A historiography of criticism of bosses and politicians. But Don Ciro was a taciturn and melancholy submarine who had emptied his head of every word he'd heard, letting them echo without a trace. As we talked, he dragged me from one end of Naples to the other, and when we said goodbye, he took a bus back to the place we'd started from. It was all part of his strategy to throw me off his trail, to keep me from forming even the slightest idea of where he lived.

For many women, marrying a Camorrista is like receiving a loan or acquiring capital. If talent and destiny are in their favor, that capital will bear fruit and the women will become entrepreneurs, managers, or generals' wives, wielding unlimited power. If things go badly, the only thing left to them will be hours in prison waiting rooms. If the clan collapses and can't pay the monthly allowance, they'll have to beg for work as a maid—competing with the immigrants—so they can pay the lawyers and put food on the table. Alliances are founded on the bodies of Camorra women, whose faces gather and display the family power. They are recognized by their black veils at funerals, their screams during arrests, the kisses they throw their men in court.

The typical image of the Camorra woman is of a female who does nothing but echo the pain and will of her men—her brothers, husband, and sons. But it's not like that. The transformation of the Camorra in recent years has also meant a metamorphosis of the female's role, which has gone from that of a maternal figure and helper in times of misfortune to a serious manager who concerns herself almost exclusively with the business and financial end of things, delegating the fighting and illegal trafficking to others.

One such historic figure is Anna Mazza. Widow of the godfather of Afragola, she headed one of the most powerful criminal and business organizations and was one of the first women in Italy to be found guilty of Mafia-related crimes. At first Anna Mazza capitalized on the aura of her husband, Gennaro Moccia, who was killed in the 1970s. The "black widow of the Camorra," as she came to be known, was the brain behind the Moccia clan for more than twenty years. She had a talent for extending her power everywhere; when the court required her to relocate to the north, near Treviso, in the 1990s, she attempted to consolidate her network of power even in total isolation and—according to investigations—made contact with the Brenta Mafia. She was accused of arming her twelve-year-old son immediately after her husband's murder to kill the person who ordered his death, but was let go for lack of proof. Anna Mazza had an oligarchic managerial style and was strongly opposed to armed uprisings. She held sway over her entire territory, as the dissolution of the Afragola city council in 1999 for Camorra infiltration shows. Politicians followed her lead and sought her support. Anna Mazza was a pioneer. Before her there was only Pupetta Maresca, the beautiful, vengeful killer who became famous in Italy in the 1950s when, six months pregnant, she decided to avenge the death of her husband, Pascalone 'e Nola.

Anna Mazza was not merely vengeful. She realized that the time warp of the Camorra would allow her to enjoy a sort of impunity reserved for women. A backwardness that made her immune to ambushes, envies, and conflicts. Her patience and fierce determination in the 1980s and 1990s made the Moccia family into one of the most important clans in the construction business; they handled contracts, controlled quarries, and negotiated the purchase of land suitable for building. The entire area of Frattamaggiore, Crispano, Sant'Antimo, Frattaminore, and Caivano was controlled by local capos tied to the Moccias. In the 1990s the Moccia clan became one of the pillars of the Nuova Famiglia, the broad cartel opposed to Raffaele Cutolo's Nuova Camorra Organizzata, and whose political and business power surpassed that of the Cosa Nostra cartels. When the political parties that had benefited from their association with clan businesses collapsed, only the Nuova Famiglia bosses were arrested and given life sentences. Not wanting to pay in place of the politicians they had helped, or to be considered the cancer of a system they'd supported and in which they'd played an active and productive, albeit criminal, role, they decided to turn state's witness. Pasquale Galasso, boss of Poggiomarino, was the first high-ranking military and business figure to collaborate with the law in the 1990s. Names, strategies, funds—

he revealed everything, a decision that the government repaid by protecting the family's assets and to a certain extent his own. Galasso told everything he knew. Of all the families in the confederation, it was the Moccias who took it upon themselves to make him shut up for good. With a few choice revelations, Galasso could have destroyed the widow's clan in no time. They tried to corrupt his bodyguards to poison him and planned to eliminate him with a bazooka. After these attempts, organized by the men, failed, Anna Mazza intervened. She sensed that the moment had arrived for a new strategy: dissociation. A concept she appropriated from the terrorism of the Red Brigades in the 1970s, when militants dissociated themselves from their armed organizations but without repenting or revealing names, without accusing instigators or perpetrators. It was an attempt to delegitimize a political stance, the official repudiation of which was enough to obtain a reduction in one's sentence; Mazza believed this would be the best way to eliminate the threat of *pentiti* while also making it seem as if the clans were unconnected to the government. If the clans could establish an ideological distance from the Camorra, they could take advantage of prison sentence reductions and improvements in conditions, but without revealing methods, names, bank accounts, or alliances. What for some observers might be considered an ideology—the Camorra ideology—for the clans was nothing more than the economic and military operations of a business group. The clans were changing: the criminal rhetoric and the Cutolo mania for the ideologization of Camorra behavior had spent itself. Dissociation could eliminate the lethal power of the *pentiti*, which, despite the inherent contradictions, is the true fulcrum of the attack on the Camorra. The widow understood the full potential of this trick. Her sons wrote to a priest, making a show of their desire to redeem themselves; as a symbolic gesture, a car filled with weapons was supposed to be left in front of a church in Acerra. Deposition of arms, just as the IRA did with the British. But the Camorra is not an independentist organization or an armed nucleus, and weapons are not its real power. That car was never left, and the strategy of dissociation conceived in the mind of a woman boss slowly lost its appeal. It was not heard in parliament or the Court and lost support among the clans as well. The *pentiti* were becoming more numerous and less useful, and Galasso's grand revelations, while disavowing the clans' military apparatuses, left nearly intact their business and political plans. Anna Mazza continued constructing a sort of Camorra matriarchy: the women as the real power center and the men as soldiers, mediators, and managers who obeyed the women's orders. The important decisions, both military and economic, were up to the black widow.

The women became clan managers, entrepreneurs, and bodyguards. They were better at business, less obsessed with ostentatious shows of power, and less eager for conflict. Immacolata Capone, one of the clan's "ladies in waiting" and the godmother of Anna Mazza's daughter Teresa, made a career for herself over the years. Immacolata didn't have the matronly look—the coiffed hair and full cheeks—of Anna Mazza; minute, and possessed of a sober elegance, her blond bob always perfectly combed, there was nothing of the shady Camorrista about her. And instead of looking for men who could confer greater authority upon her, she was sought out by men who wanted her protection. She married Giorgio Salierno, a Camorrista implicated in the attempts to thwart the *pentito* Galasso, and later became involved with a member of the Puca clan of Sant'Antimo, a family with a powerful history close to Cutolo, and made famous by Immacolata's companion's brother Antonio Puca. An address book found in her pocket contained the name of Enzo Tortora, the TV personality unjustly accused of being a Camorrista. The clan was undergoing a managerial and business crisis by the time Immacolata came of age. Prison and *pentiti* had jeopardized Lady Anna's painstaking labor. But Immacolata bet everything on cement. She also managed a brick factory in the center of Afragola. As a businesswoman she did all she could to associate with the Casalesi, the most powerful clan in the building and construction business nationally and internationally. According to the Naples DDA investigations, Immacolata Capone led the Moccia family companies back to the top of the building trade. In this she had the cooperation of MOTRER, one of the most important names in earthmoving in southern Italy. The mechanism she set up was impeccable. According to investigations, she collaborated with a local politician, who awarded contracts to a businessman who then subcontracted to Lady Immacolata. I only saw her once, I think, right as she was going into a supermarket in Afragola. Her bodyguards were young women. They followed her in a Smart, the little two-seater car all the Camorra women own, but judging by the thickness of the doors, hers was armor-plated. In our fantasies female bodyguards look like bodybuilders, every muscle bulging like a man's, bunching thighs, pectorals swallowing breasts, overgrown biceps, neck like a tree trunk. But there was nothing of the Amazon in the bodyguards I saw. One was short, with a big, flabby ass and hair dyed too black; the other was thin, frail, and bony-looking. I was struck by the fact that both were wearing fluorescent yellow, the same color as the Smart. The driver had on yellow sunglasses and the other a bright yellow T-shirt. A yellow that could not have been chosen by chance, a combination that could not have been a mere coincidence. A professional touch. The same yellow as Uma Thurman's motorcycle outfit in *Kill Bill*, the Quentin Tarantino film in which for the first time women are first-rate criminal stars. The same yellow that Uma Thurman wears in the ad for the film, with her bloody samurai sword—a yellow imprinted on your retina and maybe even on your taste buds. A yellow so unreal it becomes a symbol. A winning business must have a winning image. Nothing is left to chance, not even the color of the car or the uniform of the bodyguards. Immacolata Capone set the example, and now Camorra women of all ranks want female bodyguards, whose style and image they cultivate.

But something wasn't right. Maybe she had invaded someone else's territory, or maybe she was blackmailing someone. Immacolata Capone was killed in March 2004 in Sant'Antimo, her companion's town. She was without her bodyguards; maybe she didn't think she was in any danger. The execution took place in the center of town, and the killers operated on foot. As soon as she sensed she was being followed, she started to run; people thought she'd had her bag snatched and was chasing the thieves, but her purse was still across her shoulder. Immacolata Capone hugged it to her chest as she ran, an instinctual reaction that prevented her from dropping the thing that made running for her life more difficult. She went into a poultry shop, but the killers got to her before she could take cover behind the counter. Two shots in the nape of her neck: that was how the old-fashioned taboo of not touching women was breached. A skull shattered by bullets, facedown in a puddle of blood—this was the new direction of the Camorra. No difference between men and women. No supposed code of honor. But the Moccia matriarch had always moved slowly, was always ready to do big business, controlling her territory through shrewd investments and first-class financial negotiations, monopolizing land deals, and avoiding feuds and alliances that could have interfered with the family business.

Doubtless unknown to IKEA, the largest IKEA complex in Italy now sits on land controlled by Moccia companies, as will the biggest high-speed train construction site in southern Italy. In October 2005—for the umpteenth time—the municipal government of Afragola was dissolved for Camorra infiltration. The accusations are heavy: a group of Afragola city council members requested the president of a commercial entity to hire more than 250 people with close family ties to the Moccia clan.

Illegal building permits also contributed to the decision to dissolve the municipality. There are megastructures on boss-owned properties and talk of a hospital being constructed on land the clan acquired just as the city council was debating the issue. Land bought for very little and then, once the location for the new hospital was announced, sold for an astronomical amount. For 600 percent more than the original price. A profit only the Moccia women were able to achieve.

Women such as Anna Vollaro worked in the trenches to defend clan assets and properties. Niece of the Portici clan boss Luigi Vollaro, Anna was twenty-nine when the police showed up to seize yet another family business, this time a pizzeria. She doused herself with gasoline and lit a match, and to make sure no one could put out the flames, she ran around wildly, finally hitting a wall. The plaster turned black, as when an outlet short-circuits. Anna Vollaro burned herself alive to protest the seizure of an illicitly acquired asset that she considered the result of the normal course of business.

One tends to think that in the criminal world military success leads to a position in business. But that's not always the case. Take the feud in Quindici, a town in the province of Avellino, which has endured the constant, suffocating presence of the Cava and Graziano clans for years. In the 1970s the Cavas were a subset of the Grazianos. But the two families have been at war forever. When the 1980 earthquake destroyed the Lauro Valley, the 100 billion lire of reconstruction funds that poured in gave rise to a middle class of Camorra businessmen. The money allowed both families to establish small construction empires, both run by the women. The battle was sparked by disagreements over contracts and kickbacks from the earthquake reconstruction funds. What unfolded in Quindici was different from in the rest of Campania, however: not simply a factional conflict, but a family feud resulting in around forty savage murders that sowed mourning among the rival groups and created an undying hatred that has contaminated generations of family leaders like the plague. The town watches helplessly as the two factions continue to slaughter each other. One day when the mayor, who had been elected through Graziano backing, was in his office, a group of Cava commandos knocked at his door. They didn't open fire right away, giving him time to open the window, climb onto the roof, and escape along the tops of the houses.

The Graziano clan has produced five mayors, two of whom were murdered; the other three were removed by the Italian president for having ties to the Camorra. But there was a moment when it seemed things could change. When a young pharmacist, Olga Santaniello, was elected mayor. Only a tough woman could take on the Cava and Graziano women. She did everything she could to wash away the filth of clan power, but she didn't succeed. On May 5, 1998, a devastating flood inundated the entire Lauro Valley, turning houses into sponges that soaked up water and mud, the earth into slimy pools, and the streets into useless canals. Olga Santaniello drowned. The mud that suffocated her was doubly rewarding for the clans: the flood meant more aid money, and the power of the clans increased. Antonio Siniscalchi was elected mayor and reelected unanimously four years later. After his first electoral victory, Siniscalchi, his advisers, and his most vocal supporters marched from the polling station to the Brosagro neighborhood, passing in front of the home of Arturo Graziano, who was called *guaglione* or boy. The salutations were not directed at him, however, but at the Graziano women. Lined up in order of age, they stood on the balcony as the new mayor paid them homage now that death had definitively eliminated Olga Santaniello. In June 2002, Antonio Siniscalchi was arrested in a blitz carried out by the Naples DDA. According to the Neapolitan anti-Mafia prosecutor's office, he used the first round of reconstruction funds to redo the street and fencing surrounding the Graziano family's bunker-villa.

The villas scattered around Quindici, the secret hideaways, paved roads, and streetlamps were paid for by the town, public works that helped the Grazianos and made them immune to attacks and ambushes. The representatives of the two families lived barricaded behind insurmountable fences and under twenty-four-hour closed-circuit surveillance.

Clan boss Biagio Cava was arrested at the Nice airport as he was getting on a plane to New York. With Biagio behind bars, all the power passed to his daughter and wife. Only the women showed their faces in the town; not only were they the behind-the-scenes administrators and brains of the operation, but they also became the official symbol of the families, the faces and eyes of power. When the rival families met on the street, they would exchange ferocious looks and intense stares—an absurd game, a test of who would drop their gaze first. Tension in the town was high. The Cava women realized that the time had come to take up arms, to go from being businesswomen to killers. They trained in apartment entranceways, the music turned up loud to cover the sound of pistols being unloaded into bags of walnuts that had been gathered on their country estates. During the 2002 local elections, Maria Scibelli, Michelina Cava, and her daughters, sixteen-year-old Clarissa and nineteen-year-old Felicetta, started traveling armed. On Via Cassese the Cava women's car—an Audi 80—encountered the Graziano women's car, with twenty- and twenty-one-year-old Stefania and Chiara Graziano aboard. The Cava women started to shoot, but the Graziano women braked hard, as if they'd been expecting them. They swerved, accelerated, reversed, and escaped. Bullets shattered windows and pierced the body of the car, but didn't hit flesh. The two girls returned to their villa in hysterics. Their mother, Anna Scibelli, and clan boss Luigi Salvatore Graziano, the seventy-year-old family patriarch, decided to avenge the attack. They took off together in his Alfa, followed by an armored car carrying four people with submachine guns and rifles. They intercepted the Cava Audi, slamming into it repeatedly as the backup car blocked first the side and then the front exit, preventing any chance of getaway. The Cava women, fearful of being stopped by the carabinieri after their unsuccessful shoot-out, had relieved themselves of their weapons, so when they found a car blocking their path, they swerved, flung open the doors, and tried to escape on foot. The Grazianos got out and opened fire, showering the Cavas' legs, heads, shoulders, chests, cheeks, and eyes with lead. In a matter of seconds they were down, shoes flying and feet in the air. It seems that the Grazianos treated their bodies mercilessly, without realizing that one of them was still alive. In fact, Felicetta Cava survived. A small bottle of acid was found in one of the Cava women's purses. Perhaps in addition to shooting, they intended to disfigure their enemies by throwing acid on their faces.

Women are better able to confront crime as if it were only momentary, or someone's opinion, or a step one takes before quickly moving on. Clan women demonstrate this very clearly. They feel offended and vilified when they are called Camorristi or criminals, as if "criminal" were merely a judgment of an action, not an objective way of behaving. In fact, contrary to the men, so far not one female Camorra boss has ever repented. Not one.

Erminia Giuliano, known as Celeste for the color of her eyes, always did her utmost to defend the family's assets. According to investigations, the beautiful and ostentatious sister of Forcella bosses Carmine and Luigi was *the* decision maker for real estate and financial investments. Celeste looks like the typical Neapolitan female, the downtown Camorra woman—platinum blond hair, cold, pale eyes drowning in yolks of black eyeliner. She managed the economic and legal aspects of the clan, which had its business assets confiscated in 2004: 28 million euros, their economic lung. They owned a chain of stores in Naples and the surrounding area and a popular brand that owed its success to the clan's savvy as well as to its military and economic protection. A brand with a franchising network of fifty-six sales points in Italy, Tokyo, Bucharest, Lisbon, and Tunis.

The Giuliano clan was born in Forcella, the soft underbelly of Naples, a neighborhood shrouded in casbah mythology, the legendary rotten navel of the old city center. The Giulianos were the dominant power in the 1980s and 1990s. They'd emerged slowly from poverty, going from smuggling to prostitution, from door-to-door extortion to holdups, creating a vast dynasty of cousins, nephews, uncles, relatives. Though they reached the pinnacle of their power in the late 1980s, their charisma has not yet faded. Even today whoever wants to operate in the city center has to square it with the Giulianos. A clan that still feels poverty breathing at the back of its neck and lives in terror of going back there. One of the utterances that best conveys Forcella king Luigi Giuliano's aversion to being poor was recorded by the reporter Enzo Perez: "I like nativity scenes, I just can't stand the poverty of the shepherds!"

The face of supreme Camorra strength is increasingly female, but so are those crushed by the tanks of power. Annalisa Durante, fourteen years old, was caught in the cross fire in Forcella on March 27, 2004. Fourteen years old. Fourteen years old. Repeating it is like running a sponge soaked in ice water down your spine. I was at Annalisa Durante's funeral. I got to the church early. The flowers hadn't been delivered yet, but messages of condolence, tears, and heartrending memories from classmates were hung all over the place. Annalisa had been killed. One hot evening, probably the first really hot evening in a season of endless rain, Annalisa had decided to go to a friend's who lived downstairs in her building. Already tan, she was wearing a pretty, eye-catching dress that clung to her toned and tense figure. Evenings like this seem created for meeting boys, and fourteen is when a girl from Forcella starts selecting a boyfriend to ferry all the way to the altar. At fourteen the girls from Neapolitan working-class neighborhoods already seem like experienced women: their faces heavily made up, their breasts mutated into swollen little melons by push-up bras, and their pointy, high-heeled boots. They must be talented tightrope walkers to navigate the Neapolitan streets paved with basalt or lava stones, enemy to all feminine footwear. Annalisa was pretty. Very pretty. She was listening to music with her friend and a cousin, all three of them eyeing the boys on their motorcycles, who were doing wheelies, burning rubber, running dangerous obstacle courses amid cars and people. A courting game, atavistic and always the same. Forcella girls love to listen to neo-melodic music, a style that sells big in the working-class neighborhoods of Naples, as well as Palermo and Bari. Gigi D'Alessio is unquestionably the best. The one who managed to break out of the small time, who made it everywhere in Italy, while the others, hundreds of them, are still just little local idols in some neighborhood, building, or street. Everyone has his singer. But all of a sudden, just as the stereo is croaking out a high note, two *motorini* go by at full throttle, hot on someone's trail. He escapes, his feet devouring the pavement. Annalisa, her cousin, and friend don't understand, they think the boys are just joking around, maybe it's a dare. Then the shots. Bullets ricochet everywhere. Annalisa is on the ground, having taken two bullets. Everyone scatters, and heads start appearing on balconies, the doors of which are always left open so as to keep an ear on what is happening in the street. The cries, the ambulance, the race to the hospital, the whole neighborhood filling the streets with curiosity and anxiety.

Salvatore Giuliano is an important name, a name that already seems to mark you as a commander. But here in Forcella it's not the memory of the Sicilian bandit that gives the boy authority. Giuliano merely happens to be his last name. The situation was made worse when Lovigino Giuliano decided to talk; he repented, betraying his clan to avoid life imprisonment. But as often happens in dictatorships, even if the head is removed, only one of his men can take his place. So despite the infamy of betrayal, only the Giulianos were able to maintain relations with the big narcotraffic couriers and impose a protection racket. But over time Forcella got tired. It didn't want to be ruled by an infamous family anymore, didn't want more arrests and police. Whoever desires to take the Giulianos' place has to assert himself officially as sovereign; he has to eradicate them by crushing their new heir, Salvatore Giuliano, Lovigino's nephew. That evening had been chosen as the moment to make the new hegemony official, to do away with the scion who had begun to raise his head and show Forcella the dawning of a new dominion. They wait for him. When he's spotted, Salvatore is walking calmly, but suddenly realizes he's in their crosshairs. He bolts, the killers at his heels, looks for some alley to dart into. The shots start flying. In all probability Giuliano runs past the three girls, using them as shields, and in the turmoil pulls out his pistol and starts shooting. After a few seconds he takes off again. The killers can't catch him. Four legs run into the doorway looking for shelter. The girls turn around. Annalisa's not there. They go out again. There she is on the street, blood everywhere, a bullet in her head.

At the funeral I manage to get close to the foot of the altar, where Annalisa's coffin rests. Policemen in dress uniform stand at each of the four corners, Campania's official tribute to the girl's family. The coffin is covered with white flowers. A cell phone—her cell phone—has been placed near the base. Annalisa's father moans and frets, mumbles something, hops around, and wiggles his fists in his pockets. He comes over, even though he's not really addressing me: "And now what? Now what?" When the head of the family bursts into tears, all the women in the family start to shout, beat their chests, and rock back and forth making high-pitched shrieks. And when he stops crying, all the women once again fall silent. The benches of girls— friends, cousins, and neighbors—imitate their mothers' gestures, the way they shake their heads, the way they moan over and over, "It can't be! It's impossible!" They feel they have been given an important role, that of comforting. And yet they ooze pride. A Camorra victim's funeral is an initiation, on a par with beginning to menstruate or your first sexual encounter. As with their mothers, this event lets them take active part in the life of the neighborhood. The news cameras trained on them, the photographers—everything seems to exist just for them. Many of these girls will soon marry Camorristi. Drug dealers or businessmen. Killers or consultants. Many of them will bear children who will be killed, or they will wait in line at the Poggioreale jail to bring news and money to their husbands. But for now they are just little girls in black. It is a funeral, but they are all carefully dressed: low waist and thong underwear showing. Perfect. They weep for a friend, knowing that this death will make them women. And, despite the pain, they had looked forward to this moment. I think about the eternal return of the laws of this earth. I think about the Giulianos, who reached the peak of their power before Annalisa had even been born, when her mother was still a young girl who played with other young girls who then became the wives of Giulianos and their affiliates, who grew up and listened to D'Alessio and cheered for Maradona, the soccer player who always enjoyed Giulianos' cocaine and parties—the photo of Diego Armando Maradona in Lovigino's shell-shaped tub is unforgettable. Twenty years later, Annalisa dies as a Giuliano is chased, shot at while a Giuliano returns fire, using her as a shield, or perhaps merely running by. An identical historical trajectory, eternally the same. Perennial, tragic, ongoing.

The church is packed by now. The police and carabinieri are still nervous, though. I don't understand. They're agitated and restless and lose patience over nothing. I walk away from the church and then I understand. A carabinieri car is separating the funeral crowd from a group of well-heeled individuals astride expensive motorcycles, in convertibles, or on powerful scooters. They are the last members of the Giuliano clan, the Salvatore loyalists. The carabinieri fear a confrontation—all hell would break lose. Luckily nothing happens, but their presence is deeply symbolic. A declaration that no one can dominate the center of Naples without their approval or at least without their mediation. They show everyone that they're there and that, in spite of everything, they're still the capos.

The white casket emerges from the church, the crowd presses in to touch it, people faint, bestial cries shatter my eardrums. When the coffin passes below Annalisa's house, her mother, who couldn't bring herself to attend the church service, tries to hurl herself off the balcony. She flounders and shouts, her face red and swollen. A group of women hold her back. The usual tragic scene unfolds. Let me be quite clear—the ritual weeping and shows of sorrow are not fictions or falsehoods. Quite the opposite. Yet they reveal the confines in which most Neapolitan women still live, in which they are forced to appeal to strong symbolic behavior to declare their grief and make it recognizable to the entire community. This frenetic suffering, although terribly real, maintains the characteristics of a Neapolitan melodrama.

The journalists keep their distance. Antonio Bassolino and Rosa Russo Iervolino—the president of the region of Campania and the mayor of Naples—are terrified; they fear the neighborhood could rise up against them. But it doesn't: the people of Forcella have learned how to take advantage of politics and don't want to make any enemies. Some people applaud the forces of law and order, causing a few journalists to get excited: carabinieri cheered in the neighborhood of the Camorra. What naïveté. That applause was a provocation. Better the carabinieri than the Giulianos is what it said. Some camera crews try to collect eyewitness accounts; they approach a fragile-looking elderly woman who grabs the microphone right away and shouts, "It's their fault . . . my son will do fifty years behind bars! Assassins!" The hatred toward the *pentiti* is well known. The crowd presses in, tension runs high. Realizing that a girl is dead because she decided to listen to music with her girlfriends at the entranceway to her apartment building one spring evening makes your stomach turn. I feel nauseous. I have to keep calm. I have to understand—if that is even possible. Annalisa was born into and lived in this world. Her girlfriends had told her about motorcycle rides with clan boys, and maybe she would have fallen in love with some handsome, rich prince who would have made a career in the System, or maybe with some good old boy who would have broken his back all day long for peanuts. Maybe her destiny was to work in an underground purse factory, ten hours a day for 500 euros a month. Annalisa was moved by the stained skin of people who work with leather and had written in her diary, "The girls who make purses always have black hands, and are shut up in the factory all day long. My sister Manu's there as well, but at least her boss doesn't make her work when she doesn't feel well." Annalisa has become a tragic symbol because the tragedy ended in its most terrible and essential aspect: murder. But here there is not a minute in which the business of living does not seem like a life sentence, a penalty that must be paid for by a wild, fast, and fierce existence. Annalisa is guilty of having been born in Naples. Nothing more, nothing less. As her body is being carried away in its white coffin, a classmate calls her cell phone. The ringing on the coffin is the new requiem. Musical tones, a sweet melody. No one answers.

PART TWO

KALASHNIKOV

I ran my finger over it. I even closed my eyes as I traced the entire length from top to bottom, my fingernail catching on the holes, some of which were big enough for my whole fingertip to fit in. I touched all the windows this way. First slowly, then quickly, frantically running my hand every which way over the surface, as if my finger were a crazed worm roaming across the glass, climbing in and out of furrows and burrowing into the holes. Until I got cut. I dragged my finger across the glass, leaving a watery reddish purple trail. I opened my eyes. A sudden, sharp pain. The hole was filled with blood. I stopped acting like an idiot and began sucking my wound.

The holes that AK-47s make in the bullet-resistant glass are perfect. They dig violently, like woodworms gnawing tunnels. Seen from a distance, the shots create a strange effect, as if tiny bubbles had formed between the layers of polyurethane, in the heart of the glass. Hardly any shopkeeper replaces his windows once they have been sprayed with bullets. Some inject silicone into the cracks or cover them with black tape, but most just leave them the way they are. A bullet-resistant shop window can cost up to 5,000 euros, so it's better to stick with the violent decorations. Besides, there's a chance they'll lure curious customers to stop and ask what happened, chat with the owner, and maybe even buy a little something extra in the end. Rather than replace the damaged windows, they wait until they implode from the next burst of gunfire. At that point insurance will cover the cost, because if the owner gets there first thing in the morning and makes all the merchandise disappear, the spray from an assault rifle is labeled a robbery.

A shop window shooting is not always an intimidation, a message written in bullets, so much as a necessity. When a new shipment of AK-47s arrive, they have to be tested, to make sure they don't jam. The Camorra could try them out in peace in the countryside, shoot at old armored cars, or buy some sheet metal to blow to pieces. But no. They fire at stores—windows, doors, metal shutters—a reminder that there is nothing that does not potentially belong to them, and that everything is really granted by them, part of the economy they alone control. A momentary concession, nothing more, something that can be withdrawn at any time. There's also a side benefit: the local glass companies with the best prices on replacement windows are all related to the clan; the more broken glass, the more money they make.

Thirty or so AK-47s had arrived the night before from Eastern Europe. From Macedonia. Skopje to Gricignano d'Aversa, a quick, easy trip that filled the Camorra garages with machine guns and air rifles. As soon as the Iron Curtain fell, Camorra members met with leaders of the crumbling Communist parties. They sat at the bargaining table representing the powerful, capable, and silent West. Aware of the crisis, the clans informally acquired entire arms depots from Eastern European countries—Romania, Poland, the former Yugoslavia— paying for years the salaries of the custodians, guards, and officials in charge of maintaining their military resources. In short, the clan financed a part of those countries' defense. It turns out that the best way to hide weapons is to keep them in barracks. With Eastern Europe's arms depots at their disposal, bosses didn't have to depend on the black market, even when there were leadership turnovers, internal feuds, and crises. This time the weapons had been loaded onto NATO trucks stolen from American garages. Thanks to the writing on the side, the trucks moved about freely in Italy. The NATO base in Gricignano d'Aversa is a small and inaccessible colossus, a column of reinforced concrete dropped into the middle of a plain. Built by the Coppolas, like everything else around here. You almost never see the Americans. Checkpoints are rare. NATO trucks have complete liberty, so when they pulled into town, the drivers even stopped in the piazza for breakfast, asking around at the bar where they could find "a couple of immigrants to do some quick unloading" as they dunked croissants in their cappuccino. And everyone knows what "quick" means. Crates of guns are only a little heavier than crates of tomatoes, and the African kids who want to do a little overtime after their shifts in the fields get paid 2 euros a crate, four times what they make moving tomatoes or apples.

In a NATO magazine for the families of military personnel overseas, I once read a short article for people about to be stationed at Gricignano d'Aversa. I translated the piece and wrote it down in my diary so I wouldn't forget it:

> To understand where you will soon be stationed, imagine yourself in a Sergio Leone film. It's like the Wild West. Somebody gives orders, there are shoot-outs and unwritten yet unassailable laws. Don't be alarmed, however, for maximum respect and hospitality are extended to the townspeople and the American military. Nevertheless, leave the military compound only when necessary.

That Yankee writer taught me something about the place where I lived.

That morning at the bar, Mariano was strangely euphoric. He was really wound up, downing martinis first thing in the morning.

"What's going on?"

Everyone was asking the same thing. Even the bartender refused him a fourth round. But Mariano didn't answer, as if it were perfectly clear to everyone.

"I want to go meet him. They tell me he's still alive, but is it true?"

"Is what true?"

"How'd he do it? I'm going to use my vacation time and go meet him."

"Who? What?"

"You realize how light it is? And precise. Before you even know it, you've let off twenty, thirty shots . . . it's brilliant!" Mariano was in ecstasy. The bartender was looking at him the way he'd look at a boy who had just slept with a woman for the first time, that unmistakable expression on his face, the same that Adam must have worn. Then I realized the cause of his euphoria. Mariano had fired an AK-47 for the first time and was so impressed with the contraption that he wanted to meet Mikhail Kalashnikov, the man who invented it. Mariano had never shot at anyone; he'd been brought into the clan to handle the distribution of certain brands of coffee in the area bars. A young man with a degree in economics, he was responsible for millions of euros, given the number of bars and coffee distributors that wanted to get in on the clan's commercial network. The neighborhood capo wanted to be sure that all his men, even those with college degrees—the businessmen as well as the foot soldiers—knew how to shoot. So they'd handed Mariano an AK-47. During the night he had unloaded it into some bar windows, selecting them at random. It wasn't a warning, but even if he didn't know why he was shooting at those particular windows, the owners had come up with a valid explanation for sure. There's always some reason to feel you're in the wrong. Mariano spoke about the weapon in menacing and professional tones. AK-47: a rather simple name, where AK is short for the Russian *avtomat Kalashnikova*, "Kalashnikov's automatic," and 47 refers to the year in which it was selected as the official weapon of the Soviet Union.

Weapons often have encoded names, letters and ciphers intended to conceal their lethal power, symbols of ruthlessness. In truth they are banal labels assigned by some NCO who catalogs new weapons just as he does nuts and bolts. AK-47s are light and easy to use and require only simple maintenance. Their strength is in their size: neither so small as to lack sufficient firepower, like revolvers, nor so big as to become unwieldy or have too much recoil. They are so simple to clean and assemble that in the former Soviet Union the military trained schoolboys to do it in an average of two minutes.

The last time I had heard machine-gun fire was several years ago. Near the university in Santa Maria Capua Vetere. I don't remember where exactly, but I am certain it was at a crossroads. Four cars blocked Sebastiano Caterino's vehicle, and killed him with a symphony of AK-47s. Caterino had always been close to Antonio Bardellino, the capo of capos of the Caserta Camorra in the 1980s and 1990s. When Bardellino was killed and the leadership changed, Caterino had managed to flee, escaping the massacre. For thirteen years he had holed up in his house; he only stuck his nose out at night, used armored cars when he ventured beyond his front gate, and stayed away from San Cipriano d'Aversa, his hometown. After many years of silence he thought he had again acquired authority, that the rival clan had forgotten about the past and would not attack an old leader such as himself. So he started to raise a new clan in Santa Maria Capua Vetere, the old Roman city that had become his fiefdom. When the marshal from Caterino's town arrived on the murder scene, he had just one thing to say: "They got him really bad!" Around here the treatment you receive is evaluated in terms of how many bullets they put in you. If they kill you delicately, a single shot to the head or stomach, it is interpreted as a necessary operation, a surgical strike, no malice. Unloading more than two hundred shots into your car and more than forty into your body, on the other hand, is an absolute method of erasing you from the face of the planet. The

Camorra has a very long memory and is capable of infinite patience. Thirteen years, 156 months, four AK-47s, 200 shots—a bullet for each month of waiting. In certain places, even the weapons remember, preserving a hatred and condemnation that they spit out when the moment comes.

On the morning when I ran my fingers over the gun's decorations, I was wearing a backpack. I was leaving, going to my cousin's house in Milan. It's strange how no matter whom you're talking to, no matter about what, as soon as you say you're going away, you receive all sorts of good wishes, congratulations, and enthusiastic responses: "Good for you, you're doing the right thing, I'd leave too." You don't need to supply any details or explain what you're going to do. Whatever the reason, it will be better than the reasons you have for sticking around here. When people ask me where I'm from, I never answer. I'd like to say "the south," but that sounds too rhetorical. If someone asks on the train, I stare at my feet and pretend not to have heard because I'm always reminded of Vittorini's novel *Conversations in Sicily* and I'm afraid if I open my mouth, I will speak in the voice of the protagonist, Silvestro Ferrato. But it's not worth it. Times change, yet the voices remain the same. But that day I happened to meet a large woman who could barely jam herself into her seat. She had boarded the Eurostar in Bologna with an incredible desire to talk, as if she intended to fill the time the way she had her body. She insisted on knowing where I was from, what I did, where I was going. I was tempted to reply simply by showing her the cut on my finger. But I didn't. Instead I told her, "I'm from Naples." A city that lets loose so many words that merely uttering its name frees you from saying anything more. A place where bad becomes all bad, and good becomes total purity. I fell asleep.

Mariano called me early the next morning. He was anxious. Accountants and organizers were needed for a delicate operation some businessmen from the neighborhood were carrying out in Rome. Pope John Paul II was ill, perhaps already dead, even though the official announcement hadn't been made. Mariano asked me to join him, so I boarded a train again and headed south. Within the space of a few days, stores, hotels, restaurants, and supermarkets would need extraordinary quantities of supplies of every sort. There was a ton of money to be made. Soon millions of people would be pouring into the capital, living on the streets, and spending long hours on the sidewalks, all of them needing to drink and eat—in a word, to buy. You could triple prices, sell all day and night, squeeze the profit out of every minute. Mariano was called in. He proposed that I keep him company and offered a bit of money in return for my kindness. Nothing's free. Mariano was promised a month of vacation so he could fulfill his dream of going to Russia to meet Mikhail Kalashnikov; he'd even received guarantees from a man from one of the Russian families who swore he knew him. Mariano would be able to look Kalashnikov in the eye and touch the hands that had invented such a powerful weapon.

The day of the pope's funeral, Rome was jam-packed. It was impossible to make out what street you were on or where the sidewalk was. One gigantic sea of flesh had covered asphalt, doorways, and windows, a lava flow that oozed into every possible space and seemed to increase in volume, exploding the channels through which it ran. Human beings everywhere. Everywhere. A dog was trembling under a bus, terrorized at having all of his usual space invaded by legs and feet. Mariano and I had stopped on the steps of a building, the only shelter from a group that had decided to show their devotion by singing a little song to Saint Francis for six hours straight. We sat and ate a sandwich. I was exhausted. Mariano, on the other hand, never got tired; being compensated for every drop of energy he spent made him feel constantly charged.

All of a sudden I heard someone call my name. I knew who it was even before I turned around. My father. We hadn't seen each other in two years, and even though we lived in the same city, we never met. It was unbelievable that we ran into each other in this Roman labyrinth of flesh. My father was highly embarrassed. He didn't know what to say or even if he could greet me in the way he would have liked. But he was euphoric, the way you get on trips that promise intense emotions within the space of a few hours, beautiful experiences you know you won't have again for a long time, so you try to drink it all in quickly, fearful that you'll miss out on other joys in the brief time you have. Taking advantage of a Romanian airline's reduced fares on flights to Italy for the pope's funeral, he had bought tickets for his lady friend and her whole family. The women were all wearing veils, and rosaries wound around their wrists. It was impossible to figure out what street we were on; all I remember is a huge sheet hanging between two buildings: "Eleventh Commandment: Do not push and you will not be pushed." Written in twelve languages. My father's new relations were happy indeed to be taking part in something as important as the death of the pope. They were all dreaming of an amnesty for immigrants. For these Romanians, the best way to earn sentimental and effective Italian citizenship, even before legal citizenship, was to participate in such an immense and universal event, to suffer together for the same reason. My father adored John Paul II. He was fascinated by the man who let everyone kiss his hand, and intrigued by how he had been able to obtain such vast power and popularity without open threats or obvious stratagems. All the powerful people had knelt in front of him. For my father, this was enough to earn his admiration. He and his companion's mother knelt down, spontaneously reciting the rosary right there on the street. I saw a child emerge from the mass of Romanian relatives. I realized right away it was my father and Micaela's child. I knew that he had been born in Italy so as to receive Italian citizenship, but that he had always lived in Romania because his mother needed to be there. He was anchored to her skirt. I had never seen him before, but I knew his name. Stefano Nicolae. Stefano after my father's father, Nicolae after Micaela's father. My father called him Stefano, and his mother and Romanian relatives called him Nico. The name Nico would eventually win out, but my father hadn't given up yet. Of course the first gift Nico had received from his father when he got off the plane was a ball. This was only the second time my father had seen his little son, but he acted as if they had always been together. He scooped him up in his arms and came over to me.

"Nico's going to live here now. In this country. In his father's country."

I don't know why, but the little boy turned sad and dropped his ball. I managed to stop it with my foot before it was lost forever in the crowd.

All of a sudden the smell of salt mixed with dust, cement, and trash came back to me. A damp smell. It reminded me of when I was twelve years old and was at the shore at Pinetamare. I had just woken up when my father came into my room. Probably a Sunday morning. "Do you realize that your cousin already knows how to shoot? And what about you? Are you less good than him?"

He took me to Coppola Village on the coast between Naples and Caserta. The beach was an abandoned mine of tools devoured by sea salt and caked in calcium crust. I could have dug around there for days, unearthing trowels, gloves, worn-out shoes, and broken hoes, but I hadn't been brought there to play in the trash. My father walked around looking for targets, preferably glass. Peroni beer bottles were his favorite. He lined them up on the roof of a burned-out Fiat 127— there were lots of car carcasses because this was where the getaway cars were burned and abandoned. I can still remember my father's Beretta 92FS. It was so covered in scratches it looked gray—an old lady of a pistol. I don't know why, but everyone refers to it as an M9. I always hear it called that way: "I'll put an M9 between your eyes. Do I have to take out my M9? Hell, I have to get myself an M9." My father handed me the Beretta. It felt heavy. The butt was rough, like sandpaper, and stuck to the palm of my hand, its tiny teeth scratching my skin. My father showed me how to take the safety off, cock it, extend my arm, close my right eye, spot the target on the left, and fire.

"Robbe', your arm has to be loose but firm. Relaxed, but not flabby . . . use both hands."

I closed my eyes, hunched up my shoulders as if I were trying to cover my ears with them, and pulled the trigger as hard as I could with both my index fingers. Even today the noise of gunshots bothers me terribly. I must have a problem with my eardrums because I'm always half-deaf for a while afterward.

The Coppolas, a powerful business family, built the largest illegal urban complex in the West on Pinetamare. Eight hundred sixty-three thousand square meters of cement: the Coppola Village. They did not ask for authorization. They didn't need to. Around here construction bids and permits make production costs skyrocket because there are so many bureaucratic palms to grease. So the Coppolas went straight to the cement plants. One of the most beautiful maritime pine groves in the Mediterranean was replaced by tons of reinforced concrete. You could hear the sea from the buildings' intercoms.

When I hit the first target of my life, I felt a mixture of pride and guilt. I could shoot, I finally knew how to shoot. No one could hurt me anymore. But I had learned to use a horrendous instrument, one of those tools you can never stop using once you start. Like learning to ride a bicycle. The bottle hadn't fully exploded; it was still upright, its right side disemboweled. My father headed back to the car. I remained there, pistol in hand, but strangely I didn't feel alone even though I was surrounded by trash and metal ghosts. I stretched out my arm toward the waves and fired two more shots. I didn't see them hit and maybe they didn't even reach the water. But it seemed courageous to fire on the sea. My father came back with a leather soccer ball with the face of Maradona on it. My reward for my good aim. Then, as always, he put his face close to mine. I could smell the coffee on his breath. He was satisfied: at least now his son was not less than his brother's son. We performed the usual chant, his catechism:

"Robbe', what do you call a man who has a pistol and no college degree?"

"A shit with a pistol."

"Good. What do you call a man with a college degree but no pistol?"

"A shit with a degree."

"Good. What do you call a man with a degree and a pistol?"

"A man, papà!"

"Bravo, Robertino!"

Nico was still learning to walk. My father spoke to him nonstop, but the little boy didn't understand him. He was hearing Italian for the first time, even though his mother had been clever enough to give birth to him here.

"Does he look like you, Roberto?"

I studied him closely, and I was happy—for him, that is. He didn't look like me at all.

"Not in the least, lucky for him!"

My father gave me his usual disappointed look, which seemed to convey that I never said the right thing, not even when joking. I've always had the impression that my father was at war with someone. As if he were engaged in a battle of alliances, precautions, and big stakes. For my father, staying in a two-star hotel was like losing face. As if he had to give an account to an entity that would punish him harshly if he didn't live in style, with an authoritarian and comic attitude.

"Robbe', the best don't need anybody. Sure they have to know, but they also have to make people afraid. If you don't scare anyone, if nobody feels uneasy looking at you, well then, in the end you haven't really succeeded."

It bothered him that when we went out to eat, the waiters would often serve certain people ahead of us, even if they'd come in an hour after we did. The bosses would sit down and a few minutes later their lunch would be ready. My father would greet them, but deep down he would have liked to get the same respect. Respect that meant generating the same envy of power, the same fear, the same wealth.

"You see them? They're the ones who are really in command. They're the ones who decide everything! Some people control words, and others control things. You have to figure out who controls things, while pretending to believe the ones who control the words. But inside you always have to know the truth. You only really command if you command things." The commanders of things, as my father called them, were sitting at one of the tables. They had always decided the fate of this area. Now they were eating together, smiling, but over the years they slit each other's throats, leaving thousands of deaths in their wake, like ideograms of their financial investments. The bosses knew how to remedy the insult of their being served first; they paid for everyone else's lunch. But only on their way out, so as not to garner thanks or adulation. Everyone's lunch except for two, that is. Professor Iannotto and his wife. The couple hadn't said hello, so the bosses hadn't dared to pay for them. But they had a waiter bring them a bottle of limoncello. A Camorrista knows to take care of his loyal enemies, who are always more valuable than his false friends. Whenever my father wanted to provide me with a negative example, he would cite Professor Iannotto. They had been in school together. Iannotto lived in a rented apartment, had been kicked out of his political party, had no children, was poorly dressed, and was always in a rage. He taught high school, and I still remember him arguing with parents who asked him which of his friends they should hire to tutor their children so they would pass. To my father, Iannotto was a condemned man. One of the walking dead.

"It's like when one person decides to be a philosopher and one a doctor. Which of the two do you think is decisive in a person's life?"

"The doctor!"

"Good. The doctor. Because you can decide about another person's life. Decide whether or not to save them. You can only do good when you have the ability to do bad. If instead you're a failure, a fool, somebody who doesn't do anything, then you can only do good, but at that point it's volunteer work, leftovers. Real good is when you choose to do it even though you could do bad instead."

I didn't answer. I could never understand what he really wanted to prove to me. And I still don't understand even now. Maybe that's why I decided to major in philosophy, so I wouldn't have to decide for anyone. As a young doctor in the 1980s my father had worked on an ambulance crew. Four hundred deaths a year. In areas with up to five murders a day. They'd pull up in the ambulance, the wounded on the ground, but if the police hadn't arrived, they couldn't load him onto the stretcher. Because if word got around, the killers would come back and track down the ambulance, stop it, climb in, and finish off the job. It had happened lots of times, so the doctors and nurses knew to stand by, to wait till the killers came back to complete the operation. But once my father's ambulance was called to Giugliano, a big town between Naples and Caserta, part of the Mallardo fiefdom. They got to the scene quickly. The victim was eighteen, maybe younger. He'd been shot in the chest, but one of his ribs had deflected the bullet. The boy was gasping for breath, shouting, losing blood. The nurses were terrorized and tried to dissuade my father, but he loaded him into the ambulance anyway. Clearly, the killers hadn't been able to get off a good shot; they had probably been sent running by a passing police patrol, but they'd be back for sure. The nurses tried to reassure my father: "Let's wait, they'll come back, finish the job, and then we'll take him in."

But my father couldn't wait. There is a time for all things, even death. And eighteen didn't seem to him the time to die, not even for a

Camorra soldier. My father got him in the ambulance and took him to the hospital. The boy survived. That night the killers who hadn't hit their target dead on went to his house—to my father's house. I wasn't there, I was living with my mother, but I've been told the story so many times, always broken off in the same place, that I remember it as if I had been there and had witnessed the whole thing. My father, I believe, was beaten bloody and didn't show his face for at least two months. And for four months after that he still couldn't bring himself to look anyone in the eye. Choosing to save someone who is supposed to die means you desire to share his fate, because wanting to isn't enough to change anything around here. A decision is not what will get you out of trouble, and taking a stand or making a choice won't make you feel you're acting in the best way possible. Whatever you do, it will be wrong for some reason. This is true solitude.

Little Nico was laughing again. Micaela is more or less my age. The same thing probably happened to her when she told people she was leaving, going to Italy; they probably wished her well without asking anything, without knowing if she was going off to become a prostitute, a wife, a maid, or a factory worker. Without knowing anything more than that she was leaving. That was good fortune enough. But Nico was obviously not thinking anything, his mouth clamped to the cup of yet another fruit shake his mother had given him to fatten him up. To make it easier for him to drink, my father set the ball down near his feet, but Nico kicked it away with all his might, sending it bouncing off people's shins and shoes. My father ran to retrieve it. Knowing Nico was watching, he humorously pretended to dribble past a nun, but the ball got away from him. The little boy laughed. Maybe the hundreds of ankles that spread out before his eyes made him feel he was in a forest of legs and sandals. He liked seeing his father—our father—tire himself out chasing that ball. I raised my arm to say goodbye to him, but a wall of flesh had come between us. He would be trapped for a good half hour; there was no point in waiting. It was really late. I couldn't even make out his silhouette anymore; it had been swallowed into the stomach of the crowd.

Mariano did get to meet Mikhail Kalashnikov. He spent a month traveling around Eastern Europe. Russia, Romania, Moldavia: a reward from the clan. I saw him again in the usual bar, the bar in Casal di Principe. Mariano had a stack of photographs bound with a rubber band, like baseball cards for trading. Autographed pictures. Before coming home he had hundreds of copies printed up of Mikhail Kalashnikov wearing his Red Army uniform, his chest dripping with medals: the Order of Lenin, the medal of honor from the Great Patriotic War, the Order of the Red Star, the Order of the Red Banner of Labor. Mariano was introduced to the general through some Russians who did business with the Caserta clans.

Mikhail Timofeevich Kalashnikov lived in a rented apartment in Izhevsk, formerly Ustinov, a city at the foot of the Ural Mountains, which didn't even appear on the map until 1991. One of the many locations the USSR had kept secret. Kalashnikov was the town's big draw. He had become a sort of tourist attraction for elite visitors, so they set up a direct connection from Moscow just for him. A hotel near his house, which is where Mariano had stayed, was making a mint putting up the general's admirers, who would wait there for him to return from some Russian tour or simply for him to receive them. Mariano had his video camera in hand when he entered Kalashnikov and his wife's house, and the general had allowed him to use it as long as he didn't make the film public. Obviously Mariano agreed, knowing full well that the person who had arranged the meeting knew his address, phone number, and face. Mariano gave Kalashnikov a Styrofoam cube sealed with tape with buffalo heads on it. He had brought a box full of mozzarella di bufala all the way from the Aversa Marshes in the trunk of his car.

Mariano showed me the video of his visit to Kalashnikov's home on the little screen that folded out from the side of his camera. The images jumped around, blurred, and danced, and the zoom action deformed eyes and objects, the lens rattled by thumbs and wrists. It was like a video from a school trip, filmed while running and jumping. Kalashnikov's house resembled Arzano secessionist boss Gennaro Marino McKay's dacha, or maybe it was simply a classic version, but the only other dacha I had ever seen was his, so it looked like a replica to me. The walls were plastered with Vermeer reproductions, and the furniture was laden with crystal and wooden knickknacks. Every inch of the floor was covered with carpets. At a certain point the general placed his hand over the lens. Mariano told me that, traipsing around with his camera and a huge dose of bad manners, he had gone into a room that Kalashnikov didn't want filmed under any circumstances. In a small metal cabinet on the wall, clearly visible through the armored glass, was the first AK-47, the prototype built from the designs that, according to legend, the old general—then an unknown, low-ranking officer—had made on scraps of paper while in the hospital recovering from a bullet wound and eager to create a weapon that would make the Red Army's frozen and starving soldiers invincible. The first ever AK-47, hidden away like the first dime earned by Uncle Scrooge McDuck, the famous Number One he keeps in an armored shrine, far from the clutches of Magica De Spell. It was priceless, that model. A lot of people would have given anything for a military relic like that. As soon as Kalashnikov dies, it will end up on the auction block at Christie's, like Titian's canvases or Michelangelo's drawings.

Mariano spent the entire morning at Kalashnikov's house. The Russian who introduced him must have been quite influential for the general to treat him so warmly. The video camera was running as they sat at the table and a tiny, elderly lady opened the Styrofoam box of mozzarella. They ate with relish. Vodka and mozzarella. Mariano wanted to record it all, so he set the camera at the head of the table. He wanted proof that General Kalashnikov ate the mozzarella from his boss's dairy. In the background the lens also captured a piece of furniture covered with framed photos of children. Even though I wanted the video to end as soon as possible as I was already feeling seasick, I couldn't contain my curiosity:

"Mariano, Kalashnikov has that many children and grandchildren?"

"They're not his children! They're all photos people send him of children named after him, people whose lives were saved by a Kalashnikov or who simply admire him."

Like doctors who put pictures of children they have treated on their office shelves as mementos of their professional success, General Kalashnikov had photographs of children named after his creature in his living room. A well-known guerrilla fighter with the Popular Liberation Movement in Angola once told an Italian reporter, "I named my son Kalash because it is synonymous with liberty."

Born in 1919, Kalashnikov is now a well-preserved, sprightly old man. He's invited all over the place, a sort of movable icon that substitutes for the most famous assault rifle in the world. Before retiring from the armed services, he received a general's stipend of 500 rubles, at the time more or less $500 a month. If Kalashnikov had been able to patent his weapon in the West, he would undoubtedly be one of the richest men in the world. Approximately—for lack of concrete figures—more than 150 million Kalashnikovs of varying models have been produced, all based on the general's original design. Even if he had only earned one dollar for each weapon, he would be swimming in money now. But this tragic loss of wealth did not bother him in the least. He had given birth to the creature, had breathed life into it, and that was gratification enough. Or maybe he made a profit after all. Mariano told me about presents arriving every now and then from admirers: financial tributes, thousands of dollars deposited in his bank account, precious gifts from Africa—there was talk of a gold tribal mask from Mobutu and a canopy inlaid with ivory that Bokassa had sent him. And it is said that a train, complete with locomotive and cars, arrived from China, a gift from Deng Xiaoping, who knew of the general's difficulty in boarding airplanes. But these are merely legends, rumors that circulate among journalists who, unable to interview the general—he receives no one without an important introduction—talk instead to the employees in the arms factory in Izhevsk.

Mikhail Kalashnikov's responses were automatic, always the same answers no matter what the question was. His English, which he'd learned as an adult, was smooth, and he used it as he would a screwdriver to remove screws. To feel less nervous, Mariano posed generic and pointless questions about the AK-47. "I did not invent that weapon to make money, but only and exclusively to defend the Motherland in a moment in which she needed it. If I had to go back and do it all over again, I would do exactly the same things and live my life just as I have. I have worked all my life, and my life is my work." This is how he answers every question about his invention.

Nothing in the world—organic or synthetic, metal or chemical—has produced more deaths than the AK-47. It has killed more than the atom bombs dropped on Hiroshima and Nagasaki, more than HIV, more than the bubonic plague, more than malaria, more than all the attacks by Islamic fundamentalists, more than the total of all the earthquakes that have shaken the globe. An exponential amount of human flesh, impossible to even imagine. Only one advertisement at a convention came anywhere close to a convincing description: fill a bottle with sugar by pouring the grains from a small hole in the corner of the bag. Each grain of sugar is someone killed by a Kalashnikov.

The AK-47 can fire in the most disparate conditions. It won't jam, will shoot even when crammed with dirt or soaking wet, is comfortable to hold, and has a feather trigger that even a child can pull. Luck, error, imprecision—all the elements that might spare a life in battle—are eliminated by the certainty of the AK-47, which has prohibited fate from playing a role. Easy to use and easy to transport, it shoots with an efficiency that allows you to kill without any type of training. "It can turn even a monkey into a combatant," as Laurent Kabila, the fearsome Congolese political leader, used to say. AK-47s have been used by armies in conflicts in more than fifty countries over the last thirty years. Massacres perpetrated with AK-47s—verified by the UN—have taken place in Algeria, Angola, Bosnia, Burundi, Cambodia, Chechnya, Colombia, Congo, Haiti, Kashmir, Mozambique, Rwanda, Sierra Leone, Somalia, Sri Lanka, Sudan, and Uganda. More than fifty regular armies are supplied with AK-47s, and statistics on the irregular, paramilitary, and guerrilla groups that also use them are impossible to formulate.

Anwar el-Sadat was killed by an AK-47 in 1981, General Carlo Alberto Dalla Chiesa in 1982, and Nicolae Ceausescu in 1989. Salvador Allende was found in the Palacio de La Moneda with AK-47 bullets in his body. And these excellent cadavers are the weapon's historic PR headliners. The AK-47 has even found its way onto the flag of Mozambique and the symbols of hundreds of political groups, from Al Fatah in Palestine to the MRTA in Peru. When Osama bin Laden appears in a video, the AK-47 is his one and only menacing symbol. It has been the prop for every role: liberator, oppressor, soldier, terrorist, robber, and the special forces who guard presidents. Kalashnikov's highly efficient weapon has evolved over the years: eighteen variants and twenty-two new models, all from the original design. It is the true symbol of free enterprise. The absolute icon. It can become the emblem of anything: it doesn't matter who you are, what you think, where you come from, what your religion is, who you're for, or what you're against, as long as you do what you do using our product. Fifty million dollars will buy about two hundred thousand weapons. In other words, with $50 million, you can create a small army. Anything that destroys political bonds and mediation, that allows for enormous consumption and exponential power, is a winner on the market, and with his invention Mikhail Kalashnikov allowed every power and micropower group a military instrument. After the invention of the AK-47, no one can say they were defeated because they didn't have access to arms. He leveled the battlefield: arms for everyone, massacres for all. War is no longer the exclusive domain of armies. The AK-47 did on an international scale what the Secondigliano clans did locally by fully liberalizing cocaine and allowing anyone to become a drug trafficker, user, or pusher, thus freeing the market from pure criminal and hierarchical mediation. In the same way, the AK-47 allowed everyone to become soldiers, even young boys and skinny little girls, and transformed people who wouldn't be able to herd a dozen sheep into army generals. Buy submachine guns, shoot, destroy people and things, and go back and buy some more. The rest is only details. In every photo Kalashnikov's face, with his angular, Slavic forehead and Mongolian eyes that shrink into tiny slits as he ages, is serene. He sleeps the sleep of the righteous. He goes to bed serene if not happy, his slippers tucked neatly under his bed. Even when he is serious, his lips are pulled up like those of Leonard "Gomer Pyle" Lawrence in *Full Metal Jacket*. Kalashnikov smiles with his lips, but not with his face.

Whenever I see Mikhail Kalashnikov's portrait, I am reminded of Alfred Nobel, famous for the prize that bears his name, but also the father of dynamite. The pictures of Nobel taken after his invention— after he realized the use that his mix of nitroglycerin and clay would be put to—show a man devastated by anxiety, his fingers tormenting his beard. Maybe it's just my imagination, but when I look at the photos of Nobel, with his arched eyebrows and lost eyes, he seems to be

saying just one thing: "I didn't mean to. I intended to move mountains, crumble rocks, and create tunnels. I didn't want everything else
that happened." Kalashnikov, on the other hand, always looks serene,
like an old Russian retiree, his head full of memories. You can imagine him, the trace of vodka on his breath as he tells you about some
friend of his from the war, or whispering as you eat that when he was
young, he could make love for hours without stopping. And in my
childish imagination, Mikhail Kalashnikov's picture seems to say,
"Everything's fine, it's not my problem, all I did was invent an assault
rifle. It's no concern of mine how other people use it." A responsibility that doesn't go beyond your own skin, and is circumscribed by
your actions. Your conscience applies only to the work of your own
hands. I think this is one of the elements that makes the old general
an involuntary icon of clans around the world. Mikhail Kalashnikov is
not an arms trafficker, carries no weight in arms deals, has no political
influence, and lacks a charismatic personality, yet he embodies the
daily imperative of the man of the market: he does what he has to do
to win, and the rest is none of his concern.

Mariano had on a hooded sweatshirt and a knapsack, with KALASH-
NIKOV on both. The general had diversified his investments and was
becoming a talented businessman. No one's name was better known,
so a German businessman launched the Kalashnikov label. The general had taken a liking to distributing his name, even investing in a
company that made fire extinguishers. In the middle of his story Mariano stopped the film and ran out to his car, took a small military
suitcase from the trunk, and came back and placed it on the bar. I
was afraid he had gone completely crazy with machine-gun mystique
and had driven across Europe with an AK-47 in his trunk, which he
was about to unveil in front of everyone. Instead he held up a tiny
crystal Kalashnikov full of vodka, the cork fitted into the end of the
barrel. Very kitsch. And after his trip, every bar Mariano supplied in

the Aversa Marshes sold Kalashnikov vodka. I was already imagining the crystal reproduction sitting on a shelf behind every barkeeper from Teverola to Mondragone. The video was almost over, and my eyes hurt from squinting—an attempt to correct my nearsightedness. But the final image was truly not to be missed. Two elderly people in slippers standing on their doorstep, still chewing on the last bite of mozzarella, are waving to their young guest. A group of kids had formed around Mariano and me, and they were staring at him as if he were one of the chosen ones, a sort of hero for having met him. Someone who had met Mikhail Kalashnikov. Mariano gave me a look of false complicity, something that had never existed between us. He removed the rubber band from the pack of photographs and flipped through them. After glancing at dozens, he handed me one.

"This is for you. And don't say I never think of you."

On the portrait of the old general was written in black felt-tip pen: "To Roberto Saviano with Best Regards M. Kalashnikov."

International research institutes in economics are in constant need of data, which they serve like daily bread to newspapers, magazines, and political parties. For example, the celebrated "Big Mac" index estimates the prosperity of a country based on the cost of a McDonald's hamburger. To calculate the state of human rights, the analysts consider the price of an AK-47. The less it costs, the more human rights violations there are, an indication that civil rights are gangrening and the social structure is falling to pieces. In western Africa, an AK-47 can cost as little as $50. And in Yemen it is possible to find second- or thirdhand weapons for as low as *six dollars*. The best resource for arms traffickers are the Caserta and Naples clans, who, together with the Calabrese Mafia, with whom they are in constant contact, have their paws on the arms deposits of crumbling, Eastern European socialist countries.

The Camorra, in handling a large slice of the international arms market, could actually set the price of AK-47s, thus becoming the indirect arbiter of the state of human rights in the West. As if the level of human rights were slowly dropping, draining drop by drop as with a catheter. In the 1980s, while French and American criminal groups were using the M16, the Marine-issue assault rifle designed by Eugene Stoner—a bulky, heavy weapon that has to be oiled and cleaned to keep from jamming—AK-47s were already making the rounds in Sicily and Campania, from Cinisi to Casal di Principe. In 2003, Raffaele Spinello, a *pentito* of the Genovese clan, which ruled Avellino and the surrounding area, revealed the connection between the Basque ETA and the Camorra. The Genovese clan is allied with the Cavas in Quindici and the Caserta families. It's not a top-level clan, yet it supplied weapons to one of the principal European militant organizations. The ETA had explored various avenues of arms provisions during its thirty-year struggle, but the Campania clans became their privileged interlocutors. According to 2003 investigations by the Naples attorney's office, José Miguel Arreta and Gracia Morillo Torres, two *etarras* or ETA militants, spent ten days negotiating in a hotel suite in Milan. Prices, routes, swaps. They reached an agreement. The ETA sent cocaine and received arms in exchange. The ETA promised to steadily lower the market price of cocaine obtained through its contacts with Colombian guerrilla groups, and cover the cost and responsibility of getting the drug to Italy—anything to keep its connections with the Campania cartels, who were probably the only ones able to supply them with entire arsenals. But the ETA didn't want just AK-47s. They also requested heavy weapons, powerful explosives, and above all, missile launchers.

Relations between the Camorra and guerrilla fighters have always been prolific. Even in Peru, the adopted country of the Neapolitan narcos. In 1994, after the murder of ten or so Italians in Lima, the Court of Naples requested permission of the Peruvian authorities to carry out investigations. Investigations that aimed at revealing the connections—through the Rodriguez brothers—between Neapolitan clans and MRTA, the guerrilla warriors with red and white bandannas over their faces. Inquiries into the Mazzarella clan's connections to Somalia moved in various directions, and arms traffic was certainly a primary thread. Even warlords become tame when they need the Campania clans' weapons.

The firepower uncovered in March 2005 in Sant'Anastasia, a town at the foot of Vesuvius, was stunning. The discovery came about partly by chance, and partly by the lack of discipline of the arms traffickers, who started fighting on the street because customers and drivers couldn't agree as to the price. When the carabinieri arrived, they removed the interior panels of the truck parked near the brawl, discovering one of the largest mobile depots they had ever seen. Uzis with four magazines, seven chargers, and 112 380-caliber bullets, Russian and Czech machine guns able to fire 950 shots a minute. (Nine hundred fifty shots a minute was the firing power of American helicopters in Vietnam.) Weapons for ripping apart tanks and entire divisions of men, not for Camorra family fights on the slopes of Mount Vesuvius. Almost new, well-oiled, rifle numbers still intact, just in from Kraków. Arms trafficking is the latest way to maneuver the levers of power of the Leviathan that imposes its authority through its potential for violence. Clan armories are filled with bazookas, hand grenades, antitank mines, and machine guns, even though clans almost exclusively use Kalashnikovs, Uzis, and automatic and semiautomatic pistols. The rest is there to construct their military power and show off their strength. With all this fighting potential the clans are not opposing the legitimate violence of the state but rather monopolizing it. Campania clans, unlike the old Cosa Nostra clans, are not obsessed with a truce. Weapons are a direct extension of the dynamics related to the adjustment of capital and territory, the mix of emerging groups and competing families. It is as if they had exclusive rights to the concept, flesh, and tools of violence. Violence becomes Camorra territory, and committing violence trains you for wielding power—System power. The clans have even created new weapons, designed and built by affiliates. In 2004 police agents found a strange gun wrapped in oil-soaked cotton cloth and hidden in a hole covered over with weeds in Sant'Antimo, north of Naples. A sort of do-it-yourself lethal weapon that sells for 250 euros—nothing compared to a semiautomatic that on average goes for 2,500. The model was based on an old toy gun from the 1980s that fired Ping-Pong balls by pulling hard on the butt, thus releasing an internal spring. A toy gun, like those used by thousands of Italian children in the wars in their living rooms. But from that model—from a children's toy—comes what around here is called simply 'o tubo—the tube. It consists of two tubes, one about forty centimeters long, with a handle and a large metal screw that acts as the bolt welded inside. The second tube, smaller in diameter, can take a 20-caliber cartridge and has a side handle. Two interlocking tubes that can be transported separately, but once assembled they turn into a deadly sawed-off shot-gun for cartridges or large shots. Incredibly simple and terribly powerful. And it has the advantage of not creating complications after use: no need to rush to destroy it after an ambush; all you have to do is take it apart and it becomes two harmless cylinders, innocuous in the event of a search. Before the gun was seized by the authorities, I had heard a poor shepherd talk about it, one of those emaciated souls who still roam the bits of countryside that encircle the highway overpasses and ugly, barracklike buildings of the suburbs. His skinny Neapolitan sheep, their ribs showing, chewed on dioxin-laced grass that rotted their teeth and turned their wool gray. This shepherd would often find his animals in two pieces, their scrawny bodies split—not cut—in half. The shepherd thought it was a warning or provocation on the part of his wretched competitors with their sickly flocks. He didn't understand. It was the tube manufacturers testing firepower on animals. Sheep were the best targets for a quick control of bullet power and weapon quality, which could be measured by the way the animals flipped in the air and split in two, as in a video game.

The arms question is kept secret in the bowels of the economy, sealed in a pancreas of silence. According to figures gathered by SIPRI, the Stockholm International Peace Research Institute, Italy spends $27 billion annually on arms. More than Russia, twice as much as Israel. If these figures from the legal economy are coupled with the $3.3 billion of arms trafficking that EURISPES, the Institute of Political, Economic, and Social Research, estimates is handled by the Camorra, 'Ndrangheta, Cosa Nostra, and the Sacra Corona Unita in Puglia, we are talking about a huge proportion of the arms in circulation worldwide. The Casalesi cartel is the criminal-business group with the best international capacity to furnish not only groups but entire armies. During the 1982 Anglo-Argentine war in the Falklands, Argentina experienced its darkest period of economic isolation. So the Camorra opened negotiations with the Argentine defense, becoming the funnel through which poured weapons no one would have sold them officially. The clans outfitted themselves for a long war, but the fighting that broke out in March was over by June. Few shots, few dead, few purchases. A war of more use to politicians than to businessmen, that did more for diplomacy than for the economy. It didn't make sense for the Caserta clans to sell off their stock just to bring in immediate earnings. On the same day that the end of hostilities was declared, the British secret services intercepted a phone call between Argentina and San Cipriano d'Aversa. Just two sentences, but enough to understand the power and diplomatic potential of the Caserta families.

"Hello?"

"Hello."

"The war's over here, now what are we supposed to do?"

"Don't worry, there'll be another one."

• • •

The wisdom of power has a patience the best businessmen often lack. In 1977 the Casalesi clan had negotiated the purchase of some tanks, and the Italian secret service reported that a dismantled Leopard tank was at the train station in Villa Literno, ready to be shipped. The Camorra had long been dealing in Leopards. In February 1986 a wiretapped conversation revealed the Nuvoletta clan's negotiations for the purchase of Leopards from what was then East Germany. Even with the turnover in leadership, the Casalesi clan remained the international point of reference for groups as well as entire armies. A 1994 report from SISMI, the Italian Military Intelligence and Security Service, and the counterespionage center in Verona indicated that Željko Ražnatović, better known as Arkan, was in communication with Sandokan Schiavone, the head of the Casalesi clan. Arkan, who was killed in 2000 in a hotel in Belgrade, was one of the most ruthless Serbian war criminals, the founder of the Serb Volunteer Guard, the nationalist group that razed Muslim villages in Bosnia to the ground. The two became allies. Arkan asked for arms for his guerrilla fighters, and above all for the possibility to circumvent the embargo imposed on Serbia by bringing in capital and weapons disguised as humanitarian aid: camp hospitals, medicine, and medical supplies. According to SISMI, however, Serbia actually paid for the provisions—worth tens of millions of dollars—out of bank accounts in Austria containing $85 million. The money was then handed over to an entity allied with the Serbia and Campania clans, which purchased from interested companies the merchandise to be given as humanitarian aid, paying with money earned through illegal activities. This is where the Casalesi clans came in. They allowed the money laundering by making available companies, transportation, and goods. According to the reports, Arkan, through his intermediaries, asked the Casalesi clan to silence the Albanian Mafiosi who could have ruined his money war by attacking from the south and blocking the arms traffic. The Casalesi clan pacified its Albanian allies with arms, thus allowing Arkan a peaceful war. In exchange, clan businessmen bought up companies, stores, and farms at favorable prices, and Italian entrepreneurship spread throughout Serbia. Before going into battle, Arkan had contacted the Camorra. From South America to the Balkans, wars are fought with the weaponry of Campania families.

CEMENT

I had been away from Casal di Principe a long time. If Japan is the capital of martial arts, Australia of surfing, and Sierra Leone of diamonds, Casal di Principe is the capital of the Camorra's entrepreneurial power. Being from Casale is a sort of guarantee of immunity around Naples and Caserta. It means that you're larger-than-life, as if you emanated directly from the ferocity of Caserta's criminal organizations. You enjoy a guaranteed respect, a sort of natural fear. Even Benito Mussolini wanted to eliminate this birthmark, this criminal aura; he rebaptized San Cipriano d'Aversa and Casal di Principe with the name Albanova—new dawn. And to inaugurate a new dawn of justice, he sent in dozens of carabinieri, who were supposed to resolve the problem "with iron and fire." Today the only thing that remains of the name Albanova is the rusty train station in Casale.

Some guys spend hours hitting a punching bag, doing bench presses to sculpt their pecs, or take muscle enhancers, but for others a particular accent or a gesture is enough to bring back to life all the bodies on the ground covered with sheets. An old saying perfectly captures the lethal charge of the place's violent mythology: "You can become a Camorrista, but you're born a Casalese." Or when you get into an argument with someone. You challenge your opponent with your eyes, and a second before you start punching or stabbing, you declare your philosophy: "Life or death, it's all the same to me!" At times your roots, your hometown, comes in handy: being associated with the violence can lend you a certain fascination. You can use it as veiled intimidation to get a discount at the movies or credit from a fearful checkout girl. But it's also true that your hometown saddles you with powerful prejudices, and you don't really want to have to stand there and explain that not everyone is a clan affiliate, not everyone is a criminal; that the Camorristi are a minority. So you take a shortcut and come up with a more anonymous nearby town that will cancel any connection between yourself and the criminals: Secondigliano becomes a generic Naples, and Casal di Principe becomes Aversa or Caserta. You're either ashamed or proud, depending on the moment and the situation. Like a suit of clothing, except it's the suit that decides when to wear you.

Compared to Casal di Principe, Corleone is Disneyland. Casal di Principe, San Cipriano d'Aversa, Casapesenna. Fewer than one hundred thousand inhabitants, but twelve hundred of them have been sentenced for having ties to the Mafia, and a whole lot more have been accused or convicted of aiding or abetting Mafia activities. Since time immemorial this area has borne the weight of the Camorra, a violent and ferocious middle class led by its bloody and powerful clan. The Casalesi clan, which takes its name from Casal di Principe, is a confederation of all the Camorra families in the Caserta area: Castelvolturno, Villa Literno, Gricignano, San Tammaro, Cesa, Villa di Briano, Mondragone, Carinola, Marcianise, San Nicola La Strada, Calvi Risorta, Lusciano, and dozens of other towns. Each with its own area capo, each a part of the Casalesi network. Antonio Bardellino, the Casalesi clan founder, was the first in Italy to understand that cocaine would far surpass heroin in the long run. Yet heroin continued to be the principal merchandise for Cosa Nostra and many Camorra families. In the 1980s heroin addicts were considered to be literal gold mines, whereas coke was thought to be an elite drug. But Antonio Bardellino understood that big money was to be had by marketing a drug that didn't kill quickly, that was more like a bourgeois cocktail than a poison for outcasts. So he created an import-export company that shipped fish flour from South America to Aversa. Fish flour that concealed tons of cocaine. Bardellino peddled heroin as well; the shipments to John Gotti in America were packed in espresso filters. An American narcotics squad once intercepted sixty-seven kilos of heroin, but it wasn't a disastrous loss for the San Cipriano d'Aversa boss. A few days later he had a call put through to Gotti: "Now we're sending twice as much another way." From the marshes of Aversa was born a cartel that knew how to stand up to Cutolo, and the ferocity of that war is still imprinted in the genetic code of the Caserta clans. In the 1980s the Cutolo families were eliminated in a few extremely violent operations. The De Matteos—four men and four women—were slaughtered in a few days. The only member the Casalesi spared was an eight-year-old boy. All seven members of the Simeone family were killed almost simultaneously. In the morning the family was alive and well and powerful, but by that evening it was extinct. Butchered. In March 1982, the Casalesi positioned a field machine gun, the kind used in trenches, on a hill in Ponte Annicchino and picked off four Cutolo members.

Antonio Bardellino was affiliated with Cosa Nostra, was tied to Tano Badalamenti, and was a friend and companion of Tommaso Buscetta, with whom he had shared a villa in South America. When the Corleones swept away the Badalamenti-Buscetta power, they also tried to eliminate Bardellino, but in vain. During the rise of the Nuova Camorra Organizzata, the Sicilians also tried to eliminate Raffaele Cutolo. They sent a hit man, Mimmo Bruno, over on the ferry from Palermo, but he was killed as soon as he set foot outside the port. Cosa Nostra had always had a sort of respect and awe of the Casalesi, but when in 2002 they killed Raffaele Lubrano—the boss of Pignataro Maggiore, a man with close ties to Cosa Nostra, having been handpicked by Totò Riina—many feared a feud would explode. I remember being at a newsstand the day after the ambush and hearing the vendor murmuring to a customer about his fears:

"If the Sicilians come here to fight now too, we won't have peace for three years."

"Which Sicilians? The Mafiosi?"

"Yes, the Mafiosi."

"The Mafia should get down on their knees in front of the Casalesi and suck. That's it, just slurp it all up."

One of the declarations about the Sicilian Mafiosi that shocked me most was made by Carmine Schiavone, a *pentito* Casalesi clan member, in a 2005 interview. He talked about Cosa Nostra as if it were an organization enslaved to politicians and, unlike the Caserta Camorristi, incapable of thinking in business terms. According to Schiavone, the Mafia wanted to become a sort of antistate, but this was not a business issue. The state-antistate paradigm doesn't exist. All there is, is a territory where you do business—with, through, or without the state:

> We lived with the state. For us the state had to exist and it had to be that state, except that our philosophy was different from the Sicilians. Whereas Riina came from island isolation, an old shepherd from out of the mountains, really, we had surpassed those limits and we wanted to live with the state. If a state figure stonewalled us, we would find someone else who was willing to help us. If it was a politician, we wouldn't vote for him, and if it was an institutional figure, we would find a way to swindle him.

Carmine Schiavone, Sandokan's cousin, was the first to take the lid off the Casalesi clan's business affairs. When he decided to cooperate with the law, his daughter Giuseppina's condemnation of him was fierce, more lethal than a death sentence. Her fiery words were printed in the newspaper:

"He's a big fraud, a liar, a bad man, and a hypocrite who has sold his failures. A beast. He never was my father. I don't even know what the Camorra is."

Businessmen. That's how the Caserta Camorristi define themselves, nothing more than businessmen. A clan made up of violent company men and killer managers, of builders and landowners. Each with his own armed band and linked by common economic interests. The Casalesi cartel's force has always been its ability to handle large drug lots without needing to feed an internal market. They are present on Rome's vast drug market, but more significant is their role in the sale of huge consignments. The 2006 acts of the Anti-Mafia Commission indicate that the Casalesi were supplying the Palermo families with drugs. Alliances with Nigerian and Albanian clans meant they no longer had to be involved in direct peddling and narcotrafficking operations. Pacts with clans in Lagos and Benin City, alliances with Mafia families in Priština and Tirana, and agreements with Ukrainian Mafiosi in Leopolis and Kiev liberated the Casalesi from bottom-rung criminal activities. At the same time the Casalesi received privileged treatment in investments in Eastern Europe and in the purchase of cocaine from Nigeria-based international traffickers. New leaders and new wars. It all happened after the explosion of the Bardellino clan, the origin of the Camorra's entrepreneurial power in this area. Antonio Bardellino, having achieved total dominion in every legal and illegal economic sector, from narcotraffic to construction, settled in Santo Domingo with a new family. He gave his Caribbean children the same names as those in San Cipriano—a simple, easy way of avoiding confusion. His most loyal men held the reins of power back home. Having emerged unscathed from the war with Cutolo, they developed companies and established their authority, expanding everywhere in northern Italy and abroad. Mario Iovine, Vincenzo De Falco, Francesco Sandokan Schiavone, Francesco *Cicciotto di Mezzanotte* Bidognetti, and Vincenzo Zagaria were the capos of the Casalese confederation. In the early 1980s Cicciotto di Mezzanotte and Sandokan headed up the clan's military operations, but they were also businessmen with widespread interests, eager to control the enormous, many-headed beast of the confederation. They found that the boss Mario Iovine was too close to Bardellino, however; he did not approve of their desire for autonomy. So they devised a mysterious but politically effective strategy. They used the cantankerous nature of Camorra diplomacy in the only way that would let them achieve their goals: they sparked an internal war.

As the *pentito* Carmine Schiavone tells it, the two bosses urged Antonio Bardellino to return to Italy and eliminate Mario's brother Mimì Iovine. Mimì owned a furniture factory and was formally unconnected to the Camorra, but, the two bosses claimed, he had often acted as a police informer. To convince Bardellino, they told him that even Mario was prepared to sacrifice his brother to keep the clan's power on solid footing. Bardellino let himself be convinced and had Mimì killed as he was going to work at his furniture factory. Right after the ambush Cicciotto di Mezzanotte and Sandokan pressured Mario Iovine to eliminate Bardellino, saying that he had dared to kill his brother on a pretext, based only on rumor. A double cross calculated to pit one against the other. They started to organize. Bardellino's heirs all agreed to eliminate the capo of capos, the man who, more than anyone else in Campania, had created a criminal-business power system. Bardellino was convinced to move from Santo Domingo to the Brazilian villa; they told him that Interpol was on his tail. Mario Iovine went to see him in Brazil in 1988 on the pretext of needing to put their fish flour and cocaine business in order. One afternoon Iovine—not finding his pistol in his trousers—took a mallet and bashed in Bardellino's skull. He buried the body in a hole dug on the beach, but as it was never found, the legend was born that Antonio Bardellino was really still alive and enjoying his wealth on some South American island. Mission accomplished, Iovine immediately phoned Vincenzo De Falco to give him the news and to kick off the massacre of all the Bardellino men. Paride Salzillo, Bardellino's nephew and his true heir in the area, was invited to a summit of all the Casalese cartel managers. The *pentito* Carmine Schiavone recounts that they had Salzillo sit at the head of the table, in honor of his uncle. All of a sudden, Sandokan attacked him and started to strangle him while his cousin, also named Francesco Schiavone but known as Cicciariello, together with his cohorts Raffaele Diana and Giuseppe Caterino, held him by the legs and arms. Sandokan could have killed him with a gun or a knife to the stomach, the way the old bosses used to. But no. He had to do it with his hands: that's the way the new sovereign kills the old one when he usurps the throne. Ever since 1345 when Andrew of Hungary was strangled in Aversa, the result of a conspiracy orchestrated by his wife, Queen Joan I, and the Neapolitan nobles loyal to Charles, Duke of Durazzo, who aspired to the throne, strangulation around here has been a symbol of succession, of the violent turnover of sovereignty. Sandokan had to show all the bosses that he was the heir, that, by right of viciousness, he was the new Casalesi leader.

Antonio Bardellino had created a complex system of power, and the business cells bred in his bosom would not long remain neatly within the structures he had devised. They had matured and now needed to express their power without further hierarchical limitations. This is how Sandokan Schiavone became the leader. He developed a highly efficient, family-run system. His brother Walter coordinated the firing squads, his cousin Carmine managed economic and financial affairs, his cousin Francesco was elected mayor of Casal di Principe, and another cousin, Nicola, treasurer. Important moves for local self-assertion, which is crucial in the early phases. In the first years of his rule Sandokan's power was also solidified through strict political ties. Because of a conflict with the old Christian Democratic Party, in 1992 the clan in Casal di Principe supported the Italian Liberal Party, which experienced the biggest upswing in its history, jumping from a measly 1 to 30 percent. Nevertheless all the other top-level clan members were hostile to Sandokan's absolute leadership. In particular the De Falcos, who in addition to their business and political alliances had the police and carabinieri on their side. In 1990 there were several meetings of the Casalesi leaders. Vincenzo De Falco, nicknamed the Fugitive, was invited to one of the meetings. The bosses would have liked to eliminate him. But he didn't show. The carabinieri arrived instead and arrested the guests. Vincenzo De Falco was killed in 1991, riddled with bullets in his car. The police found him hunched over with the stereo blasting, a tape of the singer Domenico Modugno still playing. After his death there was a rift in the Casalesi confederation. On one side the families close to Sandokan and Iovine: Zagaria, Reccia, Bidognetti, and Caterino; on the other the families close to the De Falcos: Quadrano, La Torre, Luise, Salzillo. The De Falcos responded to the murder of the Fugitive by killing Mario Iovine in Cascais, Portugal, in 1991. They showered him with bullets in a phone booth. Iovine's death meant a green light for Sandokan Schiavone. There followed four years of wars and massacres, four years of continuous killings between the families close to Schiavone and those close to the De Falcos. Years of upheavals, of alliances, and shifting sides; there was no real solution but rather a division of territories and powers. Sandokan became the emblem of his cartel's victory over the other families. Afterward, all his enemies reconverted into allies. Cement, drugs, rackets, transportation, waste management, commercial monopolies, and specified suppliers: all this was Casalesi company territory under Sandokan.

Cement makers became a crucial weapon for the Casalesi clans. Every construction company is dependent on them for cement. This supply system is key for putting the clans in touch with all the contractors in the area and for linking them to every possible deal. As Carmine Schiavone frequently claimed, the clans' cement makers offered favorable prices because their ships carried not only cement but also distributed arms to Middle Eastern countries under embargo. This second level of commerce allowed them to beat out the legal prices. The Casalesi clans made money at every step of the way; they supplied cement and subcontractors, receiving bribes on big deals. These bribes were really just the beginning, since their efficient and economical companies would not work without them, and no other company could do the work for a good price and without being punished. The Schiavone family manages a turnover of 5 billion euros a year. The entire economic potential of the Casalesi cartel—consisting of real estate holdings, farms, stock, liquid assets, construction companies, sugar refineries, cement plants, usury, and drug and arms traffic—is around 30 billion euros. The Casalese Camorra has become a multipurpose company, the most dependable in Campania, players in a whole range of business activities. The amount of illegally accumulated capital often leads to subsidized credit, which allows their companies to trounce the competition through low prices or intimidation. The new Casalese Camorrista middle class has transformed extortion into a sort of additional service, the racket into participation in Camorra business. Your monthly payments fund clan operations, but they also earn you economic protection with the banks, punctual deliveries, and respect for your sales representatives. Extortion as an imposed acquisition of services. This new racket concept came to light in a 2004 investigation by the Caserta police, which ended in the arrest of eighteen people. Francesco Sandokan Schiavone, Michele Zagaria, and the Moccia clan were, at that time, the most important Campania stockholders in Cirio and Parmalat. The milk distributed first by Cirio and then by Parmalat had conquered 90 percent of the market in the Caserta region, a good part of the Naples region, all of southern Lazio, parts of the Marche, Abruzzo, and Lucania. The companies achieved this result through their close alliance with the Casalese Camorra and bribes to the clans to maintain their preeminent position. Various brands were involved, all connected to Eurolat, which in 1999 passed from Cirio, under Cragnotti's direction, to Parmalat, then run by Calisto Tanzi.

The judges ordered the seizure of three concessionaries and numerous companies connected to the distribution and sale of milk, all accused of being controlled by the Casalesi. The milk companies were registered under false names on their behalf. Cirio and Parmalat dealt directly with the brother-in-law of Michele Zagaria, the Casalesi clan regent in hiding for a decade, in order to obtain special client status, which they won above all through commercial deals. Cirio and Parmalat brands gave their distributors special discounts—from 4 to 6.5 percent, rather than the usual 3 percent—as well as various production awards, so supermarkets and retailers also received price reductions. In this way the Casalesi achieved widespread acquiescence for their commercial predominance. And where pacific persuasion and common interest didn't work, violence did: threats, extortion, destruction of transport vehicles. They beat up their competitors' drivers, plundered their trucks, and burned their depots. The fear was so widespread that in the areas controlled by the clans it was impossible not only to distribute but even to find someone willing to sell brands other than those imposed by the Casalesi. In the end, consumers paid the price: in a situation of monopoly and a frozen market, retail prices were uncontrollable due to a lack of real competition.

The big deal between the national milk companies and the Camorra came to light in the fall of 2000, when Cuono Lettiero, a Casalesi affiliate, began collaborating with the law and discussing the clans' commercial ties. The guarantee of a constant rate of sale was the most direct and automatic way of obtaining bank guarantees—the dream of every big business. In this scenario, Cirio and Parmalat were officially the "offended parties"—the victims of extortion—but investigators became convinced that the mood was relatively relaxed and that the behavior of both the national companies and the local Camorristi was mutually beneficial.

Cirio and Parmalat—at least their management at the time—never reported suffering from clan interference in Campania. Not even in 1998, when a Cirio official was the victim of an attack in his home near Caserta; he was brutally beaten with a stick in front of his wife and nine-year-old daughter because he hadn't obeyed clan orders. No rebellion, no charges filed. The certainty of the monopoly was better than the uncertainty of the market. The money to maintain the monopoly and take possession of the Campania market had to be justified on the company balance sheet. But in the country of creative financing and the decriminalization of false accounting, this was not a problem. False invoicing, false sponsorships, and false year-end awards for milk sales resolved any bookkeeping problems. To this end, nonexistent events have been paid for since 1997: the Mozzarella Festival, Music in the Piazza, even the Feast of San Tammaro, patron saint of Villa Literno. As a token of esteem for its employees, Cirio even financed the Polisportiva Afragolese, a sports club run by the Moccia clan, as well as an extensive network of music, sports, and recreation centers, demonstrating the "public spiritedness" of the Casalesi. Cirio stated that it had been forced to do so as part of a protection racket and insisted that it was the victim. (Subsequent to these investigations and the financial scandals that ensued, both Cirio and Parmalat filed for bankruptcy. Both companies have been reconstituted and continue to trade under completely new management teams.)

The power of the clan has grown extensively in recent years, extending to eastern Europe: Poland, Romania, and Hungary. Poland was where Francesco Cicciariello Schiavone, Sandokan's cousin, the squat, mustachioed boss and a principal Camorra figure, was arrested in 2004. He was wanted for ten homicides, three kidnappings, nine attempted homicides, numerous violations of arms laws, and extortion. They nabbed him as he was grocery shopping with his twenty-five-year-old Romanian companion Luiza Boetz. Cicciariello was going by the name of Antonio and seemed like a simple, fifty-one-year-old Italian businessman. But his companion must have sensed that something was amiss when, in an attempt to throw off the police bloodhounds, she had to make a long and tortuous train journey to join him in Krosno, near Kraków. They tailed her across three borders and followed her by car to the outskirts of the Polish city. They stopped Cicciariello at the supermarket checkout; he had shaved his mustache, straightened his curly hair, and slimmed down. He had moved to Hungary, but continued to meet his companion in Poland, where he had big business interests: animal farms, land purchases, deals with local businessmen. The Italian representative of SECI, the Southeast European Cooperative Initiative for Combating Trans-Border Crime, had reported that Schiavone and his men frequently went to Romania and had started important dealings in Barlad in the east, in Sinaia in the center, and in Cluj in the west, as well as along the Black Sea. Cicciariello Schiavone had two lovers: Luiza Boetz and Cristina Coremanciau, also Romanian. In Casale, word of his arrest "because of a woman" was like a slap in the boss's face. The headline of one local paper seemed to sneer at him: "Cicciariello arrested with his lover." In truth both of his lovers were crucial to his business as they were in fact managers who handled his investments in Poland and Romania. Cicciariello was one of the last Schiavone family bosses to be arrested. In twenty years of power and feuds, many Casalesi clan leaders and supporters had been locked away. All the investigations against the cartel and its branches were grouped together in the Spartacus maxi-trial, named after the rebel gladiator who had attempted the greatest insurrection Rome had ever known on this very same land.

I went to the courthouse in Santa Maria Capua Venere on the day of the sentencing. I was expecting video crews and photographers, but there were only a few, and only from local newspapers and TV stations. But police and carabinieri were everywhere. About two hundred of them. Two helicopters were hovering low over the courthouse, the noise of the propellers pounding in everyone's ears. Bomb detection dogs, police vehicles. The mood was extremely tense. And yet the national press and TV crews were absent. The media was totally ignoring the biggest trial—in terms of the number of accused and convictions requested—of a criminal cartel. Experts refer to the Spartacus trial by a number: 3615, the number assigned to the investigation in the general register, with around thirteen hundred DDA inquiries beginning in 1993, all stemming from Carmine Schiavone's testimony.

The trial lasted seven years and twenty-one days, for a total of 626 hearings. The most complex Mafia trial in Italy in the last fifteen years. Five hundred witnesses took the stand, in addition to twenty-four government witnesses, six of whom were defendants. Ninety files were deposited: acts, sentences from other trials, documents, and wiretaps. Almost a year after the 1995 blitz, the offspring investigations of Spartacus also started up: Spartacus 2 and Regi Lagni, related to the renovation of the Bourbon canals, which hadn't been properly restored since the eighteenth century. According to the accusations, the clans had piloted the renovation project for years, generating contracts worth millions. Rather than putting the money toward the canals, they channeled it into their construction businesses, which subsequently became extremely successful throughout Italy. There was also the Aima trial, related to the swindling in the famous produce collection centers, where the European community destroyed surplus production, providing subsidies to the farmers. The clans dumped trash, iron, and construction waste into the huge craters intended for the produce. But first they had it all weighed as if it were fruit. And obviously they collected the subsidies while the fruit of their lands continued to be sold. One hundred and thirty-one orders of seizure were issued regarding companies, lands, and agricultural businesses, amounting to hundreds of millions of euros. Two soccer clubs were also sequestered: Albanova, which competed in the C2 league, and Casal di Principe.

Investigations also probed the clan's imposition that public works contracts go to firms connected to their concrete and earthmoving operations, and scams regarding illegally obtained contributions in the agricultural-alimentary sector, which were injurious to the EEC, the European Economic Community. As well as hundreds of homicides and business relationships. As I awaited the sentence along with everyone else, it occurred to me that this was not just another trial, not a simple, ordinary prosecution of Camorra families in southern Italy. It seemed more like a trial of history, the Nuremberg for a whole generation of the Camorra. But unlike the high officers of the Reich, many of the Camorristi present were still in command, still the heads of their empires. A Nuremberg without victors. The accused in cages, in silence. Sandokan was on videoconference from the Viterbo prison; it would have been too risky to move him. The only sound in the courtroom was the lawyers' voices: over twenty law firms were involved and more than fifty lawyers and paralegals had studied, followed, observed, and defended. The relatives of the accused were huddled together in a small room next to the bunker wing, their eyes glued to the monitors. When the Court president, Catello Marano, picked up the thirty-page verdict, there was silence. A nervous silence, accompanied by an orchestra of anxious sounds: heavy breathing, hundreds of throats swallowing and watches ticking, dozens of muted cell phones silently vibrating. The president read the list of the guilty first, then the not guilty. Twenty-one life sentences, more than 750 years of prison. Twenty-one times the president pronounced the sentence of life imprisonment, often repeating the names of the condemned. And then seventy times he read out the years that other men, associates and managers, would spend in prison for their alliance with the terrible Casalese power. By one thirty it was almost all over. Sandokan asked to speak. He was agitated and wanted to respond to the sentence, repeat the claim of the counsel for the defense: he was a successful businessman, but a plot of envious, Marxist judges had deemed the local bourgeoisie a criminal power rather than the product of entrepreneurial and economic talent. He wanted to shout that the sentence was unjust. According to his logic,

all the dead resulted from local feuds that were part of the rural culture, and not from Camorra wars. But this time Sandokan was not allowed to speak. Silenced like an unruly schoolboy, he started to yell,
so the judges had the audio disconnected. A big, bearded man continued to squirm on the screen until the video was cut as well. The
courtroom emptied immediately, the police and carabinieri slowly dis-
persing as the helicopter hovered over the courtroom bunker. It's
strange, but I didn't have the feeling that the Casalesi clan had been
defeated. Many were thrown in jail for a few years, some bosses
would never come out alive, and perhaps a few would eventually decide to cooperate and thus regain a piece of their existence beyond
bars. Sandokan's rage must have been the suffocating anger of a powerful man who holds the entire map of his empire in his head but
cannot control it directly.

The bosses who decide not to cooperate with the authorities live
off a metaphysical, almost imaginary power, and they do everything
possible to forget about the businessmen whom they supported and
launched, those who, not being clan members, get off scot-free. If
they wanted to, the bosses could make sure they ended up in jail as
well, but they would have to talk first, and this would immediately put
an end to their supreme authority and place all their family members
at risk. But even then—something far more tragic for a boss—they
would not be able to map the routes of their money and legal investments. Even confessing and revealing their power, they would never
know exactly where all their money ended up. The bosses always
pay—they can't do otherwise. They kill, they direct firing squads,
they're the first link in the chain of the extraction of illegal capital;
this means that their crimes are always traceable, unlike the di-
aphanous economic crimes of their white-collar men. Besides, bosses
are not eternal. Cutolo gives way to Bardellino, Bardellino to Sandokan, Sandokan to Zagaria, Zagaria to La Monica, La Monica to Di
Lauro, Di Lauro to the Spaniards, and the Spaniards to God knows
whom. The economic power of the Camorra System lies exactly in its

continual turnover of leaders and criminal choices. One man's dictatorship of the clan is always brief; if the power of a boss were long-lasting, he would raise prices, create a monopoly, making rigid markets, and invest continuously in the same sectors rather than exploring new ones. Instead of value being added in the criminal economy, he would become an obstacle to business. And so, as soon as a boss takes over, new figures ready to take his place start to emerge, figures eager to expand, to stand on the shoulders of the giants they helped create. Something that the journalist Riccardo Orioles, one of the most astute observers of power dynamics, always remembered: "Criminality is not power, but a kind of power." There will never be a boss who wants a seat in government. If the Camorra had all the power, its business, which is essential to the workings of the legal and illegal scale, would not exist. In this sense every arrest and maxi-trial seems more like a way of replacing capos and breaking business cycles than an act capable of destroying a system.

The faces that were printed the next day in the newspapers, all lined up one next to another—bosses, supporters, young affiliates, and seasoned old guard—did not represent an infernal circle of criminals but pieces of a mosaic of power that no one had been able to ignore or defy for twenty years. After the Spartacus trial, the imprisoned bosses started implicitly and explicitly threatening judges, magistrates, and journalists—everyone they considered responsible for turning a group of cement and mozzarella managers into killers in the eyes of the law.

Senator Lorenzo Diana was their favorite target. They sent letters to the local papers, made explicit threats during trials. Immediately following the Spartacus sentencing, some people went to the senator's brother's trout farm and scattered the fish around, leaving them wiggling on the ground to die slowly, suffocating in the air. Some *pentiti* even reported attempts on the senator's life on the part of the organization's "hawks." Operations that were halted through the intervention of more diplomatic elements of the clan. Diana's police escort also helped dissuade them. Armed escorts are never an obstacle for the clans; they're not afraid of armored cars and policemen. But it is a sign, a signal that the man they want to eliminate is not alone, that they can't so easily rid themselves of him as they could an individual whose death would concern only his family circle. Lorenzo Diana is one of those politicians who decided to reveal the complexity of the Casalese power rather than generically denounce criminals. He was born in San Cipriano d'Aversa and experienced firsthand the emergence of Bardellino and Sandokan, the feuds, massacres, and business operations. He can speak about that power better than anyone else, and the clans fear his knowledge and his memory. They fear that from one moment to the next he can reawaken the national media's interest. They fear that the senator will report to the Anti-Mafia Commission what the press, attributing everything to local crime, ignores. Lorenzo Diana is one of those rare men who knows that fighting the power of the Camorra calls for infinite patience, the sort of patience that starts over from the beginning, again and again, that pulls the threads of the economic knot one by one to arrive at the criminal head. Slowly, but with perseverance and anger, even when your attention wanes, even when it all seems futile, when you're lost in a metamorphosis of criminal powers that change but are never defeated.

With the trial over, there was the risk of an open clash between the Bidognetti and the Schiavone families. They had been facing off through confederate clans for years, but their common business interests always prevailed over their differences. Bidognetti territory covers the northern part of the Caserta region, extending to the coast. The Mezzanotte clan has powerful hit squads who are incredibly ferocious. They burned alive Francesco Salvo, who owned and worked at a bar called The Tropicana: punishment for having dared to replace Bidognetti video poker machines with those of a rival clan. They went so far as to launch a phosphorus bomb at Gabriele Spenuso's car on the Nola–Villa Literno road. In 2001, Domenico Bidognetti ordered Antonio Magliulo eliminated because though he was married he had

dared to make advances on a cousin of a boss's. They took him to the beach, tied him to a chair facing the sea, and began to stuff his mouth and nose with sand. Magliulo tried to breathe, swallowing and spitting sand, blowing it out his nose, vomiting, chewing, and twisting his neck. His saliva, mixing with the sand, formed a kind of primitive cement, a gluey substance that slowly suffocated him. Mezzanotte ferocity was directly proportional to its business power. According to various investigations by the Naples DDA in 1993 and 2006, the Bidognettis, who were in the waste-management business, forged alliances with businessmen of the deviant P2 Masonic Lodge, for whom they illegally—and at special prices—disposed of toxic wastes. Cicciotto di Mezzanotte's nephew Gaetano Cerci, arrested in the "Adelphi" operation against the *ecomafia* or illegal-waste traffickers, was the contact between the Casalese Camorra and the Masons, and he frequently met directly with Licio Gelli, for business purposes.*
Investigators discovered the deals through the earnings—more than 35 million euros—of a single company. The bosses Bidognetti and Schiavone, both in prison serving life sentences, could take advantage of each other's conviction to unleash his own men in an attempt to eliminate the rival clan. There was a moment when everything seemed about to explode, setting off one of those wars that results in clusters of deaths every day.

In the spring of 2005 Sandokan's youngest son went to a party in Parete, in Bidognetti territory, and—according to the investigations—started flirting with a girl even though she was with someone. The Schiavone scion was without an escort, believing that the mere fact of being Sandokan's son would make him immune to any form of aggression. But that's not how it went. A small group dragged him outside and beat him up—slapping, punching, and kicking him in the ass. He

---

*Gelli was master of the Propaganda Due or P2 Masonic Lodge, which was implicated in criminal activities. The lodge was closed by Masonic authorities in 1976, and Licio Gelli was expelled from Freemasonry.—Trans.

had to go to the hospital to get his scalp sewed up. The next day fifteen or so guys on motorcycles and in cars showed up at Penelope's, the bar where the kids who had attacked Sandokan's son usually hung out. Armed with baseball bats, they wrecked the place, beating to a pulp everyone there, but they couldn't identify those responsible for insulting Sandokan. It seems they escaped through another exit; the commandos chased them and fired at them in the piazza, hitting a passerby in the stomach. In response, the next day three motorcycles pulled up at the Caffè Matteotti in Casal di Principe, where the younger Schiavone clan affiliates usually hung out. The riders got off their bikes slowly, giving passersby time to flee, then started smashing everything. Brawls and more than sixteen knifings were reported. The air was heavy: a new war was brewing.

Luigi Diana's unexpected confession increased the tension. According to a local paper, the *pentito* declared that Bidognetti was responsible for Schiavone's first arrest, that he was the one who had collaborated with the carabinieri, revealing the boss's hiding place in France. The hit squads were gearing up and the carabinieri were ready to collect the dead bodies. But Sandokan himself called a halt to the massacre with a public gesture. Despite strict prison rules, he managed to send an open letter to a local paper, which was printed on the front page on September 21, 2005. The boss, like a successful manager, resolved the conflict by contradicting the *pentito*, a relative of whose was killed just hours after his declaration.

"It has been proven that the tip-off, from the person who squealed, thus permitting my arrest in France, was given by Carmine Schiavone, and not by Cicciotto Bidognetti. The truth is that the individual who goes by the name of the *pentito* Luigi Diana speaks lies and wants to sow discord for his own personal gain."

Sandokan also "advises" the newspaper editor to report the news properly:

"I beg you to not let yourself be exploited by this mercenary and very compromised traitor, and not to fall into the error of turning your newspaper into a scandal-mongering rag that would inevitably lose credibility, as your competitor has done. I have not renewed my subscription to that paper, and many other people will follow suit. They, like me, would not buy such a manipulated newspaper."

Sandokan thus discredits the rival publication and officially elects the one to whom he sent his letter as his new interlocutor.

"I won't even bother to comment on the fact that your competitor is accustomed to writing falsehoods. The undersigned is like water from a spring: completely transparent!"

Sandokan urged his men to buy the new paper instead of the old one. Requests for subscriptions to the boss's new choice and cancellations for the old one arrived from dozens of prisons throughout Italy. The boss closed his letter of peace with Bidognetti as follows:

"Life always asks you what you are able to face. And it has asked these so-called *pentiti* to face the mud. Like pigs!"

The Casalesi cartel was not defeated. On the contrary, it even seemed reinvigorated. According to the Naples anti-Mafia prosecutor, the cartel is now run by a dyarchy: Antonio Iovine, known as *'o ninno* or "nursing baby" because he became a clan leader when he was still a kid, and Michele Zagaria, the manager boss of Casapesenna, called *capastorta*—crooked head—due to the irregularity of his face, even though it seems he now calls himself Manera. Both bosses have been in hiding for years and are on the minister of the interior's list of most dangerous Italian fugitives. Untraceable, yet they are undoubtedly in their hometowns. No boss can leave his roots for too long, because all his power is based on them, and it's there that it can all collapse.

A mere handful of miles, minuscule towns, knots of little lanes, farms lost in the countryside—and yet it's impossible to catch them. But they're here. They move along international routes, but they always go home and are here most of the year. Everyone knows it. And yet they can't nab them. Their system of cover is so efficient that it prevents their arrest. Their families and relatives continue to live in their villas. Antonio Iovine's villa in San Cipriano is in art nouveau style, whereas Michele Zagaria's vast complex, between San Cipriano and Casapesenna, has a glass cupola to allow the sunlight to reach an enormous tree that dominates the living room. The Zagaria family owns dozens of satellite companies throughout Italy and—according to the Naples DDA judges—the largest Italian earthmoving business. The most powerful of all. An economic supremacy that is born not of direct criminal activity but of the ability to balance licit and illicit capital.

These firms manage to be extremely competitive. They have full-scale criminal colonies in Emilia, Tuscany, Umbria, and the Veneto, where anti-Mafia controls and certification are less strict and thus allow for the transfer of whole branches of a company. At first the Casalesi demanded protection money from Campania businessmen working in the north, but they now manage the market directly. They control most of the construction business around Modena and Arezzo, importing a workforce that is predominantly from Caserta.

Current investigations reveal that construction companies connected to the Casalesi clan have infiltrated the TAV or high-speed-train works in the north, just as they have done in the south. A July 1995 investigation coordinated by Judge Franco Imposimato revealed that the large companies that had won bids for the Naples-Rome leg of the TAV then subcontracted the work to Edilsud, a company connected to none other than Michele Zagaria, as well as to dozens of other companies linked with the Casalese cartel. A deal that yielded about 5 billion euros.

Investigations show that the Zagaria clan had already reached an agreement with the Calabrian 'Ndrangheta about their firms' participation in the bidding in the event that the TAV were to get as far south as Reggio Calabria. The Casalesi were ready, as they are now. According to recent Naples anti-Mafia prosecutor's investigations, the Casapesenna rib of the organization has infiltrated a series of public works projects in Umbria connected to reconstruction activities after the 1997 earthquake. The Camorra companies in the Aversa area can dominate every step of every large contract and every construction site. Rental equipment, earth removal, transportation, materials, and manpower.

The Aversa-area firms are ready to intervene: they are organized, economical, fast, and efficient. Officially there are 517 construction companies in Casal di Principe. A great many of them are direct emanations of the clans, and there are hundreds more in the area, an army ready to cement over anything. The clans have not blocked development in the area, but rather rerouted the benefits into their pockets. In the past five years, veritable commercial thrones of cement have been built in just a few square miles: one of the largest movie theater complexes in Italy in Marcianise; the largest shopping center in southern Italy in Teverola; and the largest shopping center in Europe in Marcianise—all within a region with extremely high unemployment that is continually hemorrhaging emigrants. Enormous commercial complexes. Rather than nonplaces, as the ethnologist Marc Augé would have defined them, they seem to be starting places. Supermarkets where the paper money from everything bought and consumed baptizes capital that would otherwise not find a specific, legitimate origin. Places that provide the legal origin of money. The more shopping centers that go up, the more new construction sites, the more merchandise that arrives, the more suppliers who work, the more shipments that arrive, the faster the money will be able to cross from the jagged confines of illegal territories into legal ones.

The clans benefited from the structural development of the area, and they're also ready to collect the material rewards. They anxiously await the inauguration of major projects: the subway in Aversa and the airport in Grazzanise, one of the biggest in Europe, to be built near the farms that once belonged to Cicciariello and Sandokan.

The Casalesi have distributed their goods throughout the region. Just the real estate assets seized by the Naples DDA in the last few years amount to 750 million euros. The lists are frightening. In the Spartacus trial alone, 199 buildings, 52 pieces of property, 14 companies, 12 automobiles, and 3 boats were sequestered. Over the years, according to a 1996 trial, Schiavone and his trusted men have seen the seizure of assets worth 450 billion euros: companies, villas, lands, buildings, and automobiles with powerful engines, including the Jaguar in which Sandokan was found at the time of his first arrest. Confiscations that would have destroyed any company, losses that would have ruined any businessman, economic blows that would have capsized any firm. Anyone but the Casalesi cartel. Every time I read about the seizure of property, every time I see the lists of assets the DDA has confiscated from the bosses, I feel depressed and exhausted; everywhere I turn, everything seems to be theirs. Everything. Land, buffalos, farms, quarries, garages, dairies, hotels, and restaurants. A sort of Camorra omnipotence. I couldn't see anything that didn't belong to them.

One businessman more than every other possessed this absolute power, becoming the owner of everything: Dante Passarelli from Casal di Principe. He was arrested years ago for Camorra ties, accused of being the treasurer of the Casalesi clan. The prosecution asked for a sentence of eight years. Passarelli was not simply one of the countless businessmen who did deals with and through the clans. Passarelli was The Businessman, the number one, the closest, the most trustworthy. He had run a highly successful delicatessen, and according to the charges, his commercial talents were what led to his being chosen to handle the investment of a part of the clan's capital. He became a wholesaler and then an industrialist, a pasta manufacturer and a contractor, had his hand in sugar and catering, even in the soccer business. According to an estimate by the DIA, the anti-Mafia directorate, Dante Passarelli's assets were worth between 300 and 400 million euros. A good part of that wealth was the fruit of holdings and significant shares in the agricultural-alimentary sector. He owned Ipam, one of the most important Italian sugar refineries. His company Passarelli Dante and Sons, which was awarded the contract for the cafeteria hospitals in Santa Maria Capua Vetere, Capua, and Sessa

Aurunca, was the leader in meal distribution. He owned hundreds of apartments, and commercial and industrial buildings. At the time of his arrest on December 5, 1995, assets subject to seizure included: nine buildings in Villa Literno; an apartment in Santa Maria Capua Vetere; another in Pinetamare; a building in Casal di Principe; lands in Castelvolturno, Casal di Principe, Villa Literno, and Cancello Arnone; and La Balzana, an agricultural complex in Santa Maria La Fossa composed of 209 hectares of land and 40 rural buildings. As well as the feather in his cap: *Anfra III*, a luxury yacht with several cabins, parquet floors, and a whirlpool tub, docked in Gallipoli. Sandokan and his consort had taken a cruise of the Greek isles aboard *Anfra III*. Investigations were advancing toward the progressive confiscation of Dante Passarelli's assets when in November 2004 he was found dead, having fallen from the balcony of one of his houses. His wife found the body—head split open, spine shattered. The investigation is ongoing. It remains unclear whether it was an accident or a very familiar, anonymous hand that caused him to fall from an unfinished balcony. With his death, all the assets that were to go to the state returned to the family. Passarelli's destiny was that of a talented businessman who, thanks to the clan, handled sums he never would have seen otherwise, and he caused them to multiply exponentially. Then there was a snag—a judicial investigation—and that wealth was confiscated. Just as his skill as a company man brought him an empire, so the seizures brought him death. The clans do not allow for mistakes. When during a trial it was made known to Sandokan that Dante Passarelli was dead, the boss serenely replied, "May his soul rest in peace."

The clans' power remained the power of cement. It was at the construction sites that I could feel—physically, in my gut—all their might. I had worked on construction sites for several summers; to get a job mixing cement, all I had to do was let the contractor know where I was from. Campania provided the best builders in all of Italy—the most skilled, the fastest, cheapest, the least pains in the ass. It's killer work, and I have never learned to do it particularly well. A trade that might yield a considerable sum only if you are prepared to gamble all your strength, all your muscles, and all your energy. To work in all kinds of weather, wearing sometimes a ski mask, sometimes just your underwear. Getting my hands and nose near cement was the only way I knew to understand what power—real power— was built on.

It was when Francesco Iacomino died that I truly understood the workings of the building trade. He was thirty-three when they found him, in his overalls, on the ground at the intersection of Via Quattro Orologi and Via Gabriele D'Annunzio in Ercolano. He had fallen from a scaffolding. After the accident everyone fled, even the draftsman. No one called an ambulance for fear that it would arrive before they got away. So they left him lying in the street, still alive, spitting blood from his lungs. The news of yet another death, one of the three hundred construction workers who die every year on Italy's building sites, pierced my insides. Iacomino's death sparked in me a rage that was more like an asthma attack than nervous excitement. I wanted to be like the protagonist in Luciano Bianciardi's 1962 novel, *La vita agra* (*It's a Hard Life*), who goes to Milan to blow up the Pirelli building, his way of avenging the forty-eight miners from Ribolla who were killed in May 1954 in an explosion in the "Camorra well," so called because of the dreadful working conditions. Maybe I too had to choose a building—*the* building—to blow up. But before I could slip into the schizophrenia of the terrorist, Pier Paolo Pasolini's "I Know" started echoing in my ears.* Over and over, tormenting me like a jingle. And so instead of searching for buildings to blow sky-high, I went to Casarsa, Pasolini's tomb. I went alone, even if this is one of those

---

*Pasolini's famous denunciation of the Christian Democrats printed on the front page of the *Corriere della sera* on November 14, 1974.—Trans.

things you should do with others to make it less pathetic. A gang. A group of devoted readers. A girlfriend. But I stubbornly went alone.

Casarsa is a nice place, one of those places where it's easy to think of someone wanting to get by as a writer, and where, on the other hand, it's hard to think of someone leaving in order to go lower, to cross the line into hell. I didn't go to Pasolini's tomb to pay him tribute or even to celebrate. Pier Paolo Pasolini. That name—three in one, as the poet Giorgio Caproni used to say—is neither my secular saint nor a literary Christ. I felt like finding a place where it was still possible to reflect without shame on the possibility of the word. The possibility of writing about the mechanisms of power, beyond the stories and details. To reflect on whether it is still possible to name names, one by one, to point out the faces, strip the bodies of their crimes, and reveal them as elements of the architecture of authority. To reflect on whether it is still possible to sniff out, like truffle pigs, the dynamics of the real, the affirmation of powers, without metaphors, without mediation, with nothing but the cutting edge of the word.

I took the train from Naples to Pordenone, an incredibly slow train with a remarkably eloquent name—Marco Polo—for the distance it had to travel. An enormous distance seems to separate Fruili from Campania. I left Naples at ten to eight and arrived in Fruili at twenty past seven the next day, having endured a relentless night of freezing cold that kept me from sleeping. From Pordenone I took a bus to Casarsa. When I got off, I started walking with my head down, like someone who knows where he's going and can recognize the way by looking at the tips of his shoes. Obviously I got lost. But after wandering about aimlessly I found the cemetery on Via Valvasone where Pasolini is buried with all his family. On the left, just past the entrance, there was an empty flowerbed. I went over to that square of earth, in the middle of which were two small, white marble slabs. I saw his tomb. "Pier Paolo Pasolini (1922–1975)." Next to it, a bit farther on, was that of his mother. I felt less alone. I began to mumble my rage, fists clenched so tight that my fingernails pierced my palms. I began to articulate my own "I Know," the "I Know" of my day.

I know and I can prove it. I know how economies originate and where they get their odor. The odor of success and victory. I know what sweats of profit. I know. And the truth of the word takes no prisoners because it devours everything and turns everything into evidence. It doesn't need to drag in cross-checks or launch investigations. It observes, considers, looks, listens. It knows. It does not condemn to prison and the witnesses do not retract their statements. No one repents. I know and I can prove it. I know where the pages of the economy manuals vanish, their fractals mutating into materials, things, iron, time, and contracts. I know. The proofs are not hidden in some flash drive concealed in a hole in the ground. I don't have compromising videos hidden in a garage in some inaccessible mountain village. Nor do I possess copies of secret service documents. The proofs are irrefutable because they are partial, recorded with my eyes, recounted with words, and tempered with emotions that have echoed off iron and wood. I see, hear, look, talk, and in this way I testify, an ugly word that can still be useful when it whispers, "It's not true," in the ear of those who listen to the rhyming lullabies of power. The truth is partial; after all, if it could be reduced to an objective formula, it would be chemistry. I know and I can prove it. And so I tell. About these truths.

I always try to quiet the anxiety that overcomes me every time I walk, every time I climb the stairs, take the elevator, or wipe my feet on a doormat and cross a threshold. I cannot stop myself from constantly brooding over how these buildings and houses are built. And when someone is willing to listen, it's difficult for me not to recount how floor after floor gets slapped together. It's not a sense of universal guilt that comes over me, nor a moral redemption for those who have been canceled from historical memory. Instead I try to cast off the Brechtian mechanism that comes naturally to me, of thinking about the hands and feet of history. In other words, to think more about the constantly empty plates that led to the storming of the Bastille than about the proclamations of Girondists and Jacobins. I can't stop thinking about it. It's a bad habit of mine. Like someone in front of a Vermeer painting who, instead of contemplating the portrait, thinks about who mixed the colors, stretched the canvas, and made the pearl earrings. A real perversion. When I see a flight of stairs, I simply cannot forget how the cement cycle works, and a wall of windows doesn't keep me from thinking about how the scaffolding was put up. I can't pretend not to think about it. I can't see the wall without thinking about the trowel and mortar. Maybe it's just that people born at certain meridians have a particular, unique relationship with certain substances. Materials are not perceived in the same way everywhere. I believe that in Qatar the smell of petroleum and gas evokes sensations and flavors of mansions, sunglasses, and limousines. The same acid smell of fossil fuel in Minsk evokes darkened faces, gas leaks, and smoking cities, whereas in Belgium it calls up the garlic Italians use and the onions of the North Africans. The same thing happens with cement in the south of Italy. Cement. The petroleum of the south. Cement gives birth to everything. Every economic empire that arises in the south passes through the construction business: bids, contracts, quarries, cement, components, bricks, scaffolding, workers. These are the Italian businessman's armaments. If his empire's feet are not set in cement he hasn't got a chance. Cement's the simplest way to make money as fast as possible, to earn trust, hire people in time for an election, pay out salaries, accumulate investment capital, and stamp your face on the facades of the buildings you put up. The builder's skills are those of the mediator and the predator. He possesses the infinite patience of a bureaucrat in compiling documents, enduring interminable delays, waiting for authorizations that come slowly, like the dripping of a stalactite. He's like a bird of prey who flies over land no one else notices, snapping it up for a few pennies, then holds on to it until every inch and every hole can be resold for astronomical amounts. The predatory businessman knows how to use his beak and claws. And Italian banks seem made for the builders; they know to grant the builder maximum credit. And if he really has no credit and the houses he will build are not enough of a guarantee, some good friend will always back him. The concreteness of cement and brick is the only real materiality that Italian banks recognize. Their directors think that research, laboratories, agriculture, and crafts are like vaporous terrain, ethereal, and devoid of gravity. Rooms, floors, tiles, phone jacks and electrical outlets—these are the only forms of concreteness they recognize. I know and I can prove it. I know how half of Italy has been built. More than half. I am familiar with the hands, the fingers, the projects. And the sand. The sand that has constructed skyscrapers, neighborhoods, parks, and villas. No one in Castelvolturno can forget the endless rows of trucks that pillaged the Volturno River of its sand. Lines of trucks flanked by farmers who had never seen such mammoths of metal and rubber before. Farmers who had managed to stay on here, to survive instead of emigrating, watched as they carted it all away, right before their very eyes. Now that sand is in the walls of apartments in Abruzzo, in buildings in Varese, Asiago, and Genoa. Now it is no longer the river that flows to the sea, but the sea that flows into the river. Now they fish for sea bass in the Volturno, and there are no more farmers. Deprived of their lands, first they turned to raising buffalo, and then set up small construction companies, hiring the young Nigerians and South Africans who used to find seasonal employment on the farms. If they didn't join up with the clans, they met an early death. I know and I can prove it. Extraction firms are authorized to remove minimal amounts, but they actually devour entire mountains and crumble hills. Kneaded into cement, the mountains and hills are all over the place now, from Tenerife to Sassuolo. The deportation of things has followed that of people. I met Don Salvatore in a trattoria in San Felice a Cancello. Once a master builder, now he was a walking corpse. He wasn't more than fifty years old, but he looked eighty. He told me that he worked for ten years adding exhaust-fume dust to cement mixers. Companies connected to the clans use cement to hide waste, which is what allows them to come in with bids as low as if they were using Chinese labor. Now garages, walls, and stair landings are permeated by poison. Nothing will happen until a worker, some North African probably, inhales the dust and dies a few years later, blaming his ill luck for his cancer.

I know and I can prove it. Successful Italian businessmen come from cement. They're actually a part of the cement cycle. I know that before transforming themselves into fashion-model men, managers with yachts, assailants of financial groups, and purchasers of newspaper companies, before all this and under all this lies cement, subcontractors, sand, crushed stone, vans crammed with men who work all night and disappear in the morning, rotten scaffolding, and bogus insurance. The driving force of the Italian economy rests on the thickness of the walls. The constitution should be amended to say that it is founded on cement, on builders. They are the founding fathers, not Ferruccio Parri, Luigi Einaudi, Pietro Nenni, or Junio Valerio Borghese. It was the real estate speculators who pulled Italy out of the mud of financial scandals through their cement works, contracts, buildings, and newspapers.

The building trade is a turning point for affiliates. After working as a killer, extortionist, or lookout, you end up in construction or trash collecting. Rather than showing films and giving lectures at school, it would be interesting to take the new affiliates for a tour of construction sites to show them the future that awaits them. If prison and death spare them, that's where they'll end up, spitting blood and lime. While the white-collar elite the bosses believe they control are living the good life, others are dying of work. All the time. The speed of construction, the need to save on every form of safety and every sort of schedule. Inhuman shifts, nine, twelve hours a day, Saturdays and Sundays included. A hundred euros a week, plus 50 more for every ten hours of Sunday or evening overtime. The younger ones even do fifteen hours, maybe by snorting cocaine. When someone dies on a building site, a tried-and-true mechanism goes into effect. The dead body is taken away and they fake a car accident. They put the body in a car and push it off a cliff or a precipice, setting it on fire first. The insurance money is given to the family as severance. It is not unusual for the people staging the accident to also be hurt, at times seriously, especially when they have to crash a car into a wall before setting it on fire. When the boss is present, everything works smoothly. But when he's not, the workers often panic. And so they take the seriously wounded guy, the near cadaver, and leave him on the side of a road leading to the hospital. They drive him there in a car, place him carefully on the pavement, and flee. When they are feeling really scrupulous, they call an ambulance. Whoever takes part in the disappearance or abandonment of a near cadaver knows that his coworkers would do the same to him if it were his body that had been smashed up or run through. You know for sure that, in a dangerous situation, the person at your side will first assist you, then finish you off to rid himself of you. And so there's a sort of wariness on the site. The person next to you could be your executioner, or you his. He won't make you suffer, but he'll leave you to die alone on the sidewalk or burn you in a car. Every builder knows that's how it works. And the companies in the south provide better guarantees. They work and disappear and fix every mess without causing an uproar. I know and I can prove it. And the proofs have a name. In seven months fifteen construction workers died in the building sites north of Naples. They fell or ended up under a power shovel or were crushed by a crane run by workers worn out from long shifts. Work has to be quick. Even if it goes on for years, subcontractors have to make way for the next lot. Make your money, call in your debts, and move on. More than 40 percent of the firms operating in Italy are from the south. From Aversa, Naples, and Salerno. Empires can still be born in the south, the links of the economy can be strengthened, and the balance of the original accumulation is still incomplete. They should hang WELCOME signs all over the south, from Puglia to Calabria, for the businessmen who want to throw themselves into the cement arena and be invited into the inner circles in Milan and Rome a few years hence. A WELCOME sign of good luck, since many come yet only a few escape the quicksand. I know. And I can prove it. And the new builders, bank and yacht owners, princes of gossip, and kings of whores hide their profits. Perhaps they still have a soul. They're ashamed to declare where their earnings come from. In their model country, the USA, when a businessman becomes a top name in the financial world, achieving fame and success, he summons analysts and young economists to show off his skills and discloses the route he took to victory. Here, silence. Money is only money. And when asked about their success, the big businessmen from a land sickened with the Camorra respond shamelessly, "I bought at ten and sold at three hundred." Someone said that living in the south is like living in paradise. All you have to do is stare at the sky and never look down. Ever. But it's impossible. The expropriation of every perspective has even removed the lines of sight. Every perspective hits up against balconies, attics, mansards, apartments, intertwined buildings, knots of neighborhoods. Around here no one thinks something could fall from the sky. Around here you have to look down. Sink into the abyss. Because there is always another abyss in the abyss. And so when I tread up stairs and across rooms, or when I take the elevator, I can't help but notice. Because I know. And it's a perversion. And so when I find myself among the best, the really successful businessmen, I feel ill. Even though these men are elegant, speak quietly, and vote for leftist politicians. I smell the odor of lime and cement emanating from their socks, their Bulgari cuff links, and their bookshelves. I know. I know who built my town and who is building it still. I know that tonight a train will leave Reggio Calabria and at a quarter past midnight it will stop in Naples on its way to Milan. The train will be packed. And at the station the vans and dusty Punto automobiles will pick up the kids for the new construction sites. An emigration without a fixed point that no one will study or evaluate since it survives only in the footprints of cement dust, nowhere else. I know what the real constitution of my day is, and the wealth of companies. I know how much of the blood of others is in every pillar. I know and I can prove it. I take no prisoners.

DON PEPPINO DIANA

Whenever I think about the clan wars in Casal di Principe, San Cipriano, Casapesenna, and all the other territories they control from Parete to Formia, I always think about white sheets. Hanging from every balcony, railing, and window. White, all white. A cascade of pure white cloth was the angry display of mourning at Don Peppino Diana's funeral in March 1994. I was sixteen. My aunt woke me as always that morning, but with an unusual violence, yanking the sheet I'd wrapped around me as if she were unwrapping a salami. I fell out of bed. My aunt didn't say a word, but walked about noisily, as if she were venting all her irritation with her heels. She knotted the sheets so tightly to the balcony, not even a tornado would have torn them loose. She threw open the windows, letting the voices from the street in and the noises of the house out. She even opened all the cupboards. I remember the waves of Boy Scouts; they had shed their usual, easygoing manner of well-behaved kids, and a deep rage seemed to trail from their peculiar blue and green scarves; for Don Peppino was one of them. It was the only time I ever saw Scouts so nervous, mindless of the forms of orderly conduct and composure that usually define their long marches. My memories of that day are spotty, like a Dalmatian's fur. Don Peppino Diana's story is strange; once you've heard it, it becomes part of you and you have to preserve it inside you somewhere—deep in your throat, tight in your fist, near your heart, at the back of your eyes. An extraordinary story, unknown to most.

Don Peppino had studied in Rome, and that's where he should have stayed to make a career for himself. Far from here, far from his hometown and its dirty deals. But, like someone who can't shake off a memory, a habit, or a smell, he suddenly decided to return to Casal di Principe. Or maybe like someone with a burning itch to do something, and who can find no peace until he does it, or at least gives it a try. Don Peppino was the young priest of the Church of Saint Nicholas of Bari, a modern structure that seemed ideally suited aesthetically to his sense of commitment. Unlike the other priests, who wore their gloomy authority along with their cassocks, he went around dressed in jeans. Don Peppino didn't eavesdrop on family squabbles, chastise the men for their erotic escapades, or make the rounds comforting cuckolded women. He spontaneously transformed the role of the local priest. He decided to take an interest in the dynamics of power, and not merely its corollary suffering. He didn't want merely to clean the wound but to understand the mechanisms of the metastasis, to prevent the cancer from spreading, to block the source of whatever was turning his home into a gold mine of capital with an abundance of cadavers. He even smoked a cigar in public every now and then. Anywhere else that might have seemed harmless, but around here priests tended to put on a show of depriving themselves of the superfluous, while indulging their lazy weaknesses behind closed doors. Don Peppino decided just to be himself—a guarantee of transparency in a land where faces must be ready to mime what they represent, aided by nicknames that pump their bodies full of the power they hope to suture onto their skin. Don Peppino was obsessed with action. He set up a welcome center to offer room and board to the first wave of African immigrants. It was important to welcome them to keep the clans from turning them into perfect soldiers—

which is what eventually happened. He even contributed some of his own money from teaching to the project. Waiting for institutional backing can be such a slow and complicated ordeal that it becomes the biggest reason for doing nothing. As priest he had watched the succession of bosses, the elimination of Bardellino, the power of Sandokan and Cicciotto di Mezzanotte, the massacres among Bardellino's men and the Casalesi, and then among the leading businessmen.

A famous episode from that time had to do with a parade of cars through the streets of town. It was about six in the evening when ten or so cars formed a sort of carousel under their enemies' windows: Schiavone's victorious men challenging their enemies. I was just a kid, but my cousins swear they saw them with their own eyes, driving slowly through the streets of San Cipriano, Casapesenna, and Casal di Principe, windows down, men straddling the doors, one leg in the car and the other dangling out. Faces unmasked, each holding an assault rifle. The cavalcade proceeded slowly, gathering more affiliates as it went; they came out of their apartments carrying rifles and semiautomatics and fell in behind the cars. A full-blown, public, armed demonstration. They stopped in front of the houses of their enemies, those who had dared to challenge their supremacy.

"Come out, you shits! Come out . . . if you have the balls!"

The parade went on for at least an hour, continuing undisturbed as shutters on shops and bars were quickly lowered. For two days there was a complete cease-fire. No one went out, not even to buy bread. Don Peppino realized it was time to devise a plan of resistance. Time to openly delineate a path to follow. No more speaking out solo; it was time to organize a protest and coordinate a new level of local church engagement. He wrote a surprising document that was signed by all the Casal di Principe priests: a religious, Christian text with a tone of despairing human dignity that made his words universal and allowed them to reach beyond the boundaries of religion, causing the bosses to tremble; they feared his words more than an anti-Mafia division blitz, more than the impounding of their quarries and concrete mixers, more than the wiretaps that can trace a command to kill. It was a lively text with a romantically powerful title: "For love of my people I will not keep silent." Don Peppino distributed the document on Christmas Day. He did not post it on his church doors; he wasn't a Martin Luther out to reform the Roman Church. Don Peppino had other things to think about: to try to understand how to create a path that could cut through the sinews of power and cripple the Camorra clans' economic and criminal authority.

Don Peppino dug a path in the surface of the word and eroded their power with syntax; spoken publicly and clearly, words could still do such things. He lacked the intellectual apathy of those who believe that words have exhausted all their resources and merely fill the space between our ears. The word as concreteness, an aggregate of atoms that intervenes in the mechanisms of things, like mortar or a pickax. Don Peppino searched for the right word to dump like a bucket of water on the dirty looks he received. Around here keeping your mouth shut is not the simple, silent *omertà* of lowered hats and eyes. Here the prevailing attitude is "It's not my problem." But that's not all. The decision to withdraw is the actual vote that's cast in the election of the state of things. The word becomes a shout. A loud and piercing cry hurled at bulletproof glass in hopes of making it shatter.

We are powerless seeing so many families grieve as their sons miserably end up either victims or perpetrators of the Camorra's organizations . . . The Camorra today is a form of terrorism that arouses fear and imposes its own laws in an attempt to become an endemic element of Campania society. Weapons in hand, the Camorristi violently impose unacceptable rules: extortions that have turned our region into subsidized areas with no potential on their own for development; bribes of 20 percent or more on construction projects, which would discourage the most reckless businessman; illicit traffic in narcotics, whose use creates gangs of marginalized youngsters and unskilled workers at the beck and call of criminal organizations; clashes among factions that descend like a ruinous plague on the families of our region; negative examples for the entire teenage population, veritable laboratories of violence and organized crime.

Don Peppino's aim was to remind people that, in the face of clan power, it was important not to confine their reactions to the silence of the confessional. He evoked the voices of the prophets to argue urgently that taking to the streets, reporting, and reacting were essential to give some sense to their lives.

Our prophetic commitment to speak out must not and cannot falter; God calls us to be prophets.

The Prophet is a watchman: he sees injustice and speaks out against it, recalling God's original command (Ezekiel 3:16–19);

The Prophet remembers the past and uses it to gather up new things in the present (Isaiah 43);

The Prophet invites us to live, and himself lives in solidarity and suffering (Genesis 8:18–22);

The Prophet gives priority to the life of justice (Jeremiah 22:3; Isaiah 58).

We ask the priests—our shepherds and brethren—to speak clearly during the homilies and in all those occasions that require courageous witness. We ask the Church not to renounce its "prophetic" role so that the means for speaking out and declaring will result in the ability to create a new conscience under the sign of justice, an ethical and social solidarity.

The document did not aim to be amenable to social reality, nor polite toward political power, which it considered not merely supported by the clans but actually shaped by similar goals. Don Peppino didn't want to believe the clan was an evil choice a person makes, but rather the result of clear conditions, fixed mechanisms, identifiable and gangrenous causes. No church or individual in this region had ever been so determined to clarify things.

The southern Italian's wariness and distrust of the establishment because of its age-old inability to solve the serious problems that afflict the south, particularly employment, housing, health, and education;

The suspicion, not always baseless, of complicity with the Camorra on the part of politicians who, in exchange for electoral support, or to achieve common goals, guarantee cover and grant favors;

The widespread feeling of personal insecurity and constant risk resulting from insufficient legal protection of persons and possessions, from the slowness of the legal system, the ambiguity of the legislative tools . . . that not infrequently leads to an appeal for defense organized by the clans or the acceptance of Camorra protection;

The lack of clarity on the job market, so that finding a job is more a matter of Camorra-client operations than the pursuit of a right based on employment legislation;

The absence or inadequacy, even in pastoral activities, of a true social education, as if it were possible to shape a mature Christian without also shaping the man and the mature citizen.

In the late 1980s Don Peppino organized an anti-Camorra march following a mass assault on the carabinieri barracks in San Cipriano d'Aversa. Some carabinieri had dared to break up a fight between two local boys during an evening of entertainment in honor of the patron saint, so dozens of people decided to destroy their headquarters and beat up the officers. The San Cipriano barracks are tucked in a narrow alley, and the marshals and lance corporals had no means of escape. The bosses themselves had to send the neighborhood capos to put down the revolt and save the carabinieri. Antonio Bardellino was still in control at that time, and his brother Ernesto was the mayor.

> We, the priests of the churches of Campania, do not intend, however, to limit ourselves to denouncing these situations; rather, within the scope of our abilities and possibilities, we intend to help overcome them even by revising and integrating the matter and method of pastoral activity.

Don Peppino started to question the bosses' religious beliefs, to deny explicitly that there could be any harmony between the Christian creed and the business, political, and military power of the clans. In the land of the Camorra, the Christian message is not considered contradictory to Camorra activities: if the clan acts for the good of all its affiliates, the organization is seen as respecting and pursuing the Christian good. The killing of enemies and traitors is seen as a necessary, legitimate transgression; by the bosses' reasoning, the command "Thou shalt not kill" inscribed on Moses' tablets may be suspended if the homicide occurs for a higher motive, namely the safeguarding of the clan, the interests of its managers, or the good of the group, and therefore of everyone. Killing is a sin that Christ will understand and forgive in the name of necessity.

At San Cipriano d'Aversa, Antonio Bardellino made use of an old ritual that eventually disappeared: *pungitura*, which the Cosa Nostra also used in initiating new affiliates. The aspirant's right index finger would be pricked with a pin and the blood made to drip onto an image of the Madonna of Pompeii. This was then burned over a candle and passed, hand to hand, to all the clan managers who stood around a table. If all the affiliates kissed the Madonna, the candidate became officially part of the clan. Religion is a constant point of reference for the Camorra, not merely a propitiatory gesture or cultural relic but a spiritual force that determines the most intimate decisions. Camorra families, especially the most charismatic bosses, often consider their own actions as a Calvary, their own conscience bearing the pain and weight of sin for the well-being of the group and the men they rule.

At Pignataro Maggiore the Lubrano clan paid to have a fresco of the Madonna restored. It is called the Madonna of the Camorra since the town's most important Cosa Nostra fugitives from Sicily turned to her for protection. It's not really that difficult to imagine Totò Riina, Michele Greco, Luciano Liggio, and Bernardo Provenzano kneeling in front of the fresco and praying that their actions be enlightened and their getaways protected.

When Vincenzo Lubrano was acquitted, he organized a pilgrimage—several busloads of the faithful—to San Giovanni Rotondo to give thanks to Padre Pio, who, he believed, was responsible for his absolution. Life-size statues of Padre Pio and terra-cotta or bronze copies of the open-armed Christ on Pão de Açúcar in Rio de Janeiro can be found in the villa of many a Camorra boss. In the drug-warehouse laboratories in Scampia, bricks of hashish are often cut thirty-three at a time—like Christ's age. Then they halt work for thirty-three minutes, make the sign of the cross, and start up again. A way to propitiate Christ and receive earnings and tranquillity. The same happens with packets of cocaine; often before they are distributed to the pushers, the neighborhood capo blesses them with holy water from Lourdes in the hopes that they don't kill anyone, especially because he would have to answer personally for the poor quality of the stuff.

Camorra power does not involve only the flesh, nor does it merely own everyone's life. It also lays claim to souls. Don Peppino wanted to bring some clarity to words, meanings, and values.

The Camorra gives the name *family* to a clan organized for criminal purposes, in which absolute loyalty is the law, any expression of autonomy is denied, and not only defection but the conversion to honesty is considered a betrayal worthy of death;

the Camorra uses every means to extend and consolidate this type of *family*, even exploitation of the sacraments. For the Christian, shaped to the school of the Word of God, *family* means only a group of people united by shared love, in which love means disinterested and attentive service, in which service exalts him who offers it and him who receives it. The Camorra claims to have its own religiosity, and at times it manages to deceive not only the faithful, but also the inexperienced or ingenuous shepherd of souls.

The document even attempted to broach the subject of the sacraments. To keep at bay any possible confusion of Communion, marriage, and the role of the godfather, with Camorra strategies. To distance clan pacts and alliances from religious symbols. At the mere thought of saying such things the local priests would have run to the bathroom in fright with their hands on their stomachs. Who would chase away from the altar a boss eager to baptize an affiliate's child? Who would refuse to celebrate a marriage just because it was the result of an alliance between Camorra families? Don Peppino was clear:

> In the sacraments that call for a godfather, do not allow that role to be held by anyone not known for Christian maturity and honesty in his public and private life. Do not admit to the sacraments anyone who attempts to assert undue pressure in the absence of the necessary sacramental initiation.

Don Peppino's challenge to the power of the Camorra came in the moment when Francesco Sandokan Schiavone was hiding in a bunker under his villa in town, the Casalesi families were warring among themselves, and cement and waste were becoming the new frontiers of their empires. Don Peppino did not want to play the consoling priest who accompanies murdered boy soldiers to their grave and whispers, "You must be strong," to mothers in black. In an interview he stated, "We must divide the people so as to throw them into crisis." He also took a stand politically, explaining that his priority was to fight political power as an expression of criminal business power: he would give his support to concrete projects, to renovation, and he would not remain impartial. "Political parties have become confused with their representatives; often the candidates favored by the Camorra have neither policy nor party, but merely a role as player or a post to fill." The goal was not to defeat the Camorra. As Don Peppino himself would say, "Winners and losers are all in the same boat." Instead it was to understand, transform, bear witness, speak out, take an electrocardiogram of the heart of economic power to understand how to wrest the organ's muscles from the clan's control.

I have never for one instant felt pious, yet Don Peppino's words resounded with something beyond the religious. He created a new method that reestablished religious and political speech. A faith in being able to bite into reality and not let go until you rip it to pieces. A language capable of tracing the scent of money.

We tend to think that money doesn't smell, but that's true only when it is in the emperor's hands. Before it ends up between his fingers, *pecunia olet*—money does indeed smell. Like a latrine. Don Peppino toiled in a land where money carries a scent, but only for a moment—the instant in which it is extracted, before it becomes something else, before it can become legitimate. Odors we recognize only when our noses brush against what smells. Don Peppino Diana realized that he had to keep his face close to the ground, on people's backs and eyes, that he couldn't pull away if he wanted to keep seeing and pointing the finger, if he wanted to understand where and how business wealth accumulates, and how the killings and arrests, the feuds and silences, begin. He had to keep his instrument—the word—the only tool that could alter the reality of his time, on the tip of his tongue. And this word, incapable of keeping silent, was his death sentence. His killers did not pick a date by chance. March 19, 1994, was the feast of San Giuseppe, his name day. Early morning.

Don Peppino was in the church meeting room near his study. He had not yet donned his priestly robes, so it was not immediately clear who he was.

"Who is Don Peppino?"

"I am."

His final answer. Shots echoed in the nave. Two bullets hit him in the face, others pierced his head, neck, and hand, and one hit the bunch of keys hooked to his belt. They had aimed at his head, shooting from close range. A shell lodged between his jacket and his sweater. Don Peppino was getting ready to say the first mass of the day. He was thirty-six years old.

Renato Natale, Casal di Principe's Communist mayor, was one of the first to race to the church, where he found the priest's body still on the floor. Natale had been elected only four months earlier. It was no coincidence; they wanted to make that body fall during his very, very brief political tenure. He was the first Casal di Principe mayor to make fighting the clans a top priority. He had even resigned from the town council in protest because he felt it had been reduced to merely rubber-stamping decisions that were made elsewhere. The carabinieri once raided the house of Gaetano Corvino, a town councilman, finding all the top clan managers assembled while Corvino was at a council meeting at the town hall. On the one side town business, on the other business via the town. Doing business is the only reason to get out of bed in the morning; it tugs on your pajamas and gets you up and on your feet.

I had always watched Renato Natale from afar, as you do those people who unwillingly become symbols of some idea of commitment, resistance, and courage. Symbols that are almost metaphysical, unreal, archetypal. I felt a teenager's embarrassment observing his efforts to set up clinics for immigrants and speak out against the Casalese Camorra families' power and cement and waste-management operations during the dark years of the feuds. They had approached him, threatened his life, told him that if he didn't stop, his family would be made to pay for his choices, but he carried on speaking out in every way he could, even putting up posters around town that revealed what the clans had decided and enforced. The more persistent and courageous he was, the more his metaphysical protection grew. One would have to know the political history of this region to understand the real weight of terms such as *commitment* and *will*.

Since the law regarding Mafia infiltration went into effect, sixteen town councils in the province of Caserta have been dissolved, five of them twice: Carinola, Casal di Principe, Casapesenna, Castelvolturno, Cesa, Frignano, Grazzanise, Lusciano, Mondragone, Pignataro Maggiore, Recale, San Cipriano, Santa Maria la Fossa, San Tammaro, Teverola, Villa di Briano. When candidates opposing the clans manage to win in these towns, overcoming the vote-trading and economic strategies that constrain every political alliance, they have to reckon with the limits of the local administrations, extremely tight funds, and total marginality. They have to demolish, brick by brick, to face off multinational companies with small-town budgets, and rein in enormous firing squads with local troops. Such as in 1988 when the Casapesenna town councilor Antonio Cangiano opposed clan infiltration of certain contracts. They threatened him, tailed him, and shot him in the back, right in the piazza, right in front of everyone. If he wasn't going to let the Casalesi clan get ahead, then the Casalesi wouldn't let him even walk. They confined Cangiano to a wheelchair. The alleged perpetrators were acquitted in 2006.

Casal di Principe is not a town under Mafia attack in Sicily, where opposing the criminal business class is difficult, but where your actions are flanked by a parade of video cameras, famous and soon-to-be-famous journalists, and swarms of national anti-Mafia executives who somehow manage to amplify their role. Here everything you do remains within narrow perimeters and is shared with only a few. I believe that it is precisely within this solitude that what could be called courage is forged: a sort of armor that you don't think about, that you wear without noticing. You carry on, do what you have to do—the rest is worthless. Because the threat isn't always a bullet between the eyes or a ton of buffalo shit dumped on your front doorstep.

They take you slowly, one layer at a time, till you find yourself naked and alone and you start believing you're fighting something that does not exist, a hallucination of your brain. You start believing the slander that marks you as a malcontent who takes it out on successful people, whom you label Camorristi out of frustration. They play with you the way they do with Pick Up sticks. They pick up all the sticks without ever making you move, so that in the end you're all alone, and loneliness drags you by the hair. But you can't allow yourself that feeling here; it's a risk—if you lower your guard, you won't be able to understand the mechanisms, symbols, choices. You risk not noticing anything anymore. So you have to draw on all your resources. You have to find something that fuels the stomach of your soul in order to carry on. Christ, Buddha, civil commitment, ethics, Marxism, pride, anarchy, the fight against crime, cleanliness, persistent and everlasting rage, southernness. Something. Not a hook to hang on. More like a root, something underground and unassailable. In the useless battle in which you're sure to play the role of the loser, there is something you have to preserve and know. You have to be certain it will grow stronger while your wasted energy tastes of folly and obsession. I have learned to recognize that root in the eyes of those who have decided to stare certain powers in the face.

Giuseppe Quadrano and his men, who were allied with Sandokan's enemies, were immediately suspected of Don Peppino's murder. There were also two witnesses: a photographer who was there to wish Don Peppino well, and the church sexton. As soon as word got out that police suspicions were directed toward Quadrano, the boss Nunzio De Falco, known as *'o lupo* or the Wolf, called the Caserta police and asked for a meeting to clarify some questions concerning one of his affiliates. As a result of territorial divisions of power among the Casalesi, De Falco was in Granada, Spain. Two Caserta officers went to meet him there. The boss's wife picked them up at the airport and drove into the beautiful Andalusian countryside. Nunzio De Falco was waiting for them not in his villa in Santa Fe, but in a restaurant where most of the customers were probably insiders ready to intervene if the police did anything rash. The boss immediately explained that he had called them to offer his version of the story, a sort of interpretation of a historical event and not a denunciation or accusation. A clear and necessary preamble so as not to besmirch the family's name and authority. He could not start collaborating with the police. Without beating around the bush the boss declared that it had been the Schiavone family—his rivals—who had killed Don Peppino. They had done it to make suspicion fall on the De Falcos. The Wolf said that he would never have given the order to kill Don Peppino Diana because De Falco's brother Mario was close to him. The priest had even carried on a dialogue to free Mario from the Camorra system and had succeeded in keeping him from becoming a clan manager. It was one of Don Peppino's major accomplishments, but De Falco used it as an alibi. Two other affiliates, Mario Santoro and Francesco Piacenti, backed up the boss's theory.

Giuseppe Quadrano was in Spain as well. He was first a guest in the De Falco villa, then settled in a village near Valencia. He wanted to form a group and tried to use some drug shipments to accelerate the establishment of yet another Italian criminal business clan in the south of Spain. But he was unsuccessful. At heart Quadrano had always been a supporting actor. He turned himself in to the Spanish police and declared he was ready to collaborate. He contradicted Nunzio De Falco's version and situated the homicide within the feud that was unfolding between his group and the Schiavones. Quadrano was the Carinaro neighborhood capo, and Sandokan's Casalese men recently had killed four of his affiliates—two uncles and his sister's husband. Quadrano said that he and Mario Santoro had decided to kill Aldo Schiavone, Sandokan's cousin, to avenge the insult. Before taking action they called De Falco in Spain—no hit can take place without the boss's consent—but De Falco blocked everything: if his cousin was killed, Schiavone would order that all of De Falco's Campania relatives be killed. The boss announced that he would send Francesco Piacenti to implement his command. Piacenti did the drive from Granada to Casal di Principe in his Mercedes, the car that became a symbol of this area in the 1980s and 1990s. The journalist Enzo Biagi was shocked when he obtained the statistics of Mercedes sales in Italy for an article he wrote in the 1990s. Casal di Principe was among the top in Europe. But he also noticed another record: Casal di Principe was the urban area with the highest murder rate in Europe. The relation of Mercedes to murders would remain a constant of observation in Camorra territories. Piacenti—according to Quadrano's first revelation—communicated that it was necessary to kill Don Peppino. No one knew why, but they were all sure that "the Wolf knew what he was doing." According to Quadrano, Piacenti declared that he would do the killing himself on the condition that Santoro or some other clan member went with him. But Mario Santoro hesitated. He called De Falco to say that he was against the killing, but in the end he gave in. He couldn't ignore such an important order if he didn't want to lose the position the Wolf had assigned him as middleman in narcotrafficking with Spain. But he couldn't accept the murder of a priest, especially without a clear motive, as if it were just like any other task. In the Camorra system murder is necessary; it's like depositing money in the bank, purchasing a franchise, or breaking off a friendship. It's no different from the rest of your life, part of the daily routine of every Camorra family, boss, and affiliate. But killing a priest, one outside the dynamic of power, pricks your conscience. According to Quadrano, Francesco Piacenti withdrew, claiming that too many people in Casale knew him for him to take part in the murder. But Mario Santoro accepted, accompanied by an affiliate of the Ranucci clan from Sant' Antimo named Giuseppe Della Medaglia, with whom he had already executed other operations. According to the *pentito*, they organized for the next morning at six. But that night the whole commando was tormented. They were restless, couldn't sleep, and quarreled with their wives. That priest scared them more than the rival clans' guns.

Della Medaglia didn't show up at the appointed hour, but in the night he had contacted someone else to send in his place: Vincenzo Verde. The other members of the commando were not particularly pleased with his choice, as Verde often suffered from epileptic fits. There was the risk that after the shooting he would fall to the floor in convulsions, foaming at the mouth and his teeth cutting his tongue. So they tried to get Nicola Gaglione to take his place, but he refused categorically. Santoro developed an inner-ear infection and couldn't stick to any set plan, so Quadrano sent his brother Armando to go with him. A simple operation: a car in front of the church waits for the killers, who walk out slowly after doing the job. Like an early-morning prayer. The hit squad was not in a rush to flee after the execution. Quadrano was invited to go to Spain that very evening, but he refused. He felt safe since Don Peppino's murder was completely unrelated to their usual practices. And just as the motive was a mystery to them, so it would be to the carabinieri. As soon as police investigations began expanding in all directions, however, Quadrano left for Spain. He even declared that Francesco Piacenti had told him that Nunzio De Falco, Sebastiano Caterino, and Mario Santoro were supposed to kill him, perhaps because they suspected he wanted to turn state's evidence, but that the day set for the hit they saw him in his car with his young son and decided to spare him.

In Casal di Principe, Sandokan kept hearing his name connected to the elimination of the priest. So he let Don Peppino's family know that if his men got their hands on Quadrano before the police did, they would cut him in three pieces and throw them on the church grounds. This was not revenge but a clear statement to say that Sandokan was not responsible for Don Peppino's murder. Shortly after, there was a De Falco clan meeting in Spain to decide how to respond to Francesco Schiavone's claims that he had nothing to do with the murder. Giuseppe Quadrano proposed killing one of Schiavone's relatives, chopping him in pieces, and leaving him in a bag outside Don Peppino's church. A way of making the blame fall on Sandokan. Both factions, each ignorant of the other's plans, had arrived at the same solution. The best way to send an indelible message is to cut up bodies and scatter the pieces about. While Don Peppino's assassins were talking about cutting up flesh to seal their position, I was still thinking about the priest's battle and the primacy of the word. About his incredibly new and powerful desire to place the word at the center of a struggle against the mechanisms of power. Words against cement mixers and guns. And not just metaphorically. But for real. To speak out, testify, take a stand. The word, with its only armor: to be spoken. A word that is a vigilant witness, that never stops seeking the truth. The only way to eliminate such a word is to kill it.

In 2001 the court of Santa Maria Capua Vetere handed down a first verdict: life sentences for Vincenzo Verde, Francesco Piacenti, and Giuseppe Della Medaglia. Giuseppe Quadrano had already begun to try to discredit the figure of Don Peppino. During the cross-examination he mused on a series of motives for the homicide, with the intention of strangling the priest's commitment in a noose of criminal interpretations. He stated that Nunzio De Falco had given Don Peppino some weapons, which he then turned over to Walter Schiavone without authorization, and had been punished for this grave transgression. There was also talk of a crime of passion, that he had been killed because he had had designs on the cousin of a boss. Just as calling a woman a slut is enough to put a stop to every sort of fantasizing about her, the fastest way of closing the books on a priest is to accuse him of frequenting prostitutes. In the end it came out that Don Peppino was killed for not doing his job as a priest, for not wanting to celebrate in church the funeral of one of Quadrano's relatives. Unbelievable, ludicrous motives, an attempt to prevent Don Peppino from becoming a martyr, to keep his words from spreading, to turn him from a Camorra victim to a clan soldier. People unfamiliar with Camorra power dynamics often think that killing an innocent person is a terribly naive gesture on the part of the clans because it only legitimizes and amplifies the victim's example and words, a confirmation of the truths he spoke. Wrong. That's never the way it is. As soon as you die in the land of the Camorra, you're enshrouded in countless suspicions, and innocence is a distant hypothesis, the last one imaginable. You are guilty until proven innocent. In the land of the Camorra, the theory of modern rights is turned on its head.

Media attention is so limited that even the smallest suspicion is enough to keep the papers from printing that an innocent person has been killed. And if there are no further deaths, no one will focus on the case. The destruction of Don Peppino Diana's image was thus an important tactic to ease pressure on the clans, to alleviate the troublesome problem of awaking national interest.

One local paper turned the campaign to discredit Don Peppino into a sound box. The headlines were so heavy with boldface that your fingers turned black as you flipped the pages: "Don Diana was a Camorrista," and a few days later, "Don Diana in bed with two women." The message was clear: no one can go up against the Camorra. Whoever does always has some personal motive, a quarrel, a private matter that wallows in the same filth.

His old friends, his relatives, and his followers defended him, including the journalists Raffaele Sardo, who preserved his memory in articles and books, and Rosaria Capacchione, who monitored the strategies of the clans, their complex, bestial power, and the shrewdness of the *pentiti*.

A 2003 appeal questioned aspects of Giuseppe Quadrano's earlier testimony, and Vincenzo Verde and Giuseppe Della Medaglia were exonerated. Quadrano had confessed partial truths; his strategy from the very beginning was to not admit his own responsibility. But he was the killer, as identified by witnesses and confirmed by ballistic reports. Giuseppe Quadrano killed Don Peppino Diana. The hit squad had been composed of Quadrano and Santoro, who acted as the driver. Francesco Piacenti had supplied information about Don Peppino, sent directly from Spain by De Falco to guide the operation. The appeal also upheld the verdict of life imprisonment for Piacenti and Santoro. Quadrano had even recorded phone conversations with affiliates, during which he repeatedly stated that he had nothing to do with the homicide—recordings that he then turned over to the police. Quadrano understood that the order for the killing had come from De Falco, and he didn't want it revealed that he was simply the brawn of the operation. It is highly likely that all the figures in Quadrano's first version had shit in their pants and didn't want to be involved in the killing in any way. At times submachine guns and pistols are not sufficient for facing an unarmed face and plain speech.

Nunzio De Falco was arrested in Albacete while on the Valencia–Madrid intercity train. He had established a powerful criminal cartel with some 'Ndrangheta men and a few Cosa Nostra dropouts. According to Spanish police investigations, he had also attempted to organize the Gypsies in the south of Spain into a criminal group. He had built an empire. Vacation villages, gambling houses, shops, and hotels. The infrastructure of Spain's Costa del Sol improved dramatically when the Casalese and Neapolitan clans decided to turn the area into a pearl of mass tourism.

In January 2003 De Falco received a life sentence as instigator of Don Peppino Diana's murder. When the verdict was read out in the courtroom, I felt like laughing, but I managed to puff out my cheeks and contain myself. I couldn't stand the absurdity of what was happening. Nunzio De Falco's attorney was Gaetano Pecorella, simultaneously the president of the Chamber of Deputies' Justice Commission and the counsel for the defense for one of the biggest Casalese Camorra cartel bosses. I laughed because the clans were so strong that they had even reversed the axioms of nature and fable. A wolf was being defended by a lamb. But my delirium may have been the result of exhaustion and nervous collapse.

Nunzio De Falco's nickname is written on his face. He really does look like a wolf. His identification photo portrays a long face covered with a thin, prickly beard, like a carpet of needles, and pointed ears. Frizzy hair, dark skin, and a triangular mouth. He looks just like one of those werewolves in a horror film. And yet a local paper—the same one that had boasted about relations between Don Peppino and the clan—dedicated the first page to his qualities as a lover, passionately desired by women and girls. The headlines on January 17, 2005, were eloquent: "Nunzio De Falco king of the womanizers."

CASAL DI PRINCIPE (CE)

They are not handsome, but they are attractive because they're bosses; that's how it is. If one had to rank the playboy bosses of the area, first place would go to two repeat convicts from Casal di Principe, men who are certainly not good-looking, unlike Don Antonio Bardellino, the most fascinating of them all. We are talking about Francesco Piacenti, alias Big Nose, and Nunzio De Falco, alias the Wolf. People say that one had five wives and the other seven. Obviously we're not talking about actual marriages but longterm relationships that produced children. In fact Nunzio De Falco apparently has more than twelve children by various women. Another interesting detail is that not all the women in question are

Italian. One is Spanish, another English, and another Portuguese.
Like sailors, these men would make a new family in every place
they hid . . . Not by chance, some of their women were called to
testify during their trials, each of them beautiful and elegant. The
fair sex is the cause of the decline of many a boss. They are often
the ones who lead indirectly to the capture of the most dangerous
bosses. Tailing the women, investigators have been led to bosses of
the caliber of Francesco Schiavone Cicciariello . . . In other words,
women are a mixed blessing even for bosses.

Don Peppino's death was the price paid for peace between the
clans. Even the verdict makes reference to this hypothesis. An agreement had to be found between the two warring groups, perhaps
sealed on Don Peppino's flesh. Like a scapegoat. Eliminating him
meant resolving a problem for all the families while also distracting
investigations away from their affairs.

I had heard talk of Cipriano, a childhood friend of Don Peppino's
who had written a harangue to be read at the funeral, an invective inspired by one of the priest's speeches, but who didn't even have the
strength to move that morning. He had gone away many years before
and settled near Rome, having decided never to set foot in Campania
again. They told me that his grief over Don Peppino's death kept him
in bed for months. Whenever I asked one of his aunts about him,
she would automatically respond in the same mournful voice, "He's
closed up. Cipriano's closed up!"

It happens every now and then. It isn't unusual to hear someone
say such a thing around here. Every time I hear that expression, I
think of Giustino Fortunato, who in the early 1900s walked the entire
length of the southern Apennine Mountains. He wanted to know the
predicament of the towns along the ridge, and visited every one of
them, staying with farmers, listening to angry peasants, getting to
know the voice and smell of the southern question. When he later became a senator, he returned to the towns and asked about the people

he had met years earlier, the most combative of whom he wanted to involve in his political reform projects. But often the relatives would respond, "He's closed up!" To close up, become silent, practically mute: a desire to escape within yourself and stop knowing, understanding, doing. To stop resisting, a decision to retreat an instant before you dissolve in the compromises of life. Cipriano had closed up too. In town they told me it started after he went on a job interview for a human resources position in a shipping company in Frosinone. The interviewer was reading his résumé out loud, but stopped at the name of his town.

"Ah, yes, I know where you're from! The town of that famous boss . . . Sandokan, right?"

"No, the town of Don Peppino Diana."

"Who?"

Cipriano got up and walked out. He ran a newsstand in Rome to support himself. I got his address from his mother, who happened to be in front of me in the checkout line at the supermarket one day. She must have alerted him to my arrival because he didn't answer the doorbell. Maybe he knew what I wanted to talk to him about. But I waited out front for hours and was prepared to sleep on his doorstep. Cipriano finally decided to come out, but he barely said hello. We went to a small park nearby. He had me sit on a bench and opened a notebook, the kind you use in elementary school. There on the lined pages was his harangue, written out in longhand. Who knows if Don Peppino's handwriting was also there somewhere. I didn't dare ask. A speech they had both intended to sign, but then came the killers, death, slander, and unfathomable solitude. When Cipriano started to read, it was with the voice and gestures of Fra Dolcino, the medieval preacher who wandered the streets announcing the Apocalypse, and who was burned at the stake for heresy:

We will not allow our lands to become places of the Camorra, one giant Gomorrah to destroy! Men of the Camorra—not beasts, but men like everyone else—we will not allow you to find here an illicit energy in what is legitimate elsewhere, we will not allow you to destroy here what is built elsewhere. You create a desert around your villas, and only your absolute desire stands between what you are and what you want. Remember. And the LORD rained upon Sodom and upon Gomorrah brimstone and fire; he destroyed those cities, and all the plain, and all the inhabitants of the cities, and that which grew on the ground. But the wife of Lot turned to look back and she became a pillar of salt (Genesis 19:24–26). We must risk becoming salt, we must turn and look at what is happening, what is raining down on Gomorrah, the total destruction where life is added to or subtracted from your economic activities. Don't you see that this is Gomorrah, don't you see? Remember. When they see that the whole land is brimstone, and salt, and burning, and there will be no sowing, no sprouting, no grass growing, like after the destruction of Sodom and Gomorrah, Admah and Seboim, which the LORD overthrew in his anger and his wrath (Deuteronomy 29:22). Men die for a yes or a no, give their lives for someone's order or decision; you spend decades in jail to achieve the power of death, you earn mountains of money that you invest in houses where you will never live, in banks you will never enter, in restaurants you do not run, in companies you do not manage; you control a deadly power in order to dominate a life you spend hidden underground, surrounded by bodyguards. You kill and are killed in a chess game, but you are not kings. The kings are those who get rich off you, making you eat one another until no one can call checkmate and only a pawn remains on the board. And it will not be you. What you devour here you will spit out elsewhere, far away, like birds that vomit food into the mouths of their chicks. But those you are feeding are not chicks but vultures, and you are not mother birds but buffalos ready to destroy yourselves in a place where blood and power are the terms of victory. *It is time we stopped being a Gomorrah* . . .

Cipriano stopped reading. It seemed as if he had imagined all the faces into which he would have liked to hurl those words. His breath was strangled, like an asthmatic's. He closed his notebook and left without saying good-bye.

HOLLYWOOD

In Casal di Principe there is now a Foster Children's Center in Don Peppino Diana's memory. It is housed in a sumptuous, spacious villa seized from Casalesi clan affiliate Egidio Coppola. AGRORINASCE, the agency for the renewal, development, and safety of Casapessena, Casal di Principe, San Cipriano d'Aversa, and Villa Literno, has transformed confiscated Camorra assets into community facilities. Sequestered villas continue to bear the mark of the bosses who built and lived in them unless they're put to some other use. Even abandoned, they remain symbols of sovereignty. A trip across the Aversa Marshes offers a catalog of the last thirty years of architectural styles. The most imposing villas, belonging to contractors and landowners, provide the inspiration for office workers' and shopkeepers' houses. If the former is enthroned with four Doric columns in reinforced concrete, the latter will be adorned with two columns half their size. This imitation game has filled the area with villas competing to be the most impressive, complicated, and impregnable, mansions striving for eccentricity and uniqueness, such as one with a gate that replicates the geometry of a Mondrian painting.

Camorra villas are pearls of cement tucked away on rural streets, protected by walls and video cameras. There are dozens and dozens of them. Marble and parquet, colonnades and staircases, granite fireplaces with the boss's initials. One, the most sumptuous, is particularly famous, or perhaps it has merely generated the most legends. Everyone calls it Hollywood. Just saying the word makes you understand why. Hollywood was the home of Walter Schiavone, Sandokan's brother, who ran the clan's cement business for years. It's not difficult to guess the reason for the name, easy to imagine the spaces and splendor. But that's not the whole of it. Walter Schiavone's villa really does have a link to Hollywood. People in Casal di Principe say the boss told his architect he wanted a villa just like Tony Montana's, the Miami Cuban gangster in *Scarface*. He'd seen the film countless times and it had made a deep impression on him, to the point that he came to identify with the character played by Al Pacino. With a bit of imagination, Schiavone's hollowed face could actually be superimposed on the actor's. The story has all the makings of a legend. People say Schiavone even gave his architect a copy of the film; he wanted the *Scarface* villa, exactly as it was in the movie. It seemed like one of those stories that embellish every boss's rise to power, of aura blending with legend, an authentic urban myth. Anytime anyone mentioned Hollywood, someone would say he'd seen it being built when he was young, a bunch of kids on bikes contemplating Tony Montana's villa as it rose right off the screen into the middle of the neighborhood. Which is rather odd, because in Casale, villa construction starts only after high walls are built to close off the site. I never did believe in the Hollywood version. From the outside, Schiavone's villa looks like a bunker surrounded by thick walls topped with threatening bars. Armored gates protect every access. There's no way to tell what's behind the walls, but they make you think it must be something extravagant.

There's only one external sign, silently celebrated at the main entrance. The red gate, which otherwise looks like that of a country farm, is framed by Doric columns and a tympanum that clash with the disciplined sobriety of the thick walls and gate. The neo-pagan tympanum is actually the family emblem; it sends a message to anyone who already knows the place. The mere sight of it was enough to convince me that the legendary villa was actually for real. I had thought about going to see it for myself dozens of times, but it seemed impossible. Even after Hollywood was seized by the authorities, clan sentinels still guarded it. One morning, almost before I realized what I was doing, I got my courage up and went inside. I used a side entrance, safe from prying eyes that would not have appreciated my intrusion. The villa was stately and luminous, and the monumental facade awe-inspiring. Columns supported a double pediment with a cropped semicircle in the center. The front hall was an architectural delirium: two enormous staircases, like marble wings, soaring up to the second-floor balcony, which looked onto the large hall below. Just like Tony Montana's. There was even a study off the balcony, just as in the final scene of *Scarface*, which ends in a torrent of bullets. The villa is a triumph of Doric columns, the interior ones in pink plaster and the external ones in aquamarine. On the sides are double colonnades with expensive wrought-iron trim. The entire property covers nearly an acre, and the three-storied villa is almost nine thousand square feet. At the end of the 1990s it was worth about $3.5 million, but now the same building would go for about $5 million. The rooms on the ground floor are huge, each with at least one bath, some large and luxurious, others small and cozy. In the children's room, posters of singers and soccer players still hang on the walls, along with a small, blackened painting of two little angels, which probably hung at the head of the bed. A newspaper cutting: "Albanova sharpens its weapons." Albanova was the local soccer team—a toy team for the bosses, backed by clan money—and disbanded by the Anti-Mafia Commission in 1997. Those scorched clippings clinging to the rotting plaster were all that remained of Walter's son, who died in a car accident as a teenager. From the balcony you can see the front yard— palm trees and even an artificial lake with a wooden bridge leading

to a tiny, verdant island encircled by a stone wall. When the Schiavones lived here, their dogs ran about in the yard: mastiffs, yet
another display of power. In the backyard, palm trees shaded an elegant, obliquely elliptical swimming pool from the summer sun.
The garden was copied from the bath of Venus, the jewel of the
English Garden at the royal palace at Caserta. The statue of the
goddess floats on the surface of the water with the same grace as
the one designed by Luigi Vanvitelli. The villa was abandoned after
the boss's arrest, which occurred in 1996, right in these rooms.
Walter did not do what his brother did; when Sandokan went into
hiding, he built a large and princely hideout under his enormous
Casal di Principe villa: a blockhouse devoid of doors and windows,
with underground passages and natural grottoes for emergency escape
routes. But there was also a thousand-square-foot, fully furnished
apartment.

A surreal apartment, with neon lights and white majolica-tiled floors.
A video intercom system and two entrances completely invisible from
the outside. There seemed to be no way in: the doors were walls of
cement that slid open along tracks. When there was the risk of a
search, the boss could go through a trapdoor in the dining room to a
network of interconnected tunnels—eleven all together—that formed
a sort of underground redoubt or final refuge, where Sandokan had
set up camp tents. A bunker within a bunker. To catch him, in 1998
the DIA staked out the place for a year and seven months, finally using an electric saw to cut through the wall into his hiding place. Only
after Francesco Schiavone had given himself up were they able to
identify the principal access amid the empty plastic crates and garden
tools in the storage room of a villa in Via Salerno. The hideout lacked
for nothing: two refrigerators were stocked with food to feed at least
six people for a fortnight. A sophisticated home entertainment center—stereo, VCRs, and projectors—took up one whole wall. It took
the Forensic Division of the Naples Police Department ten hours to
check the alarm and lock systems controlling the two accesses. There

was even a whirlpool tub in the bathroom. Schiavone lived underground, in a rabbit warren, amid trapdoors and secret passageways.

Walter, on the other hand, did not squirrel himself away. As a fugitive, he'd still show up in town for the most important meetings, returning home in the light of day, accompanied by his bodyguards, secure in the inaccessibility of his villa. The police arrested him almost by chance. They were performing the usual controls. Police and carabinieri usually go to a fugitive's home eight, ten, twelve times a day; they check up on the family members, pay visits, search, and above all attempt to wear down their nerves and undermine their support for their relative's decision to go into hiding. Signora Schiavone always greeted the police with courtesy and defiance, always serene as she offered them tea and cookies, which they systematically refused. One afternoon, however, Walter's wife was already tense when they rang the bell, and by the slowness with which she opened the gate, they suspected immediately that something was up. Mrs. Schiavone kept right on their heels as they moved about the villa, rather than shouting to them from the bottom of the stairs as she usually did, her words echoing throughout the house. They found freshly ironed men's shirts too big for her son folded on the bed. Walter was there. He'd come home. The police fanned out to search for him, catching him as he tried to scale the wall. The same wall he had had built to make his villa impregnable now prevented his quick escape. Nabbed like a petty thief flailing about in search of a hold on a smooth wall. The villa was sequestered immediately, but no one really took possession of it for six years. Walter ordered everything possible removed. If he couldn't use it, it shouldn't exist. Either his or no one's. He had the doors taken off their hinges, the windows removed, the parquet taken up, the marble pulled off the stairs, the expensive fireplace mantels disassembled. Ceramic bathroom fixtures, wood railings, light fixtures, and kitchen appliances were removed, and antique furniture, china closets, and paintings carried off. He gave orders to strew the house with tires and set them on fire, ruining the plaster and damaging the columns. Even so, he managed to leave a message. The only thing left untouched was a bathtub, sitting on three wide steps in the living room. A princely version, with a lion's face that roared water. The boss's great indulgence. The tub sat right in front of a Palladian window that looked directly onto the garden. A sign of his power as builder and Camorrista, like an artist who cancels out his painting but leaves his signature on the canvas.

As I wandered through those blackened rooms, I felt my chest swell, as if my insides had become one giant heart. It beat harder and harder, pumping through my entire body. My mouth had gone dry from the deep breaths I took to calm my anxiety. If some clan sentinel had jumped me and beaten me to a pulp, I could have squealed like a butchered pig but no one would have heard me. Evidently no one saw me enter, or maybe no one was guarding the villa anymore. A pulsating rage rose up inside me. Flashing in my mind, like a giant swirl of dismantled visions, were the images of friends who had emigrated, joined the clan or the military, the lazy afternoons in these desert lands, the lack of everything except deals, politicians mopped up by corruption, and empires built in the north of Italy and half of Europe, leaving behind nothing but trash and toxins. I needed to vent, to take it out on someone. I couldn't resist. I stood on the edge of the tub and took a piss. An idiotic gesture, but as my bladder emptied, I felt better. That villa was the confirmation of a cliché, the concrete realization of a rumor. I had the absurd sensation that Tony Montana was about to come out of one of the rooms and greet me with a stiff, arrogant gesture: "All I have in this world is my balls and my word, and I don't break them for no one, you understand?" Who knows if Walter dreamed of dying like Montana too, riddled with bullets and tumbling into his front hall rather than ending his days in a prison cell, consumed by Graves' disease, his eyes rotting and his blood pressure exploding.

It's not the movie world that scans the criminal world for the most interesting behavior. The exact opposite is true. New generations of bosses don't follow an exclusively criminal path; they don't spend their days on the streets with the local thugs, carry a knife, or have scars on their faces. They watch TV, study, go to college, graduate, travel abroad, and are above all employed in the office of the mechanisms of power. The film *Il Padrino, The Godfather*, is an eloquent example. Before the film came out, no one in the Sicilian or Campania criminal organizations had ever used the term *padrino*, derived from a philologically incorrect translation of the English word *godfather*. The term for the head of the family or an affiliate had always been *compare*. After the film, however, ethnic Italian Mafia families in the United States started using *godfather* instead of *compare* and its diminutive, *compariello*, which were falling out of use. Many young Italian-Americans with Mafia ties adopted dark glasses, pin-striped suits, and solemn speech. John Gotti himself wanted to become a flesh-and-blood version of Don Vito Corleone. And even Cosa Nostra boss Luciano Liggio jutted his chin like Marlon Brando in *The Godfather* when posing for photographs.

Mario Puzo's inspiration was not a Sicilian but Alfonso Tieri, boss of Pignasecca in downtown Naples, who became the head of the leading Italian Mafia families in the United States after the death of Charles Gambino. In an interview for an American newspaper, Antonio Spavone *'o malommo*, or "bad man," the Neapolitan boss linked to Tieri, stated, "If the Sicilians showed how to keep their mouths shut, the Neapolitans showed the world how to behave when you're in command. To convey with a gesture that commanding is better than fucking." Most of the criminal archetypes, the acme of Mafia charisma, were from a few square miles of Campania. Even Al Capone was originally from here; his family came from Castellammare di Stabia. Capone was the first boss to measure himself against the movies. His nickname, Scarface, from a scar on his cheek, was used by Brian De Palma for his 1983 film about Tony Montana, but Howard Hawks had used it previously for his 1932 movie about Capone. Capone and his escort would show up on the set every time there was an action scene or location shot he could watch. The boss wanted to make sure that Tony Camonte, the Scarface character he inspired, did not become trite. And he wanted to be as much like Tony Camonte as possible; he knew that after the film's release, Camonte would become the emblem of Capone, rather than the other way around.

Movies are the source for forms of expression. In Naples, Cosimo Di Lauro is a good example. His clothes are reminiscent of Brandon Lee's in *The Crow*. Camorristi look to the movies to create for themselves a criminal image they often lack. They model themselves on familiar Hollywood masks, a sort of shortcut to make themselves into figures to fear. Cinematographic inspiration even conditions technical choices such as the way you handle or shoot a gun. A veteran of the Naples Forensic Division once told me how Camorra killers imitate the movies:

"Ever since Tarantino, these guys don't know the right way to shoot! They don't keep the barrel straight anymore. Now they hold it crooked, like in the movies, which makes for disaster. They hit the guts, groin, or legs, seriously wounding but not killing. And so they have to finish the victim off with a bullet to the nape of the neck. A pool of pointless blood, a barbarism completely superfluous to the goal of execution."

Female bosses have bodyguards who dress like Uma Thurman in *Kill Bill*: blond hair and phosphorescent yellow outfits. Vincenza Di Domenico, a woman from the Quartieri Spagnoli who collaborated with the authorities for a short while, had the eloquent nickname of Nikita, like the heroine killer in Luc Besson's film. Movies, especially American movies, are not distant lands where aberrations occur or the impossible happens, but places very close to home.

• • •

I left the villa quietly, freeing my feet from the brambles and weeds that had overgrown the English Garden so dear to the boss. I left the gate open. Just a few years earlier, getting anywhere near here would have meant being spotted by dozens of sentinels. But now I walked out with my hands in my pockets and my head down, as when you leave the movie theater, still dazed by what you've seen.

It's not hard to understand why Giuseppe Tornatore's film *Il camorrista* left such a powerful mark on the imagination in Naples. All you have to do is listen to people's banter, the same lines repeated for years:

"Tell the professor I didn't betray him."

"I know who he is, but I also know who I am!"

"Malacarne's a weakling!"

"Who sent you?"

"The one who can save your life, or take it from you."

The film's sound track has become a sort of Camorra theme song, whistled when a neighborhood capo walks by, or just to make a shop-keeper nervous. *Il camorrista* even made it to the discos, where people can dance to three different mixes of the most famous utterances of Raffaele Cutolo, played in the film by Ben Gazzara.

Two kids from Casal di Principe, Giuseppe M. and Romeo P., knew the *Il camorrista* dialogues by heart and would act out various scenes:

"How much does a *picciotto** weigh? As much as a feather in the wind."

They started hassling groups of kids their age in Casale and San Cipriano d'Aversa even before they were old enough to drive a car.

---

*The lowest-ranking Mafioso.—Trans.

They were bullies. Braggarts and buffoons, they'd go out to eat and leave a tip twice the amount of the check. Shirts unbuttoned to show off hairless chests, a theatrical swagger, as if claiming every step. Chin high, an ostentatious display of confidence and power, real only in their minds. They were inseparable. Giuseppe played the boss, always one step ahead of his *compare*. Romeo acted as his bodyguard, his right-hand man and loyal friend. Giuseppe often called him Donnie, after Donnie Brasco. Even though Brasco was a police infiltrator, he becomes a real Mafioso in his soul and that saves him from his original sin in the eyes of his admirers. In Aversa, Giuseppe and Romeo would terrorize the kids who had just gotten their licenses. They liked young couples best. They'd run their *motorino* into the couple's car, and when they got out to ask for insurance papers, Giuseppe or Romeo would spit in the girl's face, provoking the boyfriend to react. Then they'd beat him to a pulp. They also challenged adults, even adults who really counted, invading their territory and doing whatever they wanted. Giuseppe and Romeo came from Casal di Principe, and in their minds that was enough. They wanted to convey that they were to be feared and respected; anyone who came near them was supposed to stare at the ground, unable to find the courage to look them in the face. But one day they aimed too high. They went out armed with a submachine gun, picked up from who knows which clan armory, and fired on a group of kids. They must have practiced a lot because they were careful not to hit a single one, but they let them smell the gunpowder and hear the voice of the weapon. Before they opened fire, one of them recited something. No one understood what he blathered, but one witness said it sounded like the Bible; perhaps Giuseppe and Romeo were preparing for confirmation. But taking apart their words, it was clear that this was no confirmation text. It was the Bible, however. A passage not from the catechism but from Quentin Tarantino. The verses Jules Winnfield delivers in *Pulp Fiction*, right before he kills the guy who had made Marsellus Wallace's precious suitcase disappear:

"The path of the righteous man is beset on all sides by the in-equities of the selfish and the tyranny of evil men. Blessed is he who, in the name of charity and goodwill, shepherds the weak through the valley of darkness, for he is truly his brother's keeper and the finder of lost children. And I will strike down upon thee with great vengeance and furious anger those who attempt to poison and destroy my brothers. And you will know my name is the Lord when I lay my vengeance upon you."

Giuseppe and Romeo recited it just as in the film and then opened fire. Giuseppe's father was a Camorrista, a *pentito* who went back to the Quadrano–De Falco organization after it was defeated by the Schiavones. So a loser. But he'd thought that maybe the film of his life could change if he just played the right role. The two boys knew all the best lines of every crime movie by heart. Most of the time they'd start fights over a glance. In the land of the Camorra a look is a question of territory; it's an invasion of one's private space, like break-ing down the door and violently entering someone's home. A look is something more than an insult. To stare someone in the face for too long is already somehow an open challenge:

"You talkin' to me? You talkin' to me? You talkin' to me?"

They'd repeat the famous monologue from *Taxi Driver*, then start fighting, landing punches on the sternum, the kind that make a noise and echo in your chest.

The Casalesi bosses took the problem seriously. The brawls, alter-cations, and threats were not easily tolerated: too many nervous mothers, too many complaints. So they sent a warning through a neighborhood capo, a sort of call to order. The capo meets them in a bar and tells them the bosses are losing patience with them. But Giuseppe and Romeo keep acting in their imaginary film, beating up whomever they feel like, pissing in gas tanks of the neighborhood kids' motorcycles. So the bosses have them sent for again. They want to talk to them directly; the clan can't accept such behavior. The paternalistic tolerance common to these parts translates into the need to punish; the boys need a beating, a brutal public spanking to make them toe the line. But Giuseppe and Romeo snub the bosses' summons and continue sprawling about at the bar, playing video poker or glued to the TV, watching their favorite films on DVD, hours spent memorizing lines, imitating body language, expressions, and wardrobe choices. They think they can stand up to anyone. Even the big guys. In fact, they believe that precisely by standing up to the big guys they'll be feared for real. Like Tony and Manny in *Scarface*, they set no limits. They don't listen to anyone, but their continual raids and intimidations make them feel they're the viceroys of Caserta. Giuseppe and Romeo had not chosen to join the clan. They didn't even try. That path was too slow and regimented, they didn't want to rise silently through the ranks. Besides, for years the Casalesi had been placing the really good members in the organization's economic sectors and not in the hit squads. Giuseppe and Romeo were the complete opposite of the new Camorra soldier. They thought they could ride the wave of the area's bad reputation. They weren't affiliates, but wanted to enjoy the privileges of Camorristi. They expected the bars to serve them for free, assumed that gas for their *motorini* was their due, and that their mothers would receive free groceries; when someone dared to rebel, they would descend upon them immediately, smashing windows and beating up greengrocers and salesgirls. So in the spring of 2004 some clan emissaries set up a meeting with them on the outskirts of Castelvolturno, in the Parco Mare area, where sand, sea, and trash all flowed together. If the bosses couldn't get to them with negative proposals, they'd try with positive ones. Some tempting deal, or maybe even the chance to participate in a killing. The first real hit of their lives. I pictured them racing full throttle on their *motorini*, replaying in their minds all their favorite movie scenes, in which the big guys are forced to yield to the ostentation of the new heroes. Young Spartans went to war with the feats of Achilles and Hector in their heads, but around here you go to kill and be killed thinking of *Scarface, GoodFellas, Donnie Brasco*, and *The Godfather*. Every time I go by Parco Mare, I imagine the scene that the police reconstructed, that was reported in the newspapers. Giuseppe and Romeo arrived on their *motorini* way ahead of the set time. Burning with anxiety. They were there waiting when the car pulled up. A group of men got out. The two kids went over to greet them, but they grabbed Romeo right away and started beating up Giuseppe. Then they pointed the barrel of an automatic at his chest and fired. I'm sure that the scene from *GoodFellas* flashed before Romeo's eyes, the scene where Tommy DeVito is invited to take part in the management of Cosa Nostra in America, but instead of welcoming him in a hall crowded with bosses, they take him to an empty room and shoot him in the head. It's not true that films are a lie, that you can't live as in the movies, that as soon as you stick your head out of the theater, you realize things are not the same. Only one moment is different: the moment when Al Pacino gets up from the fountain into which his double, mowed down by machine-gun fire, has fallen, and dries his face, wiping off the color of blood. The moment when Joe Pesci washes his hair and stops the fake bleeding. But you don't want to know that part, so you don't understand it. When Romeo sees Giuseppe on the ground, I'm sure—though I can never confirm it— that he understood the exact difference between movies and reality, between a staged scene and the smell in the air, between his own life and a script. Then it was his turn. They shot him in the throat, finishing him off with a bullet to the head. The sum of their ages was barely thirty. That was how the Casalesi clan resolved the problem of this micro-criminal excrescence nourished on movies. They didn't even make an anonymous call to the police or ambulance. They left the boy cadavers there, their hands to be pecked at by seagulls and their lips and noses nibbled by stray dogs that roam the trash-covered beaches. But that's something the movies never show. They end just the minute before.

• • •

There's no real difference between movie audiences in the land of the Camorra and elsewhere. Cinematographic references everywhere create mythologies of imitation. If elsewhere you may like *Scarface* and secretly identify with him, here you can *be* Scarface, but you have to be him all the way.

The land of the Camorra is also filled with people passionate about art and literature. Sandokan had an enormous library in his villa bunker, with dozens of volumes, all on two topics: the Kingdom of the Two Sicilies, and Napoléon Bonaparte. Sandokan was attracted to the Bourbon state's importance, bragging that his ancestors were officers in southern Italy, the Terra di Lavoro. He was fascinated by the genius of Bonaparte, who rose from a low military rank to conquer half of Europe; he saw similarities to his own life, for he'd started at the bottom and was now generalissimo of one of the most powerful clans in Europe. Sandokan, who had once been a medical student, preferred to pass his time in hiding painting religious icons and portraits of Napoléon and Mussolini. They're still for sale today, in Caserta shops that are above suspicion: extremely rare holy images, Sandokan's own face inserted in place of Christ's. He also liked reading epics. Homer, the Arthurian legends, and Walter Scott were his favorites. It was his love of Scott that inspired him to baptize one of his numerous children with the grandiloquent, proud name of Ivanhoe.

But the names of the sons always bear a trace of the passions of the father. Giuseppe Misso, boss of the Sanità neighborhood clan, has three grandchildren: Ben Hur, Jesus, and Emiliano Zapata. When on trial, Misso always assumed the attitude of political leader, conservative thinker, and rebel; he recently wrote a novel, *I leoni di marmo*, "The Marble Lions." Several hundred copies were sold in a few weeks in Naples. Told with a mangled syntax but in a furious style, it is the story of Naples in the 1980s and 1990s, the story of the boss's formation, his emergence as lone warrior against the Camorra of rackets and drugs, in defense of a chivalrous but vaguely defined code of robbery and theft. Each time he was arrested in his long criminal career, he was found with books by Julius Evola and Ezra Pound.

Augusto La Torre, the boss of Mondragone, is a student of psychology, an avid reader of Carl Jung, and an expert on Sigmund Freud. A glance at the titles of the books he requested in prison reveals a lengthy bibliography of scholars of psychoanalysis, and in court, his quotations of Lacan are interwoven with his reflections on the Gestalt school of psychology. A knowledge the boss utilized in his rise to power, an unexpected managerial and military weapon.

Even one of Paolo Di Lauro's most loyal men is a lover of culture: Tommaso Prestieri produces many neo-melodic singers and is a connoisseur of contemporary art. Many bosses are art collectors. Pasquale Galasso's villa housed a private museum with about three hundred antiques; the jewel of the collection was the throne of the Bourbon king Francis I. And Luigi Vollaro, known as 'o califfo or the caliph, owned a painting by his favorite artist, Botticelli.

The police were able to arrest Prestieri because of his love of music. He was caught at the Teatro Bellini in Naples when he went to hear a concert while a fugitive. After his sentencing, Prestieri declared, "In art I am free, I don't need to be released from prison." Painting and song offer equilibrium and impossible serenity to an unlucky boss such as Prestieri, who has lost two brothers, both killed in cold blood.

ABERDEEN, MONDRAGONE

The psychoanalyst boss Augusto La Torre was one of Antonio Bardellino's favorites. He had taken his father's place when he was young, becoming the sole leader of the Chiuovi clan, as it was called in Mondragone, which ruled in northern Caserta, southern Lazio, and along the Domitian coast. The La Torre clan had sided with Sandokan Schiavone's enemies, but their management and business savvy, the only elements powerful enough to alter conflictual relationships among Camorra families, eventually reconciled them to the Casalesi, with whom they worked while still maintaining their autonomy. Augusto didn't come by his name by chance. La Torre family tradition was to name the firstborn after a Roman emperor. But in this case they inverted history; instead of Augustus being followed by Tiberius, the father bore the second emperor's name and the son the first.

Scipio Africanus's villa near Lake Patria, Hannibal's battles at Capua, and the unassailable might of the Samnites, the first warriors in Europe to attack the Roman legions and then flee to the mountains—these are legends in local Camorra families; they consider themselves connected to these stories out of the distant past. The clans' historical fantasies clashed with the widespread image of Mondragone as the

mozzarella capital of Italy. My father used to stuff me full of mozzarelle from Mondragone, but it was impossible to decide which
area's mozzarella was the best. The flavors were too diverse: the light,
sickly sweetness of Battipaglia, the heavy saltiness of Aversa, or the
purity of Mondragone. But the Mondragone mozzarella masters had a
way to tell. A good mozzarella leaves an aftertaste, what country folk
call 'o ciato 'e bbufala or buffalo breath. If there's no buffalo aftertaste,
the mozzarella isn't any good. I liked to stroll back and forth on the
Mondragone wharf, one of my favorite summer destinations before it
was knocked down. A tongue of reinforced concrete, boat moorings
built out over the sea. A useless, unused construction.

Mondragone suddenly became the place for all the kids around
Caserta and the Pontine Marshes who wanted to emigrate to the UK.
Emigration, the chance of a lifetime, a way to finally get out, but not
as a waiter, a scullery boy in a McDonald's, or a bartender paid in
pints of dark beer. They went to Mondragone to try to make contacts
with the right people, who could get you a good rent and an in with
employers. In Mondragone there were people who could get you a job
in insurance or real estate, and who helped the desperate, chronically
unemployed find a decent contract and respectable work. Mondragone was the door to Great Britain. Starting in the late 1990s, having
a friend in Mondragone all of a sudden meant you'd be valued for
what you're worth, without needing recommendations or connections. A rare thing indeed, impossible in Italy, especially in the south.
Around here, you always need a protector, someone who can at least
get your foot in the door, if not the rest of you. Presenting yourself
without a protector is like showing up without arms and legs. With
something missing. But in Mondragone they'd take your résumé and
see whom to send it to in the UK. Your skills mattered and, even
more, the way you used them. But only in London or Aberdeen. Not
in Campania, the most provincial of the provinces of Europe.

My friend Matteo decided to give it a try, to leave once and for all.
He'd graduated cum laude and was tired of doing internships and

supporting himself working construction sites. He'd put aside some money and got the name of a guy in Mondragone who would help him line up some job interviews in Britain. I went with him. We waited for hours at the beach where Matteo's contact had told him to meet. It was summer. Mondragone's beaches are invaded by vacationers from all over Campania, the ones who can't afford the Amalfi coast or a summer rental on the shore, so they commute from the hinterland. Till the mid-1980s mozzarelle were sold on the beach, in wooden pails overflowing with boiling buffalo milk. The bathers ate them with their hands, the milk dripping all over. Kids would lick their hands, salty from the sea, then take a bite. But no one sells them anymore, now it's grissini and coconut slices. Our contact was two hours late. When he finally showed up, tanned and wearing only a skimpy bathing suit, he explained that he'd eaten breakfast late, so had gone for a swim late and had dried himself off late. That was his excuse—it was the sun's fault. He took us to a travel agency. That was all. We thought we were going to meet some big middleman, but instead we were merely introduced at an agency, and not a particularly elegant one at that. Not one of those agencies with hundreds of brochures, just an ordinary hole-in-the-wall kind of place. But you needed a local contact to access their services. To anybody just walking in, it functioned like a normal travel agency. A young woman asked Matteo for his résumé and told us the first available flight to Aberdeen. That's where they were sending him. They handed him a list of businesses where he could go for an interview, and for a small fee they'd even set up appointments with the secretaries of the people in charge of hiring. Never had a temp agency been so efficient. Two days later we boarded the plane for Scotland, a quick and affordable trip from Mondragone.

Aberdeen felt like home, though this Scottish city couldn't have been more different from Mondragone. The third-largest city in Scotland, dark, dirty, and gray, but it rains less than in London. Before the Italian clans arrived, Aberdeen didn't know how to exploit its resources for recreation and tourism, and the restaurant, hotel, and entertainment businesses were organized in the sad English manner. The same old thing, people packed into pubs once a week. According to the Naples anti-Mafia prosecutor, it was Antonio La Torre, the boss Augusto's brother, who set up a series of commercial activities in Scotland, which in the space of a few years became the feather in the cap of Scottish entrepreneurship. Most La Torre clan activities in Britain are perfectly legal: acquisition and management of properties and businesses, commerce in foodstuffs with Italy. Enormous turnover, difficult to place a figure on. In Aberdeen, Matteo sought everything he'd been denied in Italy. We walked around feeling pleased; for the first time in our lives being from Campania seemed sufficient to guarantee some measure of success. At 27/29 Union Terrace, I found myself in front of Pavarotti's, a restaurant registered in Antonio La Torre's name and listed on tourist websites. Aberdeen had become chic, an elegant address for fine dining and important dealings. At Italissima, the gastronomic fair held in Paris, clan businesses even marketed themselves as the height of Made in Italy. Antonio La Torre advertised his own brand of catering activities there. His success had made him one of the top Scottish businessmen in Europe.

Antonio La Torre was arrested in Aberdeen in March 2005. There was an Italian warrant for his arrest on account of Camorra criminal conspiracy and extortion, but for years his British citizenship and the fact that the authorities did not recognize his alleged crimes shielded him and he had been able to avoid extradition. Scotland didn't want to lose one of its most brilliant entrepreneurs.

In 2002 the Court of Naples issued preventive-detention orders for thirty people connected to the La Torre clan. It emerged from the order that extortion, contracts, and control of economic activities were earning the clan vast sums of money, which they then invested overseas, particularly in Britain, where an actual clan colony had formed. The colonists hadn't invaded or introduced bearish competition in the workforce; instead they infused the city with economic energy, revitalized the tourist industry, inspired new import-export activities, and injected new vigor in the real estate sector.

The international energy from Mondragone was personified by Rockefeller. That's what people here call him because of his obvious talent for making deals and his control of vast sums of money. Rockefeller is Raffaele Barbato, sixty-two years old, a native of Mondragone. Maybe even he has forgotten his real name. He has a Dutch wife, and until the late 1980s he did business in Holland, where he owned two casinos that drew international big shots, such as the brother of Bob Cellino, who'd set up casinos in Las Vegas, and Miami-based, Slavic Mafiosi. His partners were a certain Liborio, a Sicilian with Cosa Nostra connections, and Emi, a Dutchman who later moved to Spain, where he opened hotels, residences, and discos. According to Mario Sperlongaro, Stefano Piccirillo, and Girolamo Rozzera—all *pentiti*—it was Rockefeller, together with Augusto La Torre, who hatched the idea of going to Caracas to try to meet Venezuelan narcotraffickers, whose coke prices beat those of the Colombians who supplied the Neapolitans and Casalesi. And it was Rockefeller who found a comfortable place for Augusto to sleep when he went into hiding in Holland: the skeet-shooting club. Even though he was far from the Mondragone countryside, the boss could keep in shape firing at flying clay pigeons. Rockefeller had an enormous network. He was one of the best-known businessmen not only in Europe but also in the USA; through his gambling houses he made contacts with Italian-American Mafiosi who were slowly being squeezed out by the Albanian clans taking over in New York. As a result the Mafiosi were increasingly allied to Campania Camorra families and eager to traffic in drugs and invest in European markets, restaurants, and hotels through Mondragone's open door. Rockefeller is the owner of Adam and Eve, renamed La Playa, a beautiful holiday village on the Mondragone coast, where, according to the magistrates, many fugitive affiliates vacationed. The more comfortable the hideout, the less the temptation to turn state's witness and put an end to life on the run. La Torre was fierce with *pentiti*. Francesco Tiberio, Augusto's cousin, phoned Domenico Pensa, who had testified against the Stolder clan, and in no uncertain terms invited him to leave town.

"I heard from the Stolders that you collaborated against them. Given as how we don't want informants in this town, you'd better leave Mondragone or else someone will come and cut your head off."

Augusto's cousin had a knack for making terrorizing telephone calls to whoever dared collaborate with the authorities or leak information. With Vittorio Di Tella, he was more explicit, inviting him to purchase his funeral suit.

"If you have to talk, you'd better buy yourself a black shirt, fucker, because I'm going to kill you."

Before clan affiliates started turning state's witness, no one would have imagined the vast scope of Mondragone dealings. One of Rockefeller's friends was a certain Raffaele Acconcia. Like Rockefeller, he was born in Mondragone but moved to Holland, where he owned a restaurant chain and, according to *pentito* Stefano Piccirillo, was an important international drug trafficker. The La Torre treasure is still hidden somewhere in Holland, perhaps in a bank—millions of euros the magistrates have never been able to locate, taken in through mediation and commerce. In Mondragone this alleged stash in a Dutch bank has become a symbol of absolute wealth, trumping all other references to international riches. People no longer say, "He thought I was the Bank of Italy," but, "He thought I was the Bank of Holland."

With backing in South America and Holland, the La Torre clan planned to take over cocaine traffic in Rome. For all Caserta Camorra families, the capital city is the number one spot for drugs and real estate investments. Rome has become an extension of the province of Caserta. The La Torres could count on the supply routes on the Domitian coast. The villas there were essential, first for contraband cigarettes, and then for all sorts of merchandise. The actor Nino Manfredi had a villa there. Clan representatives went and asked him to sell it. Manfredi resisted in every way he could, but clan pressure increased; his house was located on a strategic point for mooring the motorboats. They stopped asking him to sell and forced him to hand it over at a price they set. Manfredi even appealed to a Cosa Nostra boss, disclosing the news to *Radio News 1* in January 1994, but no Sicilian stepped in to mediate against the powerful Mondragonesi. Only by going on TV and attracting national media attention was he able to make known the pressure the Camorra applied for the sake of strategic interests.

Drug traffic followed on the heels of other commercial routes. Enzo Boccolato, a cousin of the La Torres' and owner of a restaurant in Germany, decided to export clothing. Together with Antonio La Torre and a Lebanese businessman, he purchased clothing in Puglia—the Campania garment industry was already monopolized by the Secondigliano clans—and resold them in Venezuela through a middleman, a certain Alfredo, who investigations indicated was one of the most important diamond traffickers in Germany. Thanks to Campania Camorra clans, diamonds—which have significant price fluctuations but always maintain a nominal value—quickly became the asset of choice for money laundering. Enzo Boccolato was known in the Venezuela and Frankfurt airports, where he had protectors among the merchandise inspectors; they probably not only did not check the clothing shipments, but were also preparing a giant cocaine network. It might seem that the clans, once they've accumulated substantial capital, would stop their criminal activities, unravel their genetic code somehow, and convert it to legality. Just like the Kennedy family, who had earned enormous amounts selling liquor during Prohibition and later broke all criminal ties. But the strength of Italian criminal business lies precisely in maintaining a double track, in never renouncing its criminal origins. In Aberdeen this system is called scratch. Like the rappers and DJs who put their finger on the record to keep it from spinning normally, Camorra businessmen momentarily stop the movement of the legal market, *scratch*, then make it spin even faster.

Various inquiries by the Naples Anti-Mafia Public Attorney's Office revealed that when the La Torre legal track was in crisis, the criminal one was immediately activated. If cash was short, they had counterfeit bills printed; if capital was needed in a hurry, they sold bogus treasury bonds. They annihilated the competition through extortions and imported merchandise tax-free. Scratching the record of the legal economy means that clients get steady prices, bank credits are always honored, money continues to circulate, and products continue to be consumed. Scratching reduces the separation between the law and economic imperative, between what regulations prohibit and what making money demands.

Foreign deals meant that British participation in various levels of La Torre clan activity was indispensable; some Brits even became affiliates. One of these is a British Camorrista, incarcerated in Great Britain. His name cannot be spoken in the Queen's land because association with the Mafia is not recognized as a crime in Great Britain, because it is very easy for someone there who belongs to a Mafia organization to hide behind the law that protects citizens from libel. And since Great Britain doesn't recognize the crime, it often doesn't recognize the accusations either. An immaculate criminal record means that words must be mute. And yet this British Camorrista receives a stipend from Mondragone every month, Christmas bonus included. In addition to physical protection, affiliates are normally guaranteed a salary, legal assistance, and clan cover if needed. Yet to receive assurances directly from the boss, this Camorrista had to have played a vital role in clan business, unquestioningly the number one British Camorrista in Italian criminal history.

I'd heard talk of this British Camorrista for years, even though I'd never seen him, not even in a photograph. When I got to Aberdeen, I couldn't help but ask about him, Augusto La Torre's trustworthy ally, the Scottish Camorrista, the man who, knowing only the syntax of business and the grammar of power, effortlessly dissolved any residual relations with ancient Highlands clans in order to join the Mondragonesi. There was always a bunch of local kids hanging out at the La Torre pubs—not the lazy, rebellious, petty-criminal types nursing a pint of beer, waiting for a punch-up or a purse snatching, but quick-witted kids involved at various levels of legal businesses. Transportation, advertising, marketing. When I asked about him, I didn't get hostile stares or vague answers, as I would have if I'd asked in Campania about an affiliate. It seemed they'd known him forever, but he'd probably become a mythical figure everyone talks about. The English boss was the man who had made it. Not like them, not just someone with a steady salary, an employee in a restaurant, company, store, or real estate agency. The British Camorrista was more than that. He had fulfilled many a Scottish young person's dream not to simply work legally, but to become part of the System, a working member of the clan. To become a Camorrista in every respect—despite the disadvantage of a Scottish birth, which means believing that the economy has just one route, belonging to everyone, the banal economy of rules and defeats, of mere competition and prices. I was shocked to discover that in Scotland my English, spoken with a fat Italian accent, did not make me an emigrant in their eyes, the skinny deformation of Jake La Motta—the Raging Bull—or a criminal invader, come to suck money out of their land; they heard instead the grammar of the economy's absolute power, a power that decides everything about everything, un-limited even by life in prison or death. It seemed impossible, yet they clearly knew Mondragone, Secondigliano, Marano, Casal di Principe; they'd heard about these places, as if in an epic of a faraway land, from the bosses who'd come through here or eaten at the restaurants where they worked. For my Scottish peers, to be born in the land of the Camorra was an advantage; it meant you had something that en-abled you to perceive the existence of an arena where entrepreneurship, arms, and even your own life are only and exclusively a means to money and power, the things that make living worthwhile, that put you at the center of your day, without having to worry about anything else. The British Camorrista had done it, even without being born in Italy, even without ever seeing Campania or driving for miles past construction sites, dumps, and buffalo farms. He had become a man of real power. A Camorrista.

This grand organization of international commerce and finance did not earn the clan flexibility at home, however. Augusto La Torre wielded his power harshly in Mondragone. He had to be ruthless to create such a powerful cartel. Weapons, hundreds of them, were ordered from Switzerland. His political tactics varied from aggressive contract management to alliances to sporadic contacts; he allowed his deals to solidify, making sure politics fell in line with his business. Mondragone was the first Italian town whose government was dissolved in the 1990s because of Camorra infiltration. Over the years, politics and the clan never really separated. In 2005 a Neapolitan fugitive found hospitality in the home of a candidate in the outgoing mayor's party. And for a long time, the daughter of a traffic police officer accused of collecting La Torre bribes represented the majority party on the town council.

Augusto was harsh on politicians as well. All who opposed the family business received cruel exemplary punishments. The method for physically eliminating La Torre enemies was always the same, and in criminal jargon it came to be referred to as Mondragone-style. The technique consists in brutally beating the body, throwing it in a country well, then tossing in a hand grenade, so the body is torn to shreds and the earth covers the remains, which sink into the water. This is what Augusto La Torre did to Antonio Nugnes, the Christian Democrat deputy mayor who disappeared into thin air in 1990. Nugnes represented an obstacle in the clan's desire to directly manage municipal contracts and intervene in all political and administrative matters. Augusto La Torre didn't want allies. He wanted to run everything himself. Military decisions were not heavily pondered then. First you shot and then you reasoned. Augusto was young when he became the boss of Mondragone. He wanted to become a stockholder in a private clinic that was being built, and Nugnes held a significant number of shares. The Incaldana clinic was one of the most prestigious in Lazio and Campania, and a stone's throw from Rome; it would attract a good number of businessmen from southern Lazio, thus solving the problem of the lack of quality hospitals on the Domitian coast and in the Pontine Marshes. Augusto insisted the clinic's board of directors accept his dauphin, another clan businessman who had gotten rich running a dump, whom Augusto wanted to represent the family. Nugnes was opposed; he realized that La Torre's strategy was more than simply about getting in on a huge deal. So Augusto sent an emissary to the deputy mayor to try to soften him up, convince him to accept his terms. For a Christian Democrat to have contact with a boss and reckon with his business and military power wasn't all that scandalous. Clans were the primary economic force in the area; refusing a relationship with them would be like the deputy mayor of Turin refusing to meet with the top management of Fiat. Augusto La Torre's idea wasn't to buy shares at a good price, as a more diplomatic boss would have done. He wanted them for free. In exchange he would guarantee that all his companies that won contracts for service, cleaning, catering, transportation, and guarding would do their job professionally and at favorable fees. He even assured Nugnes his buffaloes would produce better milk. On the pretense of a meeting with the boss, Nugnes was picked up at his agricultural business and taken to a farm in Falciano del Massico. According to Augusto's testimony, waiting with him for Nugnes were Girolamo Rozzera, known as Jimmy, Massimo Gitto, Angelo Gagliardi, Giuseppe Valente, Mario Sperlongano, and Francesco La Torre. All waiting for the ambush. The deputy mayor got out of the car and went to say hello to the boss. Augusto confessed to the judges that as he put out his hand to greet Nugnes, he mumbled to Jimmy:

"Come, Uncle Antonio's here."

A clear, unequivocal message. Jimmy shot Nugnes twice in the head. The boss finished him off himself. They dumped the body in a forty-meter well in the middle of the countryside and threw in two grenades. For years nothing was known about Antonio Nugnes. People would call in saying they'd spotted him in every corner of Italy, but he was actually at the bottom of a well, buried under tons of dirt. Thirteen years later, Augusto and his most trusted men told the carabinieri where to find the deputy mayor who had dared to oppose the growth of La Torre business. When the carabinieri started to collect the remains, they realized they were not just of one man. Four tibiae, two skulls, three hands. For more than ten years, Nugnes's body lay next to that of Vincenzo Boccolato, a Camorrista connected to Cutolo, but who joined the La Torres after Cutolo's defeat.

Boccolato was condemned to death because he deeply offended Augusto in a letter he sent to a friend from prison. The boss came across it by chance as he wandered around in an affiliate's living room. Flipping through some letters and papers, his eye caught his name. Curious, he read the heap of insults and criticisms Boccolato dumped on him. Even before finishing the letter, the boss decided he had to die. He sent Angelo Gagliardi, another former Cutolo affiliate, to kill him; Boccolato would get in his car without suspecting anything. Friends make the best killers. They do a clean job, no need to chase after a target who runs off screaming. Silently, when you least suspect it, they point the barrel of a gun at your neck and pull the trigger. Augusto La Torre wanted executions to be carried out with a friendly intimacy. He couldn't bear being ridiculed and didn't want anyone to laugh when his name was uttered. No one should dare.

Luigi Pellegrino, whom everyone knew as Gigiotto, was one of those people who enjoyed gossiping about the city's powerful figures.

Lots of kids in the land of the Camorra whisper about the sexual preferences of bosses, the orgies of neighborhood capos, and the whoring daughters of clan businessmen. The bosses usually put up with it, though. They've got other things to think about, and after all, it's inevitable that the people in command give rise to quite a bit of talk. Gigiotto spread rumors about the boss's wife, saying he'd seen her with one of Augusto's most trusted men. Seen the boss's driver take her to meet her lover. The La Torre clan's number one, the man who controlled everything, had a wife who was cheating on him right under his nose, and he didn't even realize it. Gigiotto repeated his stories, always with more details, always with slight variations. Lie or no lie, by now everyone was telling the funny story of the boss's wife's affair with her husband's right-hand man. They were careful to mention the source: Gigiotto. One day Gigiotto was walking in downtown Mondragone when he heard a motorcycle coming a little too close on the sidewalk. He started to run as soon as it slowed down. Two shots were fired, but Gigiotto, zigzagging among people and lampposts, fled while the killer, stuck behind the motorcyclist, unloaded his entire charger. So he chased Gigiotto on foot, to a bar where he was trying to hide. He pulled out his pistol and shot him in the head in front of dozens of people who vanished quickly and silently a moment later. According to the investigations, it was Giuseppe Fragnoli, clan regent, who had wanted Gigiotto eliminated; without even asking for authorization, he decided to silence the tongue wagger who was sullying the image of the boss.

In Augusto's mind, Mondragone, the surrounding countryside, coastline, and sea were nothing more than the clan's workshop, a laboratory for him and his colleagues, an area from which to extract material to be churned into profit by their companies. He categorically prohibited drug dealing in Mondragone and along the Domitian coast, with the severest level of command that Caserta bosses issue to their subordinates, or anyone. The command was morally motivated: to save his fellow townspeople from heroin and cocaine—but it was more to keep the clan's unskilled pushers from gaining an economic foothold in his territory, from growing rich within the bosom of power and being able to oppose his leadership. Drugs from Holland, sold on the Roman market by the Mondragone cartel, were absolutely forbidden. People from Mondragone had to get in the car and drive all the way to Rome to buy pot, coke, and heroin, sold through the Neapolitans, Casalesi, and Mondragonesi themselves. The clan formed an antidrug group called GAD, which would call the police switchboard and claim responsibility for its actions. If they caught you with a joint in your mouth, they'd break your nose. If a wife discovered a packet of cocaine, all she had to do was let the GAD know, and after being kicked and punched in the face, after the gas stations refused to fill his tank for the drive to Rome, her husband would change his mind.

An Egyptian boy, Hassa Fakhry, paid heavily for being a heroin addict. He raised pigs. Black Caserta pigs, a rare breed. Darker than buffaloes, squat and hairy, accordions of fat from which lean sausages, tasty salami, and flavorful chops were made. Being a swineherd is a horrendous job. Constantly shoveling manure, slitting the animals' throats, hanging them upside down, and letting the blood drip into basins. Hassa had been a driver in Egypt, but he came from a family of farmers so he knew how to handle animals. But not pigs. To a Muslim, pigs were doubly disgusting. But better to take care of pigs than spend the whole day shoveling buffalo manure as the Indians do. Pigs don't shit half as much, and pigsties are tiny compared to bovine stalls. Every Arab knows this, so they go for pigs rather than ending up faint with exhaustion from the buffalo. Hassa started doing heroin. He'd take the train to Rome, make his purchase, and return to the pigsty. He became a serious addict and never had enough cash, so his pusher suggested he try peddling in Mondragone, a city with no drug market. Hassa accepted and started pushing outside the Bar Domizia. He established a clientele and could earn in ten hours what he'd make in six months as a swineherd. All it took was one phone call on the part of the bar owner to put an end to his activity. That's how it works around here. You call a friend who calls his cousin who tells his *compare* who relays the news to whoever needs to know. A chain of which only the beginning and end points are known. After a few days La Torre's men, the self-proclaimed GAD, went right to Hassa's hovel and knocked at the door. They pretended to be police officers so he wouldn't escape amid pigs and buffalo, forcing a chase in the mud and shit. They loaded him into the car and started to drive away, but they didn't take the road to headquarters. As soon as Hassa realized they were about to kill him, he suffered a strange allergic reaction. His body started to swell up, as if someone were forcing him full of air—as if fear had sparked an anaphylactic shock. Augusto La Torre himself, when he told the story to the judges, was aghast at the metamorphosis: the Egyptian's eyes became tiny, as if being sucked into his head, his pores exuded a thick, honey sweat, and his mouth foamed ricotta. There were eight killers, but only seven fired. The *pentito* Mario Sperlongano stated, "It seemed completely pointless to shoot at a dead body." But that's how it always was. Augusto seemed intoxicated by his own imperial name. Every one of his legionnaires had to stand behind him and all his actions. Murders that could be taken care of by one or two men were instead carried out by all his most trusted legionnaires, who were usually expected to fire at least one shot, even if the person was already dead. One for all and all for one. Augusto required full participation, even when it was superfluous. The constant fear that someone could pull back made him always act in a group. Clan dealings in Amsterdam, Aberdeen, London, and Caracas might make some affiliate lose his head and think he could go out on his own. Here savageness is the true value of commerce: to renounce it is to lose everything. After they killed Hassa Fakhry, they stuck hundreds of insulin syringes, the kind heroin addicts use, in his body. A message on his flesh, which everyone in Mondragone and Formia would immediately understand.

The boss wasn't concerned about other people. When Paolo Montano, known as Zumpariello, one of the most reliable men in his hit squad, started doing drugs and couldn't break his cocaine habit, Augusto had one of his faithful friends summon him to a meeting on a farm. When they arrived, Ernesto Cornacchia was supposed to unload his entire charger into Zumpariello, but the boss was standing too close and Cornacchia was afraid he would also hit him. Seeing Ernesto hesitate, Augusto took out his pistol and killed Montano himself. The shots pierced his body, hitting Cornacchia as well, but he preferred to take a bullet rather than risk wounding the boss. Zumpariello was thrown in a well and blown up, Mondragone-style.

Augusto's legionnaires would do anything for him. They even followed him when he turned state's witness. In January 2003, after his wife's arrest, the boss decided to take the big step. He accused himself and his men of forty or so homicides, gave the locations of the wells where they'd exploded people, and charged himself with dozens and dozens of extortions. A confession that focused more on military than economic aspects. His most loyal men—Mario Sperlongano, Giuseppe Valente, Girolamo Rozzera, Pietro Scuttini, Salvatore Orabona, Ernesto Cornacchia, Angelo Gagliardi—soon followed him. Once in jail, silence becomes the bosses' best weapon for holding on to authority, for formally maintaining power, even if the harsh prison routine removes them from hands-on management. But Augusto La Torre is a special case: by confessing and having all his men follow suit, there was no fear that someone would kill his family as a result of his defection. Nor did collaborating with the authorities seem to undermine the Mondragone cartel's economic empire. His confession only helped reveal the logic of the killings and the history of power along the Caserta and Lazio coast. Like many Camorra bosses, Augusto La Torre spoke of the past. Without *pentiti*, the history of power could not be written. Without *pentiti* the truth of the facts, details, and mechanisms is only discovered ten, twenty years later, as if a man were to understand how his vital organs worked only after he is dead.

• • •

Collaboration on the part of Augusto La Torre and his chiefs of staff presents a certain risk; they could receive substantial sentence reductions in exchange for confessing about the past and be released a few years later. After delegating military power to others, above all the Albanian crime families, they could maintain their legal economic power. It's as if they decided to tell the whole truth and nothing but the truth, to use their knowledge as a way of living on their legal activities only and to avoid life sentences and internal feuds in the process. Augusto had never been able to stand being locked up; unlike the great bosses who'd trained him, he was incapable of surviving decades of incarceration. He expected the prison cafeteria to serve vegetarian food. And as he loved movies but wasn't allowed a VCR in his cell, when he felt like seeing *The Godfather*, he'd ask a local broadcaster to air it in the evening, before he went to bed.

For the magistrates, La Torre's collaboration is laden with ambiguity, for he did not renounce his role as boss. That his revelations were an extension of his power is shown in a letter Augusto had delivered to his uncle, in which he reassures him that he "saved" him from any possible involvement in clan affairs, but, good storyteller that he is, he also does not fail to threaten him and two other relatives, thus averting the possibility that an alliance against him could develop in Mondragone:

"Your son-in-law and his father feel protected by the walking dead."

The boss, even as a *pentito*, still asked for money from his jail cell in the Aquila prison. He got around the System by delivering commands and requests for cash in letters he gave to his mother or driver, Pietro Scuttini. According to the magistrates, those requests were actually extortions. A polite, courteous letter to the owner of one of the largest cheese makers on the Domitian coast proves that Augusto still considered him under his control.

"Dear Peppe, I need to ask you a huge favor, because I've been ru-ined. If you would like to help me—but I only ask in the name of our old friendship and not for any other reason, and even if you say no, don't worry, I'll always look out for you! I am in urgent need of ten thousand euros. You also have to tell me if you can give me a thou-sand euros a month, which I need to live with my children."

The standard of living the La Torre family was used to was way above the level of economic assistance the state provides to those who collaborate with the authorities. I only managed to understand the family dealings after reading the documents of the mega-sequester carried out under the Santa Maria Capua Vetere Court or-ders in 1992. They seized properties worth about 230 million euros, nineteen companies worth 323 million euros, as well as manufactur-ing equipment and machinery worth 133 million euros. Numerous factories located along the coast between Naples and Gaeta, includ-ing a dairy, a sugar refinery, four supermarkets, nine seaside villas, buildings, and lands, as well as big cars and motorcycles. Every com-pany had about sixty employees. The judges also ordered sequestered the company that had won the trash-collection contract in Mondrag-one. A huge operation that annulled a vast economic power, but mi-croscopic compared to actual clan operations. A grandiose villa near Ariana di Gaeta, whose fame had reached all the way to Aberdeen, was also seized. Four stories, right on the cliffs, a swimming pool complete with underwater labyrinth, designed after the villa of Tiberius—not the founder of the Mondragone clan, but the Roman emperor who had retired to the island of Capri. I never did get inside; legends and court documents were the lens through which I learned of the existence of this imperial mausoleum, sentinel of the clan's Italian properties. The coastal zone could have been a sort of infinite space, inspiring every architectural fantasy imaginable. Instead over time it became a hodgepodge of houses and small villas, thrown up quickly to attract tourists to southern Lazio and Naples. No zoning regulations, no permits. As a result, groups of African immigrants were crammed into cottages from Castelvolturno to Mondragone, and the parks that were planned, the grounds that were supposed to contain new conglomerations of vacation homes, became unregulated dumps. None of the coastal towns had a purification plant. Now a brownish sea bathes beaches covered in trash. In a few years, even the most remote remembrance of beauty had been canceled out. In the summertime some nightclubs turned into regular brothels. Friends, preparing for the evening's activities, would show me their empty wallets. Empty not of cash, but of thin foil packets with a circular soul—condoms. They were letting it be known that it was safe to go to Mondragone to fuck without protection: "Tonight we go without!"

Augusto La Torre was Mondragone's condom. The boss decided to keep watch over the health of his subjects. Mondragone became a sort of temple completely safe from the most dreaded of sexually transmitted diseases. While the rest of the world was plagued with HIV, northern Caserta was completely under control. The clan was meticulous, tracking everyone's test results. To the extent possible, the clan kept complete lists; they did not want their territory infected. And so when a man close to Augusto tested positive for HIV, they found out immediately. Fernando Brodella frequented the local girls; he could be dangerous. Unlike the Bidognetti clan, who sent their affiliates to the best doctors and paid for surgery in the top hospitals in Europe, the La Torres didn't even consider sending Brodella to a good doctor or paying for his treatment. They killed him in cold blood. Clan orders: eliminate the sick to stop the epidemic. An infectious disease, especially one transmitted sexually, through the least controllable act, could only be stopped by removing those who were infected once and for all. The only way to be sure they would not infect anyone was to end their lives.

Capital investments in Campania also had to be safe. They even bought a villa in Anacapri that housed the local carabinieri headquarters. With carabinieri as tenants, they were guaranteed not to run into any difficulties. When the La Torres realized the villa would bring in more money with tourists, they evicted the carabinieri and divided it into six apartments with a yard and parking spaces—before the anti-Mafia division arrived and seized the whole place. Clean, safe investments, with no speculative risks.

After Augusto turned state's witness, the new boss, Luigi Fragnoli, a La Torre loyalist, started having problems with some affiliates such as Giuseppe Mancone, also known as Rambo. Rambo bore a vague resemblance to Stallone, his body pumped up from weight lifting. The drug market he'd established was gaining in importance; soon he would be able to kick out the old bosses, whose reputation had been shattered by the *pentiti*. According to the anti-Mafia prosecutor, the Mondragone clans asked the Birra family from Ercolano to hire the killers. Two hit men arrived in Mondragone to take out Rambo in August 2003. They showed up on one of those big motor scooters—not terribly maneuverable, but so menacing they couldn't resist using it for the ambush. They'd never set foot in Mondragone, but didn't have any problems spotting their victim; he was at the Roxy Bar, as always. The motorbike came to a halt. One of them got off, walked decisively up to Rambo, unloaded an entire charger into him, then returned to the bike.

"Everything all set? You did it?"

"Yeah, I did it, go go go."

There was a group of kids near the bar, deciding what to do for the August 15 *ferragosto* holiday. As soon as they saw the guys from Ercolano, they realized what was going on; there was no mistaking the sound of an automatic for fireworks. They all lay down, face to the ground, fearing to be seen by the killer as potential witnesses. Only one person didn't look away. One person stared at the killer without lowering her eyes, without pressing her chest to the tarmac or covering her face with her hands. A thirty-five-year-old schoolteacher. The woman testified, made identifications, reported the killing. Among the many reasons for keeping quiet, for pretending nothing happened, for going home and living as before, are the fear of intimidation and, even more, futility—one killer arrested was one out of many. And yet among the slag heap of reasons to keep quiet, the Mondragone schoolteacher found one motivation to speak: the truth. A truth that seems natural, like an everyday, habitual gesture, an obvious and necessary act, like breathing. She testified without asking anything in return. She didn't expect a stipend or police protection, didn't set a price on her word. She told what she'd seen, described the killer's face, his angular features and thick eyebrows. After the shooting, the motor scooter sped off, but it made several wrong turns, heading down dead-end streets and having to turn around. They seemed more like schizophrenic tourists than killers. In the trial that resulted from the schoolteacher's testimony, Salvatore Cefariello, the twenty-four-year-old killer considered to be in the pay of the Ercolano clans, was condemned for life. The judge who took the teacher's testimony called her "a rose in the desert," blooming in a land where truth is always the powerful people's version of things, where it is almost never stated, a rare commodity to be bartered for a profit.

And yet her confession made her life difficult. It was as if she had snagged a thread, and her entire existence unraveled along with her courageous testimony. She had been engaged, but her fiancé left her. She lost her job and was transferred to a protected location where she received a small state stipend, just enough to survive. Some family members took their distance from her, and a profound loneliness descended upon her. A loneliness that explodes violently in her daily life when she wants to dance and has no one to dance with, when cell phones are never answered, when friends stop calling and eventually disappear. It wasn't testifying in itself that generated such fear, or her identifying a killer that caused such a scandal. The logic of *omertà* isn't so simple. What made the young teacher's gesture scandalous is that she considered being able to testify something natural, instinctive, and vital. In a land where truth is considered to be what gets you something and lying what makes you lose, living as if you actually believe truth can exist is incomprehensible. So the people around you feel uncomfortable, undressed by the gaze of one who has renounced the rules of life itself, which they have fully accepted. And accepted without feeling ashamed, because in the end that's just how things are and have always been; you can't change it all on your own, and so it's better to save your energy, stay on track, and live the way you're supposed to live.

In Aberdeen my eyes were confronted with the material success of Italian entrepreneurship. It's odd to see the distant branches if you know the roots. I don't know how to describe it, but seeing the restaurants, offices, insurance firms, and buildings was like being grabbed by the ankles, turned upside down, and flung about until everything—house keys and small change—fell out of my pockets and mouth, even my soul, if that can be commercialized. The cash flows radiate in all directions, sucking energy from the center. Knowing this is not the same as seeing it. I went with Matteo to a job interview. They hired him, obviously. He wanted me to stay in Aberdeen as well.

"Here all you have to do is be yourself, Robbe'."

Matteo had to be from Campania to have that aura, to have his résumé, degree, and desire to work be appreciated. The very origins that in Scotland allowed him to become a full-fledged citizen classified him in Italy as little more than a waste of a man, devoid of protection and importance, defeated right from the start because he hadn't set his life on the proper track. Matteo suddenly burst into a happiness never seen before. The more his spirits soared, the more I was weighed down by a bitter melancholy. I've never been able to take enough distance from the place I was born and the behavior of people I hated; I've never felt myself truly different from the fierce dynamics that crush lives and longing. Being born in certain places means you're like a hunting dog, born with the smell of the hare already in your nose. You chase after the hare even against your own will, even if, once you catch it, you snap your jaws and let it go. I was able to follow the routes, streets, and paths with unconscious obsession, with a cursed ability to understand completely the conquered territories.

I wanted to get out of Scotland, go away and never set foot in that country again. I left as soon as I could. I had trouble sleeping on the plane; the lack of air and the darkness outside my window grabbed my throat, as if I were wearing a tie that was too tight, pressing against my Adam's apple. Perhaps my claustrophobia wasn't caused by a tiny seat on a minuscule plane, or by the darkness outside, but by the sensation of being crushed in a reality like a chicken coop crammed full of starving birds, ready to eat and be eaten. As if everything were just one territory with one dimension and one syntax, understood everywhere. A feeling of no exit, of being constrained to join the big battle or not exist. I returned to Italy thinking about the tracks on which high-speed trains travel; the capital flowing into the great European economy rushes in one direction, while in the other—southbound—comes everything that would be infectious elsewhere, entering and exiting through the forced nets of the open and flexible economy, creating—in the continuous cycle of transformation—wealth elsewhere, but without ever triggering any form of development in the lands where the metamorphosis began.

Rubbish has swollen the belly of southern Italy, stretching it like a pregnant belly, but the fetus never grows; it aborts money, then immediately becomes pregnant again, only to abort and conceive again, to the point where the body is ruined, the arteries are clogged, the lungs filled, the synapses destroyed. Over and over and over again.

LAND OF FIRES

It's not hard to imagine something, not hard to picture in your mind a person or gesture, or something that doesn't exist. It's not even complicated to imagine your own death. It's far more difficult to imagine the economy in all its aspects: the finances, profit percentages, negotiations, debts, and investments. There are no faces to visualize, nothing precise to fix in your mind. You may be able to picture the impact of the economy, but not its cash flows, bank accounts, individual transactions. If you try to imagine it all, you risk shutting your eyes to concentrate and racking your brains till you start seeing those psychedelic distortions painted on the backs of your eyelids.

I kept trying to construct in my mind an image of the economy, something that could convey the idea of its process and production, its buying and selling. But it was impossible to come up with a flow chart, something of precise iconic compactness. Perhaps the only way to represent the workings of the economy is to understand what it leaves behind, to follow the trail of parts that fall away, like flaking of dead skin, as it marches onward.

The most concrete emblem of every economic cycle is the dump. Accumulating everything that ever was, dumps are the true aftermath of consumption, something more than the mark every product leaves on the surface of the earth. The south of Italy is the end of the line for the dregs of production, useless leftovers, and toxic waste. If all the trash that, according to the Italian environmental group Legambiente, escapes official inspection were collected in one place, it would form a mountain weighing 14 million tons and rising 47,900 feet from a base of three hectares. Mont Blanc rises 15,780 feet, Everest 29,015. So this heap of unregulated and unreported waste would be the highest mountain on earth. This immense mountain is how I came to imagine the DNA of the economy, its commercial transactions and profit dividends, the additions and subtractions of accountants. It is as if this mountain had exploded and scattered over the south of Italy, in particular in Campania, Sicily, Calabria, and Puglia, the regions with the greatest number of environmental crimes. These same regions head the list for the largest criminal associations, the highest unemployment rate, and the greatest number of volunteers for the military and the police forces. Always the same list, eternal and immutable. In the last thirty years, the area around Caserta, between the Garigliano River and Lake Patria—the land of the Mazzoni clan—has absorbed tons of ordinary and toxic waste.

Hardest hit by the cancer of traffic in poisons are the outskirts of Naples—Giugliano, Qualiano, Villaricca, Nola, Acerra, and Marigliano—and the nearly 115 square miles comprising the towns of Grazzanise, Cancello Arnone, Santa Maria La Fossa, Castelvolturno, and Casal di Principe. On no other land in the Western world has a greater amount of toxic and nontoxic waste been illegally dumped. In the last five years the trash business has shown an overall increase of 29.8 percent, a growth comparable only to that of the cocaine market. The Camorra clans became the European leaders in waste disposal in the late 1990s; together with their middlemen, they have lined their pockets with 44 billion euros in proceeds in four years. In 2002 the parliamentary report from the minister of the interior noted a shift from rubbish collection to a pact among certain insiders in the business, aimed at exercising full control over the entire cycle. Waste management has become such big business that, despite continuous tensions, the two branches of the Casalesi clan, headed by Sandokan Schiavone and Francesco *Cicciotto di Mezzanotte* Bidognetti, have shared the vast market without arriving at a head-on collision. But the Casalesi are not alone. The Mallardo clan of Giugliano distributes an immense quantity of refuse throughout its territory and swiftly apportions its revenues. An abandoned quarry in the area was discovered to be completely overflowing with trash—the equivalent of twenty-eight thousand tractor trailers. Imagine a line of trucks, bumper to bumper, that runs from Caserta all the way to Milan.

The bosses have had no qualms about saturating their towns with toxins and letting the lands that surround their estates go bad. The life of a boss is short; the power of a clan, between vendettas, arrests, killings, and life sentences, cannot last for long. To flood an area with toxic waste and circle one's city with poisonous mountain ranges is a problem only for someone with a sense of social responsibility and a long-term concept of power. In the here and now of business, there are no negatives, only a high profit margin. Most trafficking in toxic waste runs in just one direction: north to south. Eighteen thousand tons of toxic waste from Brescia have been dumped around Naples and Caserta since the late 1990s, and a million tons ended up in Santa Maria Capua Vetere over four years. Refuse from northern treatment facilities in Milan, Pavia, and Pisa has been shipped to Campania. The public prosecutor's offices in Naples and Santa Maria Capua Vetere, led by Donato Ceglie, discovered that in 2003 more than sixty-five hundred tons of refuse from Lombardy arrived in Trentola Ducenta near Caserta over the space of forty days.

The countrysides around Naples and Caserta are veritable maps of garbage, litmus tests of Italian industry. The destiny of countless Italian industrial products can be seen in the local landfills and quarries. I've always liked riding my Vespa along the dumps, on country roads that have been cemented over to facilitate truck traffic. I feel I'm moving among the remains of civilization or the strata of commercial transactions, flanking pyramids of production or the record of distances traveled; here the geography of things creates a varied and multiform mosaic. Every scrap of production, the leftovers from every activity, end up here. One day a farmer was plowing a newly purchased field on the line between Naples and Caserta when all of a sudden the tractor motor stalled, as if the earth were unusually compact in that spot. Bits of paper started sprouting up on either side of the plow. Money. Thousands, hundreds of thousands of bills. The farmer threw himself from his tractor and began frenetically collecting the loot hidden by some unknown thief, the fruit of some unknown heist. But it was merely shredded and faded scraps. Minced money from the Banca d'Italia, bales of consumed currency, now out of circulation. The temple of the lira had ended up underground, the bits of old paper currency leaching lead into a cauliflower field.

Near Villaricca the carabinieri identified a piece of land where paper towels from hundreds of dairy farms in the Veneto, Emilia-Romagna, and Lombardy had been dumped: towels used for cleaning cow udders. Farmhands have to clean the udders constantly—two, three, four times a day—every time they attach the suction cups of the automatic milker. As a result the cows often develop mastitis and similar diseases and begin to secrete pus and blood. They're not allowed to rest, however. Their udders are simply cleaned every half hour so that the pus and blood do not get into the milk and ruin an entire can. Maybe it was just my imagination, or perhaps the heaps of yellowish udder paper distorted my senses, but they smelled like sour milk. The fact is that the trash, accumulated over decades, has reconfigured the horizons, created previously nonexistent hills, invented new odors, and suddenly restored lost mass to mountains devoured by quarries. Walking in the Campania hinterlands, one absorbs the odors of everything that industry produces. Seeing the earth mixed with the arterial, poisonous blood from an entire region of factories, I am reminded of a plasticine ball, the kind children make, using every available color. For decades the city of Milan's trash was dumped near Grazzanise; all the trash collected in the city's garbage bins or swept up each morning by the street cleaners was shipped here. Eight hundred tons of waste from the province of Milan end up in Germany every day, yet the total trash production is thirteen hundred tons. Five hundred tons are missing from official records. Where they end up is unclear, but it's highly probable that this phantom refuse is scattered about the south of Italy. Printer toner also fouls the land, as the 2006 operation coordinated by the Santa Maria Capua Vetere public prosecutor's office and entitled *Madre Terra*—Mother Earth—discovered. At night, trucks officially transporting compost or fertilizer were dumping toner from Tuscan and Lombard offices in Villa Literno, Castelvolturno, and San Tammaro. Every time it rained, a strong, acid smell blossomed: the land had become saturated with hexavalent chromium. Once inhaled, it lodges in the red blood cells and hair and causes ulcers, respiratory and kidney problems, and lung cancer.

Every foot of land has its own type of trash. A dentist friend of mine once told me that a group of boys had brought him some skulls. Real human skulls. They wanted him to clean the teeth. Like so many little Hamlets, each boy held a skull in one hand and a wad of money to pay for the dental work in the other. The dentist threw them out of his office and then called me, agitated. "Where the hell do they get those skulls? Where do they find them?" He was imagining apocalyptic scenes, satanic rites, boys initiated in the language of Beelzebub. I just laughed. It wasn't hard to figure out. I once got a flat tire passing Santa Maria Capua Vetere on my Vespa; I'd run over what looked like a sharp stick. First I thought it was a buffalo femur, but it was too small. It was a human femur. Cemeteries periodically perform exhumations, removing what younger gravediggers call the superdead, those buried for more than forty years. The cemetery directors are supposed to call specialized firms to dispose of the bodies, caskets, and everything else, down to the votive lamps. Removal is expensive, so the directors bribe the gravediggers to throw everything together on a truck: dirt, rotting caskets, and bones. Great-great-grandparents and great-grandparents, ancestors from who knows where, were piling up in the Caserta countryside. In February 2006 the Caserta NAS—the branch of the carabinieri in charge of monitoring food adulteration and protecting public health—discovered that so many dead had been dumped in Santa Maria Capua Vetere that people crossed themselves when they passed by, as if it were a cemetery. Young boys would steal the rubber gloves from their mothers' kitchens and dig with hands and spoons for skulls and intact rib cages. Flea market vendors pay up to 100 euros for a skull with white teeth. A rib cage with all the ribs in place could bring up to 300 euros. There's no market for shin, thigh, or arm bones; hands, yes, but they decompose easily in the soil. Skulls with blackened teeth are worth 50 euros. There's not much of a market for them; potential buyers are not repulsed by the idea of death, apparently, but by tooth enamel that eventually starts to decay.

The clans manage to drain all sorts of things from north to south. The bishop of Nola called the south of Italy the illegal dumping ground for the rich, industrialized north. Dross from the thermal metallurgy of aluminum; smoke-abatement dust from the steel and iron industry; derivatives from thermoelectric plants and incinerators; paint dregs; liquids contaminated with heavy metals; asbestos; polluted soil from reclamation projects that then pollutes other, previously uncontaminated soil; toxic waste from old petrochemical companies such as the old Enichem of Priolo; sludge from tanning factories near Santa Croce sull'Arno; and sediment from the purifiers of primarily publicly owned companies in Venice and Forlí.

Large companies as well as small businesses eager to rid themselves cheaply of material from which they can no longer extract anything except costs are the first step in illegal disposal. Next come the warehouse owners who shuffle the documents and collect the waste;

often they dilute the toxic concentration by mixing it with regular trash, thereby registering the whole as below the toxic level set by the CER, the waste catalog of the European Community. Chemicals are essential for rebaptizing toxic waste as innocuous trash. Many operators supply false identification forms and deceptive analytic codes. Then there are the carriers who haul the waste to the selected dump site. Finally there are the people who allow for disposal: managers of authorized landfills or compost facilities where waste is turned into fertilizer, as well as owners of abandoned quarries or farmlands given over to illegal dumping. Any space with an owner can become a dump site. Fundamental to the success of the whole operation are public officials and employees who do not check or verify procedures or who allow people clearly involved in organized crime to manage quarries or landfills. The clans do not need to make blood pacts with politicians or ally themselves with political parties. All it takes is one official, one technician, one employee—one individual who wants to add to his salary. And so the business is conducted, with extreme flexibility and quiet discretion, and turns a profit for every party involved. But its architects are the stakeholders; they are the real criminal geniuses of illegal toxic-waste management. The best Italian stakeholders are shaped here, in Naples, Salerno, and Caserta. Stakeholders in business jargon are entrepreneurs who are involved in an economic project in such a way as to directly or indirectly influence its outcome. Toxic-waste stakeholders have come to constitute a regular managerial class. During the stagnant stretches of my life when I was out of work, it was not unusual for someone to say to me, "You have a college degree and the skills, why don't you become a stake?"

In southern Italy, at least for college graduates whose fathers are not lawyers or accountants, becoming a stakeholder is a sure path to enrichment and professional satisfaction. Educated and presentable, they study environmental policy in the United States or England for a few years and then become middlemen. I knew one. One of the first. One of the best. His name was Franco. Before listening to him and watching him work, I understood nothing of the treasure trove of trash. I met him on the train on the way back from Milan. He had graduated from the Bocconi—Italy's most prestigious business school —and in Germany had become an expert in environmental renewal policy. One of the stakeholder's prime skills is knowing the European Community's waste catalog by heart and understanding how to maneuver within it, so as to work around the regulations and to find hidden shortcuts into the business community. Franco was originally from Villa Literno, and he wanted to involve me in his trade. The first thing he told me about his work was the importance of physical appearance, the dos and don'ts of the successful stakeholder. If you have a receding hairline or a bald spot, it is strictly forbidden to wear a toupee or grow your hair long to comb it across your scalp. For a winning image, you should shave your head, or at least keep your hair short. According to Franco, if a stakeholder is invited to a party, he must avoid skirt-chasing and always be accompanied by a woman. If he doesn't have a girlfriend or a suitable date, he should hire an escort, a companion of the elegant, deluxe sort.

Stakeholders approach owners of chemical plants, tanneries, and plastics factories and show them their price list. Waste removal is an expense that no Italian businessman feels is necessary. The stakes all say exactly the same thing: "The crap they shit is worth more to them than trash, which they have to drop heaps of money to get rid of." Stakeholders must never give the impression that they are offering a criminal service, however. They put the industrialists in touch with the clans' trash disposers, then coordinate every step of the process from a distance.

There are two types of waste producers: those whose only objective is to save on price and who have no concern for the trustworthiness of the removal companies, considering their responsibility complete as soon as the poison leaves their premises; and those directly implicated in the operations, who illegally dispose of the waste themselves. Yet in both cases stakeholder mediation is necessary to guarantee transportation and identify a dump site, and for help in contacting the right person to declassify the waste. The stakeholder's office is his car, and he moves hundreds of thousands of tons of waste with a phone and a portable computer. He earns a percentage on the contracts relative to the number of kilos slated for removal. His prices vary. For example, thinners, when handled by a stakeholder with ties to the clans, go for from 10 to 30 eurocents a kilo. Phosphorus sulfide is 1 euro a kilo. Street sweepings 55 cents; packaging with traces of hazardous substances, 1.40 euros; contaminated soil up to 2.30 euros; cemetery remains 15 cents; fluff, or nonmetallic car parts, 1.85 euros, transportation included. The clients' needs and the difficulty of transport are factored into the prices. The quantities handled by stakeholders are enormous, their profit margins exponential.

Operation Houdini, carried out in 2004, revealed that just one establishment in the Veneto illegally managed about two hundred thousand tons of waste a year. The market price for legal disposal ranges from 21 to 62 cents a kilo, while the clans provide the same service at 9 or 10 cents a kilo. In 2004 the stakeholders in Campania saw to it that eight hundred tons of soil contaminated with hydrocarbon from a chemical company were handled at 25 cents a kilo, transportation included—a savings of 80 percent on regular prices.

The real strength of the stakeholders who work with the Camorra is their full-service guarantee, whereas those employed by legitimate enterprises offer higher prices that do not include transportation. Yet stakeholders hardly ever become clan members. There's no reason to. Their nonaffiliation is an advantage to both parties: they work freelance for several families, have no hit-squad obligations or specific duties, and do not become battle pawns. A few are nabbed in every roundup, but the sentences are light: it's difficult to prove their direct responsibility because they do not formally participate in any step of the illegal dumping.

Over time I learned to see with the eyes of a stakeholder. A different point of view from that of a builder. A builder sees empty space as something to be filled and tries to occupy the void; a stakeholder looks for the empty space in what is already full. When walking about, Franco did not look at the landscape but thought instead about how to insert something in it. He'd search the land as if it were a giant carpet, look at the mountains and fields for the corner he could lift up and sweep things under. Once when we were walking together, Franco noted an abandoned gas station and realized immediately that the underground tanks could hold dozens of drums of chemical waste. A perfect tomb. Such was his life—an endless search for emptiness. Franco later gave up stakeholding; he stopped chewing up the miles in his car, meeting with businessmen from the northeast, being called all over Italy. He set up a professional training course. Franco's most important students were Chinese, from Hong Kong. Asian stakeholders learned from their Italian counterparts how to do business with European companies, offering good prices and speedy solutions. When the cost of waste removal in England increased, Chinese stakeholders educated in Campania moved in to offer their services. In March 2005 the Dutch port police in Rotterdam discovered a thousand tons of English urban trash that had officially been passed off as pulp paper for recycling. Every year a million tons of high-tech waste from Europe are unloaded in China. The stakeholders relocate the waste in Guiyu, northeast of Hong Kong. Entombed, shoved underground, drowned in artificial lakes. Just as in Caserta, Guiyu has been contaminated so quickly that the groundwater is now completely polluted, and drinking water must be imported from neighboring provinces. The Hong Kong stakeholders' dream is to make the port of Naples the hub for European refuse, a floating collection center where the gold of trash can be crammed into containers for burial in China.

The stakeholders from Campania are the best; with the clans' help, they beat out the Calabrese, Pugliese, and Roman competition by turning the region's landfills into one enormous, unlimited discount store. In thirty years of trafficking they've managed to confiscate and dispose of all sorts of things, with one sole objective: to bring down the costs so as to contract for greater quantities. King Midas, a 2003 investigation that took its name from an intercepted phone call—"As soon as we touch the trash, it turns into gold"—revealed that every step of the waste cycle makes a profit.

When Franco and I were in the car together, I'd listen to his phone conversations. He'd supply instant advice on how and where to dump toxic waste. He'd discuss copper, arsenic, mercury, cadmium, lead, chrome, nickel, cobalt, and molybdenum, move from tannery residues to hospital waste, from urban trash to tires, and explain what to do, carrying in his head entire lists of people and places to turn to. When I thought about poisons mixed in with compost, about tombs of highly toxic waste carved out of the body of the countryside, I went pale. Franco noticed.

"Does this job disgust you? Robbe', do you know that the stakeholders are the ones who made it possible for this shit country to enter the European Union? Yes or no? Do you know how many workers' asses have been saved because I fixed it so their companies didn't spend a fucking cent?"

Franco's birthplace had trained him well, ever since his boyhood. He knew that in business you earn or you lose—there's no room for anything else—and he didn't want to lose or make the people he worked for lose. He justified his actions—to himself and to me—with fierce statistics, which completely altered my previous understanding of toxic waste management. By combining all the data from the Naples and Santa Maria Capua Vetere public prosecutors' investigations from the late 1990s to the present, it is possible to calculate the economic advantage for businesses that turn to the Camorra for waste removal as 500 million euros. I knew that these investigations reflected only a percentage of the actual infractions, and it made my head spin. With the dead weight of disposal costs lightened by

Neapolitan and Casertan clans, many northern businesses were able to expand, hire workers, and make the entire industrial fabric of the country competitive, which was what pushed Italy into the European Union. Schiavone, Mallardo, Moccia, Bidognetti, La Torre, and all the other families offered a criminal service that relaunched and energized the Italian economy. The 2003 Operation Cassiopea revealed that every week forty tractor trailers filled with waste left the north and headed south; according to the investigators' reconstructions, they dumped, buried, or otherwise disposed of cadmium, zinc, paint residue, purification-plant sludge, various plastics, arsenic, steel mill by-products, and lead. North-south is the traffickers' privileged route. Through stakeholders, many a business in the Veneto and Lombardy has adopted a territory in Naples or Caserta and transformed it into an enormous dump site. It's estimated that in the last five years around 3 million tons of waste has illegally been dumped in Campania, 1 million alone in the province of Caserta, an area specifically designated for this purpose in the clans' urban development "plans."

Tuscany, the most environmentally conscious region of Italy, plays a significant role in the geography of the illicit traffic. According to at least three investigations, King Midas in 2003, and Fly and Organic Agriculture in 2004, numerous steps of the process, from production to brokering, are concentrated here.

Not only do enormous quantities of illegally managed waste come from Tuscany, the region is also a regular base of operations for a whole host of persons involved in these criminal activities, from stakeholders to cooperating chemists to owners of compost sites who allow waste to be mixed with the compost. But the domain of toxic waste recycling is expanding. Further investigations have revealed activity in Umbria and Molise, regions that had seemed immune. In Molise, the 2004 Operation Fly, coordinated by the federal public prosecutor's office of Larino, brought to light the illegal removal of 120 tons of special waste from the metallurgy, steel, and iron industries. The clans ground up 320 tons of old road surface with an elevated tar density and had identified a compost site ready to mix it with fill so as to hide it in the Umbrian countryside. Such recycling metamorphoses generate exponential earnings at every step. It's not enough to disguise the toxic content; further gains can be had by transforming the poisons into fertilizer and selling it. Four hectares of land near the Molise coast were tilled with fertilizer derived from tannery wastes; nine tons of grain with elevated concentrations of chrome were recovered. The traffickers had chosen the Molise coast—the section between Termoli and Campomarino—to illegally dump dangerous and special wastes from northern Italian businesses. But according to recent investigations by the Santa Maria Capua Vetere public prosecutor's office, the true center for stockpiling is the Veneto, which has fed illegal traffic nationwide for years. The foundries in the north carelessly dispose of their dross, mixing it with the compost used to fertilize hundreds of agricultural fields.

The Campania stakeholders often make use of the clans' drug-trade routes to discover new territories to hollow out, new tombs to fill. The 2003 Midas investigation reported that waste disposal traffickers were already making contacts in Albania and Costa Rica. But every channel is open now: to the east, to Romania, where the Casalesi have hundreds and hundreds of hectares of land; to Africa, to Mozambique, Somalia, and Nigeria, where the clans have always had backing and contacts. During the tsunami, one of the things that shocked me was seeing the worried, tense faces of Franco's colleagues. As soon as they saw the photos on the news, they turned pale, as if each one of them had a wife, a lover, or a child in danger. In truth, something much more precious was at risk: their business. After the tidal wave, hundreds of drums of hazardous or radioactive waste from the 1980s and 1990s were found on the beaches in Somalia, between Obbia and Warsheik. Media attention could have blocked the stockholders' new deals and outlets. But the danger was immediately averted. The charity campaigns for refugees diverted attention from the barrels of poison floating alongside the cadavers. Even the ocean has become a place for endless dumping. Traffickers increasingly fill ship holds with waste, then simulate an accident, letting the ship sink. They make money twice: the insurance covers the accident and the waste is entombed in the deep.

The clans find space everywhere for waste, but the regional administration of Campania, run for ten years by an external commission because of Camorra infiltrations, was unable to dispose of its own trash. While waste from every part of Italy was finding its way illegally to Campania, Campania trash was being shipped to Germany at fifty times the removal price the clans offered their clients. Investigations indicate that in the Naples area alone, of eighteen waste management firms, fifteen are directly tied to the Camorra clans.

The south is flooded with trash and it seems impossible to find a solution. For years the waste has been made into eco-bales, enormous cubes of ground-up garbage wrapped in white. Just to dispose of the eco-bales already accumulated would take fifty-six years. The only solution ever proposed is incineration. Such as at Acerra, where the very idea of building an incinerator generated rebellion and fierce opposition. The clans are ambivalent about incinerators. On the one hand they're opposed, since they would like to continue to live off landfills and fires, and the state of emergency also allows them to speculate on lands for eco-bale disposal, lands they themselves rent. Yet they're ready to subcontract construction and management if an incinerator were to be approved. Although the judiciary investigations have not yet reached their conclusions, the people have. They're terrorized, nervous, frightened. Afraid that in the clans' hands, incinerators will become perpetual furnaces for half of Italy's trash, and that all guarantees of environmental safety would be thwarted by the burning of poisons. Thousands of people are on the alert every time a defunct landfill is ordered reopened. Fearing that toxic waste passed off as ordinary trash will arrive from all over the place, they resist till the end rather than risk having their hometown become an uncontrolled depot for new dregs. When in February 2005 the regional commissioner attempted to reopen the landfill at Basso dell'Olmo near Salerno, townspeople spontaneously formed picket lines to impede the arrival of the trucks and block access to the dump. A continuous and constant defense, at all costs. Carmine Iuorio, thirty-four years old, died from exposure as he kept watch one terribly cold night. When they went to wake him in the morning, his beard was frozen and his lips were blue. He'd been dead for at least three hours.

The image of a landfill, pit, or quarry is increasingly a concrete and visible synonym for deadly danger for nearby residents. The Giugliano-Villaricca-Qualiano triangle near Naples has come to be known as the Land of Fires. Thirty-nine landfills, twenty-seven of which contain hazardous waste. An area with a 30 percent annual increase in landfills. When a site approaches capacity, the trash is set on fire. A tested technique, practiced regularly. Gypsy boys are the best at it. The clans give them 50 euros for each mound burned. The technique is simple. They circumscribe each hill with videocassette tapes, pour alcohol and gas all over it, twist the tape ends to form an enormous fuse, then move away, putting a cigarette lighter to the fuse. In a few seconds there's a forest of flames, as if they'd launched napalm bombs. They throw foundry remnants, glue, and naphtha dregs into the fire. Dense black smoke and flames contaminate every inch of land with dioxins. The local agriculture, which used to export fruit and vegetables as far as Scandinavia, is collapsing. Plants sprout diseased, and the land grows infertile. But this disaster and the farmers' rage are only the umpteenth advantage for the Camorra: desperate landowners sell off their fields, and the clans acquire new landfill sites at low—very low—costs. Meanwhile people are constantly dying of tumors. A slow and silent massacre, difficult to monitor since those who want to live as long as possible flee to the hospitals in the north. The Italian Superior Health Institute has reported that the cancer mortality rate in Campania cities with substantial toxic waste sites has increased by 21 percent in recent years. The lungs fester, the trachea starts to redden, a trip to the hospital for a CAT scan, where the black spots betray the presence of a tumor. Ask the ill of Campania where they're from and often the entire path of toxic waste is revealed.

I once decided to cross the Land of Fires on foot. I tied a handkerchief over my mouth and nose, the way the Gypsy boys do when they set fires. We looked like a gang of cowboys in a desert of burned garbage. I walked through lands devoured by dioxins, dumped on by trucks, and so gutted by fire that the holes would never completely be erased.

The smoke around me wasn't dense, but more like a sticky patina on the skin, making me feel damp. Not far from the fires was a series of houses, each one sitting on an enormous X of reinforced concrete. Homes resting on closed landfills and unauthorized dumps, their potential exhausted now that they'd been filled to the point of exploding and everything combustible had been burned. Yet the clans managed to reconvert them to building zones. After all, officially they were pasture and farmlands. And so they built charming clusters of small villas. The terrain was unstable, however; landslides could occur and chasms suddenly open, so a fretwork of reinforced concrete propped up the dwellings, securing them. The houses were affordable; everyone knew they were standing on tons of trash. But given the chance to own their own home, office clerks, factory workers, and retirees don't look a gift horse in the mouth.

The Land of Fires looks like a constant and repeated apocalypse—

routine—as if nothing else could surprise it in its disgust of leachate and old tires. Investigations have revealed the clans' method for safeguarding their activity from interference by policemen and forest rangers. An ancient method, used by guerrilla warriors and partisans in every corner of the world. Shepherds grazing their sheep, goats, a few cows, are used as lookouts. Rather than watching over their flocks, the best are hired to watch out for intruders. They sound the alarm as soon as they spot a suspicious car. Glances and cell phones are unassailable weapons. I often see them wandering about, trailed by their shriveled and obedient flocks; once I joined them to see where the kids practice driving trucks. The 2003 inquiry Eldorado found that minors are increasingly employed for these operations. Truck drivers no longer want to haul loads all the way to the dump site; they don't feel safe coming in close contact with toxic waste. It was a driver, after all, who set off the first important inquiry into waste trafficking in 1991. Mario Tamburrino had gone to the hospital with eyes like egg yolks, so swollen his lids couldn't close. He had gone completely blind, and the outer layer of skin on his hands had burned away, as if gasoline had been ignited on his palms. A drum of toxins had opened near his face; that was enough to blind him and nearly burn him alive. A dry burn, for there were no flames. After that incident the truck drivers asked to use tractor trailers; with the drums at a distance behind the kingpin, they'd never even have to touch them. The most dangerous trucks are the ones hauling adulterated compost, fertilizer mixed with toxins. Just inhaling the fumes could permanently damage the entire respiratory system. The final step— unloading the drums onto smaller trucks to be taken directly to the pit—is the riskiest. No one wants to do it. Piled one on top of another, the drums often get dented, allowing fumes to escape. So when the tractor trailers arrive, the drivers don't even get out. They let the kids unload and haul the drums to their final destination. A shepherd showed me a slope where the kids practice driving before a shipment arrives. Two pillows under their butts so as to reach the pedals, they learn how to brake on the way down. Fourteen, fifteen, sixteen years old. Two hundred fifty euros a trip. They're recruited in a bar. The bar owner knows and doesn't dare protest, but he offers his opinion to anyone who'll listen as he serves coffee and cappuccino.

"That stuff they make them haul, the more they breathe it in, the sooner they'll drop dead. They send them to die, not to drive."

The more the young drivers hear it said that theirs is a dangerous and deadly job, the more they feel up to such an important mission. They stick out their chests, arrogance glinting behind their sunglasses. They feel fine, better all the time. None of them could imagine, not for an instant, that in ten years time they'll be getting chemotherapy, vomiting up bile, their stomachs, livers, and intestines reduced to a pulp.

It kept on raining. The ground, unable to absorb anything else, quickly turned soggy. The shepherds, unperturbed, went and sat like three emaciated holy men under a makeshift shelter of sheet metal. They kept their eyes on the road while the sheep sought safety by clambering up on a trash heap. One of the shepherds used his walking stick to tilt the roof so that it wouldn't buckle under the weight of the rain and come crashing down on their heads. I was soaked to the skin, but all that water wasn't enough to extinguish the burning sensation rising from my stomach and radiating up my neck. I tried to fathom whether human feelings were able to withstand such a vast power machine, if it was possible to act in a way, in any way, that would permit me to live outside of the dynamics of power. I tormented myself trying to grasp if it was possible to try to understand, to discover, to know, without being devoured or destroyed. Or if the choice was between knowing and being compromised, or ignoring— and thus living serenely. Perhaps the only option was to forget, to not see. To listen to the official version of things, to half-listen, distractedly, and respond with nothing more than a sigh. I asked myself if there was anything that held out the possibility of a happy life, or if perhaps I just had to stop dreaming of emancipation and anarchic freedoms and throw myself into the arena, stick a semiautomatic in my underwear and start doing business for real. Convince myself to be part of the connective fabric of my day, to gamble everything, to command and be commanded, to become a beast of profit, a raptor of finance, a samurai of the clans; to turn my life into a battlefield where you don't hope to survive but merely to go down after a good fight.

I was born in the land of the Camorra, in the territory with the most homicides in Europe, where savagery is interwoven with commerce, where nothing has value except what generates power. Where everything has the taste of a final battle. It seemed impossible to have a moment of peace, not to live constantly in a war where every gesture is a surrender, where every necessity is transformed into weakness, where everything needs to be fought for tooth and nail. In the land of the Camorra, opposing the clans is not a class struggle, an affirmation of a right, or a reappropriation of one's civic duty. It's not the realization of one's honor or the preservation of one's pride. It's something more basic, more ferociously carnal. In the land of the Camorra, knowing the clans' mechanisms for success, their modes of extraction, their investments, means understanding how everything works today everywhere, not merely here. To set oneself against the clans becomes a war of survival, as if existence itself—the food you eat, the lips you kiss, the music you listen to, the pages you read—were merely a way to survive, not the meaning of life. Knowing is thus no longer a sign of moral engagement. Knowing—understanding—becomes a necessity. The only necessity if you want to consider yourself worthy of breathing.

My feet were deep in the mire. The water had risen to my thighs. I could feel my heels sinking. A huge refrigerator floated in front of me. I threw myself on it, clutching it tightly with my arms, and let myself be carried. I thought of the final scene of *Papillon*, based on the novel by Henri Charrière and starring Steve McQueen. I felt like Papillon, who escapes French Guiana on the tide, floating away on a sack of coconuts. It was an absurd thought, but at certain moments there's nothing else to do but humor your own delirium as something you don't chose but simply endure. I wanted to shout, to scream, to tear my lungs out like Papillon. I wanted to howl from deep down in my gut, my throat exploding with all the voice left in me: "Hey, you bastards, I'm still here!"